THE
PRESSURE COOKER
COOKBOOK FOR
WEIGHT LOSS

125 Easy and Healthy Recipes

Sukaina Bharwani

PHOTOGRAPHY BY HELENE DUJARDIN

ROCKRIDGE PRESS

For my family, their endless words of encouragement, and willingness to try everything I create in the kitchen.

Copyright © 2020 by Rockridge Press, Emeryville, California

No part of this publication may be reproduced, stored in a retrieval system or transmitted in any form or by any means, electronic, mechanical, photocopying, recording, scanning or otherwise, except as permitted under Sections 107 or 108 of the 1976 United States Copyright Act, without the prior written permission of the Publisher. Requests to the Publisher for permission should be addressed to the Permissions Department, Rockridge Press, 6005 Shellmound Street, Suite 175, Emeryville, CA 94608.

Limit of Liability/Disclaimer of Warranty: The Publisher and the author make no representations or warranties with respect to the accuracy or completeness of the contents of this work and specifically disclaim all warranties, including without limitation warranties of fitness for a particular purpose. No warranty may be created or extended by sales or promotional materials. The advice and strategies contained herein may not be suitable for every situation. This work is sold with the understanding that the Publisher is not engaged in rendering medical, legal, or other professional advice or services. If professional assistance is required, the services of a competent professional person should be sought. Neither the Publisher nor the author shall be liable for damages arising herefrom. The fact that an individual, organization, or website is referred to in this work as a citation and/or potential source of further information does not mean that the author or the Publisher endorses the information the individual, organization, or website may provide or recommendations they/it may make. Further, readers should be aware that websites listed in this work may have changed or disappeared between when this work was written and when it is read.

For general information on our other products and services or to obtain technical support, please contact our Customer Care Department within the United States at (866) 744-2665, or outside the United States at (510) 253-0500.

Rockridge Press publishes its books in a variety of electronic and print formats. Some content that appears in print may not be available in electronic books, and vice versa.

TRADEMARKS: Rockridge Press and the Rockridge Press logo are trademarks or registered trademarks of Callisto Media Inc. and/or its affiliates, in the United States and other countries, and may not be used without written permission. All other trademarks are the property of their respective owners. Rockridge Press is not associated with any product or vendor mentioned in this book.

Interior and Cover Designer: Diana Haas
Photo Art Director/Art Manager: Michael Hardgrove
Editor: Alyson Penn
Production Editor: Ashley Polikoff
Photography © 2020 Helene Dujardin. Food styling by Anna Hampton.
Author photos courtesy of © Zaheer Molu of Z Molu.

ISBN: Print 978-1-64611-983-7 | eBook 978-1-64611-984-4
R0

Contents

INTRODUCTION IX

CHAPTER ONE
Electric Pressure Cooker and Weight Loss—A Perfect Pair 1

CHAPTER TWO
The Electric Pressure Cooker Guide 9

CHAPTER THREE
Breakfast 21

CHAPTER FOUR
Sides and Snacks 43

CHAPTER FIVE
Sandwiches and Bowls 63

CHAPTER SIX
Chilis, Soups, and Sauces 85

CHAPTER SEVEN
Meatless Mains 109

CHAPTER EIGHT
Poultry and Seafood 131

CHAPTER NINE
Beef, Lamb, and Pork 157

CHAPTER TEN
Desserts and Drinks 183

MEASUREMENT CONVERSIONS 207

INDEX 208

Introduction

GROWING UP, health and wellness was never something we thought about in my house. We ate what we wanted, and weight loss was something we didn't discuss. It wasn't until I reached my mid-twenties that I started to think more about health. I got that token gym membership, which I made use of maybe once a week, and started trying some of those crazy fad diets (don't get me started on the cabbage soup diet!).

It was after my kids were born that I started experiencing some health issues that prompted me to take a closer look at what I was eating and how it was affecting my health. As I focused on eating more whole foods and avoiding processed foods, I noticed a positive change in my overall health and wellness and realized that by eating better for my health, I was also able to shed those stubborn 10 pounds.

To help me overcome my health issues, I had to remove gluten and refined sugars from my diet, but my family could still eat those foods and I didn't want to restrict their eating. In order to make everyone happy, I ended up making two meals for dinner every night and soon started feeling overwhelmed because it seemed I was spending all my time in the kitchen. All that changed when I got my electric pressure cooker up and running. Now I had this multifunctional machine that I could use to cook my meals and not have to stand watch over them, giving me extra time to prep other ingredients and meals, reducing the time I spent in the kitchen.

In this cookbook you'll find tasty, easy-to-follow recipes that are lower in calories and higher in nutrients and can all be prepared in your electric pressure cooker. Not sure how to start your weight loss journey? At the end of chapter 2, you will find a two-week meal plan designed to help you get started with recipes found right here in this book. By the end of the two weeks, it's my hope that you will have a better understanding of what to eat and how preparing your meals in an electric pressure cooker reduces the time you spend in the kitchen, leaving you with more time to focus on other things. While following this meal plan, remember that weight loss is about more than just the foods we eat. Make sure you're moving daily, getting enough sleep, and finding ways to reduce your stress.

As you make your way through the recipes in this book, you'll notice that I have included a variety of international cuisines. I love exploring the various flavor profiles from all over. I am of East Indian and East African descent and I have shared some recipes of foods that I grew up eating and that bring me comfort and joy. Most of these recipes have the same flavor profiles as the traditional versions, but have been modified slightly to fit into my healthy-eating lifestyle with more vegetables, more whole grains, and no refined sugars. Due to my religious beliefs and personal restrictions, you'll notice in chapter 9, the recipes in the pork section have not been written by me. Having never eaten pork, I was unable to create these recipes, but recipe developer Sandy Gluck kindly contributed her recipes for us to share with all of you: Pork Carnitas (page 178), Pork and Broccoli (page 179), and Pork Barbacoa (page 181).

There is no reason why you can't enjoy delicious meals as you work on eating healthier and losing weight. I'm excited for you to make your way through this cookbook and try all the simple, healthy recipes that I have shared. Healthy eating and sustainable weight loss can be easy and delicious, and with the help of an electric pressure cooker, it can be less stressful and time consuming. My hope is that these recipes bring you as much joy and comfort as they do me.

CHAPTER ONE

Electric Pressure Cooker and Weight Loss—A Perfect Pair

Why all the hype about electric pressure cookers? When used correctly with the right recipes, electric pressure cookers can produce healthy meals with minimal fuss and can encourage a healthier lifestyle. Not only do electric pressure cookers help reduce the amount of time spent in the kitchen, they make creating healthy meals quick and easy. With the help of these machines, you can say goodbye to processed convenience foods and create more nutritiously balanced meals that the whole family can enjoy.

Benefits of Pressure Cooking for Weight Loss

Congratulations, you've made the decision to eat better and start your weight loss journey! Now we move to the next step, the step that many find the most intimidating—learning what to eat and how much. Following a weight loss plan can be easy to start and maintain with the help of some handy tools—and an electric pressure cooker is one of them. We know that one of the main changes you'll have to make is to your food intake, ensuring that you're eating the right nutrients. This is where many people get discouraged. Healthy meals seem to come with a preconceived notion that they take a lot of time to prepare and cook. Yes, cooking something like brown rice on the stove can take up to 40 minutes, but in an electric pressure cooker you can have your rice ready to go in about 25 minutes—less time, and you don't have to watch the pot during the process. The ease with which you can prepare healthy, low-calorie meals in these machines can result in less takeout and processed meals for you and your family, already putting you on a healthier path. The number of healthy, family-friendly electric pressure cooker recipes available is endless—from breakfast, appetizers, meals, and desserts—there are bound to be recipes that even the pickiest eaters will enjoy. This variety of recipes can help ensure that you won't be eating the same boring foods every night, making your weight loss journey more sustainable and enjoyable for all.

HEALTHY EATING

A common question asked by many is "What should I eat if I want to lose weight?" With so many food choices available, it is hard to know what foods are nutritious and most beneficial to us. The main focus should be on whole foods that can assist with weight loss, disease prevention, and overall good health, while avoiding processed foods that are high in excess sugars and sodium. The goal should be to include meals that consist of fiber-rich foods, whole grains, vegetables, and clean sources of protein. This is where electric pressure cookers shine, as they reduce the cook time for beneficial whole foods, such as whole grains, beans, legumes, lean meats, chicken, seafood, and vegetables, making them easier to enjoy without having to be fried, coated in oil, or microwaved. Another great benefit of using an electric pressure cooker in your weight loss journey is that you can add all the important components of a healthy meal—fiber, vegetables, proteins—in one pot and have a nutritious one-pot meal ready in about 30 minutes that everyone can enjoy and benefit from.

Portion Control and Leftovers

Portion control is an important aspect of any weight loss plan. Having portion and calorie amounts in mind makes it easier to stay focused and not overeat. Try portioning out your meal before you start eating; that way you know when you're done. Remember that not all portion sizes of foods are equal—for successful weight loss, focus on having a larger portion of vegetables, which will add bulk to your meals and help you stay fuller for a longer period of time. Include a smaller portion of carbohydrates, which tend to be higher in calories. When preparing my meals in an electric pressure cooker, I try to make a little more than we need, so we end up with leftovers that we can enjoy for lunch in the following day or two. This prep helps reduce the temptation to pop out and buy a lunch, which saves me time and money and ensures I'm eating something healthy and nutritious.

EASY PREP MEANS MORE FREE TIME

Life is busy. Sometimes it seems like we have a million things to get done in a day, then comes that dreaded question, "What's for dinner?" That's when you turn to your electric pressure cooker for help. There is minimal prep time required when using an electric pressure cooker—maybe some quick chopping, mixing, or sautéing—and with so many one-pot recipes available, you can add all your ingredients, set your timer, and you're pretty much done. Not having to watch the pot while your food is cooking and knowing that you will be alerted with multiple beeps when your meal is ready means you have more time to focus on other things, like squeezing in a quick workout or taking a time-out for yourself with some meditation or a relaxing cup of tea. The possibilities of what you can do with some extra minutes in your day are endless.

CANNED AND FROZEN FOODS

Forgot to defrost your ingredients for dinner? No problem. There are some frozen foods that you can add right into your pot. However, there are a few things to keep in mind. First, when using frozen foods in your electric pressure cooker, it will take a little longer to heat up and for the pressure to build, which means adding a few extra minutes to your original cook time. Also, when cooking frozen foods, try not to overlap the foods or to overfill the pot; the extra space is needed to achieve even heating and cooking throughout. Finally, keep in mind that certain foods, like frozen vegetables, will not require as much time to cook as their fresh counterparts, as they soften while defrosting. Some popular foods to cook from frozen include chicken, ground beef, meatballs, soups and broths, salmon, vegetables, and fruits. Canned foods also make cooking in an electric pressure cooker a breeze. Some popular canned foods to use are tomatoes, beans (be sure to rinse these out well before use to help with digestion), fruit, coconut milk, and chiles. Like frozen foods, canned vegetables, fruits, and beans take less time to cook, so make the necessary time adjustments. Finally, when using packaged frozen or canned foods, make sure to read the labels and watch out for any extra added ingredients and sodium.

Healthy Eating as a Lifestyle

Losing weight and leading healthier lifestyles are goals for many of us, and once we view the foods necessary for weight loss as nourishing instead of restrictive, these goals are attainable. One of the keys to staying on track with healthy eating is finding healthier alternatives to favorite comfort foods. This book includes recipes for everyday snacks and meals that are health focused, using whole-food ingredients. Not having the time to prepare healthy home-cooked meals is a common reason for not eating well. This is why electric pressure cookers are so ideal, as they reduce the prep and cook time needed to create healthy meals. The focus of this cookbook is not on dieting. Rather, it's designed to provide the tools necessary to make healthy lifestyle changes that are sustainable and can assist you in reaching your weight loss goals.

Substitutions

I have tried to include healthy ingredients that should be easy to locate at your local grocery store. If you are unable to find these ingredients or find that they may be a little costly, then use the familiar option for similar results.

Avocado oil or olive oil instead of canola oil: Oils are very important when preparing your meals, but it is important to use oils that are beneficial to your health and are able to withstand high temperatures. Electric pressure cookers do not use high temperatures to cook, so oils with lower smoke points, like extra-virgin olive oil, can be used.

Coconut aminos instead of tamari or low-sodium soy sauce: Coconut aminos is made from coconut sap with no added ingredients. Plus, it's gluten-free and has the same flavor profile as soy sauce, making it a great addition to Asian-inspired meals.

Cauliflower rice instead of white rice: This is a great low-carbohydrate and low-calorie option to replace regular white or brown rice. The mild flavor of cauliflower makes this substitute hardly noticeable. If you feel you have a hard time digesting cauliflower, as some people do, or would rather not try it, you can use your rice of choice instead. Riced cauliflower can be found in the fresh produce or freezer section of most grocery stores.

Steel-cut oats instead of quick oats: Steel-cut oats are higher in fiber and lower on the glycemic index than quick oats, but they do take a little longer to cook. Rolled or quick oats can be used instead of steel-cut oats with a reduced cook time.

Almond flour, oat flour, and brown rice flour instead of whole-wheat flour: These flours are gluten-free, whole-grain options and are more beneficial to our digestion and health than processed white or wheat flours.

Coconut sugar, pure maple syrup, and honey instead of white and brown sugar: These sweeteners are more natural forms of sugar that have fewer calories and do not cause blood sugar spikes as processed white or brown sugars do.

EXERCISE

Exercise plays an integral part in any wellness journey. It not only helps strengthen the body, but it strengthens the mind as well. Keep things interesting with your workouts: add a variety of exercises that you enjoy—cardio, strength training, and stretching—and plan on exercising at least three to five times a week. The great thing about regular exercise is that your body is not only burning calories during your workouts but also for hours after. Stay on track and motivated with a workout buddy or a group program; this will help you stay accountable and committed to your goals.

SLEEP AND STRESS

A healthy lifestyle is more than eating the right foods and exercising. Sleep and stress play essential roles as well. Studies have shown that getting an average of seven to eight hours of sleep and reducing stress can have a significant impact on weight loss. It's while we sleep that our bodies convert fat to muscle and our cells regenerate.

Stress, on the other hand, can be detrimental to weight loss. To help reduce stress, try some deep breathing, meditation, a walk out in nature, or any activity that you enjoy and helps you relax. This cookbook is designed to help take the stress out of your time in the kitchen and make it more enjoyable.

Beyond the Scale

Scales are helpful for giving you a rough idea of how much you weigh, but do not rely on those numbers! Did you know that your body weight can fluctuate up to five pounds in one day? There are so many factors that can affect the number on the scale—water retention, digestion, hormones, muscle growth, clothing—it's in no way an accurate figure. Some more beneficial ways to keep track of your progress are to take body measurements, take pictures of yourself, or find an outfit that you want to fit into and keep trying it on. The most important thing to keep in mind is that you're adopting a healthy lifestyle for the long term. Celebrate all your victories, big or small.

5 Basic Rules for Weight Loss

The key to successful weight loss is adopting a healthy lifestyle that suits your individual needs and is sustainable long-term. Forget the fad diets—here are five rules to keep in mind to help you see the results you want.

1. **Make healthy lifestyle changes.** Focus on making lifestyle changes that are realistic and sustainable to you. Eat well-balanced meals, move daily, get enough sleep, and find ways to help reduce stress, as these are the foundations for good health.

2. **Stay hydrated.** I can't stress enough how important water is to our overall health! Try to drink half your body weight in ounces of water daily. Thirst can often mask itself as hunger, making you think you're hungry when all you really need is some water.

3. **Eat a well-balanced plate.** Keep your plate balanced with protein, fiber, vegetables, and a healthy fat source. Protein helps the body form lean muscle, burn fat, and feel fuller for longer. Fiber-rich foods aid in digestion and proper elimination. Fill at least half your plate with vegetables and include a variety in various colors. Eat the rainbow for added antioxidant benefits. Healthy fats help you feel fuller for longer, but keep portion control and moderation in mind.

4. **Avoid refined sugars and refined carbohydrates.** Focus on natural forms of sugar in your meals, drinks, and baking. Refined sugars and carbohydrates are addicting, full of added calories and fats, and can wreak havoc on your overall health.

5. **Be easy on yourself.** Long-term success will take time. Avoid comparing your weight loss journey with anyone else's. We are all so different. If you're craving a certain food, go ahead and enjoy it, in moderation without regrets. This will help avoid binge eating, feelings of regret, and make your journey more sustainable in the long term.

Vegetable Pad Thai, page 119

CHAPTER TWO

The Electric Pressure Cooker Guide

In this chapter we will discuss electric pressure cookers and what makes them so popular. We compare some popular brands, the basic functions of an electric pressure cooker, and some important safety rules to always keep in mind. We share more about the delicious recipes included in this book and some of the descriptive labels attached to them. This chapter ends with an easy-to-follow, two-week meal plan designed to help you start your weight loss journey with simple and delicious recipes from this book.

Your Electric Pressure Cooker

A pressure cooker is a sealed pot that cooks food from the steam and pressure that builds up inside the pot at a higher temperature than regular pots on the stove. Newer, electrical versions have multicooking features, allowing you to pressure cook, slow cook, sauté, and steam all in one pot, making meal preparation easy and convenient. The convenience of adding all your ingredients into a pot, setting a timer, and being free to complete other tasks while your meal cooks is just one of the reasons why these machines are loved by so many.

It took a while for me to get an electric pressure cooker. I was skeptical of all the hype and didn't need another small appliance sitting unused in my cabinet. Then, one of my nieces decided I needed an Instant Pot in my life and ordered one for me. After a couple of weeks of nervously staring at the box, I finally opened it up and decided to give it a go. Once I took the time to figure out all the functions and tried a few basic recipes, I was hooked. I am an electric pressure cooker junkie.

HOW TO USE IT

No matter which electric pressure cooker you own, the basic functions are the same across the brands and they offer similar conveniences, even though some of the function names may vary along with included tools.

Most standard electric pressure cookers look similar with common parts, features, and safety measures. The base units contain the control panels, there's a removable inner pot for the cooking, a heavy-duty lid that contains a silicone ring to aid with sealing the pot, and a steam release valve.

The recipes in this book use the function names of the Instant Pot Duo. If your machine does not have a function that I mention, reread your owner's manual for the term that your brand uses.

Basic Functions of the Electric Pressure Cooker

Many electric pressure cookers are referred to as multicookers because they perform a variety of functions in the one machine. Here, I have shared a few of the basic functions found in common electric pressure cooker brands and a brief explanation on how they work and when to use them.

- **Manual/Pressure:** This is the function used most because of the flexibility it provides and the speed at which it cooks most foods like beef, beans, and grains. The level of pressure can be adjusted from high to low and the cook time can be manually adjusted, depending on ingredients being used.

- **Sauté:** Want to brown meats, sauté vegetables, or simmer ingredients in the pot? This is the function that can do all that. The sauté setting can be adjusted to low for simmering, normal for sautéing, and high for browning meats. It's the perfect function for prepping ingredients before pressure cooking them.

- **Slow Cook:** This function allows foods to be cooked at a lower temperature for a longer time, such as braised beef, chilis, or stews. With this function, there is no need to lock in the steam, so a clear glass lid that fits the pot can be used instead of the regular machine lid.

- **Steam:** You can steam vegetables and other foods with this function, a much faster process then stovetop steaming. To steam anything in your pot, you will need to add some water to the base of the inner pot then add a steamer basket or trivet with the ingredients to be steamed. Keep in mind that foods will steam faster in the electric pressure cooker than on the stove—and will retain more of their nutrients.

- **Keep Warm/Cancel/Off:** This button performs three functions: Use it to keep your food warm at a low temperature, to cancel a function, or to turn off your machine altogether.

Tips for Your Electric Pressure Cooker

When you first unbox your electric pressure cooker, you may feel a little overwhelmed. I know I was, and that's okay. These machines are unique, and there is a learning curve to overcome, but once you figure it all out, using it will begin to feel easy and natural. Here are some basic tips that can be helpful for beginners and a general refresher for all.

SAFETY INSTRUCTIONS

Most electric pressure cookers have various safety features built in to keep you safe. Here are a few basic tips to keep in mind.

- **Always stay** near your machine when using the sauté function. The machines can heat up very quickly and burn contents.

- **Keep ingredients** and liquids below the max fill line—two-thirds full is good to prevent overflowing.

- **Always keep** at least ¾ to 1 cup of liquid in the pot during cook time to achieve the steam needed and avoid burning food.

- **Be careful** when releasing the steam. Use a glove, spoon, or towel to turn the steam valve to avoid getting burned by the steam being released. Always open the pot with the lid turned away from your face.

- **Never force** open the lid, even if it seems that all the steam has been released, give it a few seconds and try again. Always wait until the steam valve pin has dropped before trying to open the lid.

- **Read over** the instruction manual that came with your specific electric pressure cooker and familiarize yourself with all the safety rules and functions to avoid any problems.

CLEANING AND CARING

With a little extra care, you can enjoy your electric pressure cooker for many years to come.

- After every use, wash out the lid and silicone sealing ring and clean the antiblock shield and inner pot—all are dishwasher safe.

- Wipe the outer pot base with a wet cloth to clean. Do not submerge the base into water; it's where all the electrical components are housed.

- Always use a nonabrasive cleaning solution and soft sponge when handwashing any parts.

- The sealing ring can become warped over time. Replace it every one to two years, depending on usage, and make sure it's fully inserted back into the lid before each use.

- Only use silicone or wooden utensils while cooking to avoid scratching the cooking surface of the inner pot.

ALTITUDE ADJUSTMENTS

Did you know that as altitude increases, atmospheric pressure and the boiling point of water decrease? This is an important fact to keep in mind for anyone using an electric pressure cooker at higher elevations, as cook times need to be increased. The recipes and times in this cookbook have been created for those living at sea level, but for those living at a higher altitude, I have included a chart below with altitudes and appropriate cook time adjustments.

ALTITUDE	COOK TIME
3000 ft	+ 5%
4000 ft	+ 10%
5000 ft	+ 15%
6000 ft	+ 20%

Other Gadgets

As wonderful as I find electric pressure cookers, I have found that with the use of some additional tools, these machines can do even more. Here's a list of some of my favorite easy-to-find and affordable items that I use with my Instant Pot and are used in some recipes within this cookbook.

Trivet or stand: These are included with some electric pressure cookers or can be purchased separately. They are beneficial for steaming and pot-in-pot cooking. In the recipes that call for the use of a trivet/stand, the standard ones that come with your electric pressure cooker are all that you need. However, some recipes call for a long-legged stand that can be purchased separately and will provide more space for pot-in-pot cooking.

Steamer basket: Perfect for setting in the base of the pot and filling with vegetables to steam.

6- or 7-inch springform pan: Can be placed on a trivet/stand in the electric pressure cooker to make cakes, casseroles, and frittatas.

Egg steamer rack: Makes boiling eggs simple, and the stand can also be used as a long-legged stand for pot-in-pot cooking.

Wooden or silicone tongs and spatulas: Can help reduce any scratching to the inner pot.

Oven-safe dishes in various sizes: You can use any glass, ceramic, or metal dishes for pot-in-pot cooking, as long as they are oven-safe and fit in the inner pot.

An extra lid-sealing ring: It's nice to have a ring dedicated to savory foods and one that's used for desserts.

Silicone oven mitts: Allows you to safely and easily remove dishes from the machine.

Hand blender: An immersion blender makes creating soups, sauces, and other pureed foods in one pot easy.

About the Recipes

The recipes in this book have been created with one important thing in mind—healthy living! That's why they all include healthy, whole-food ingredients beneficial to your weight loss journey and overall good health. I have tried to use simple, easy-to-find ingredients to produce quick-and-easy meals that are full of flavor.

As you read through the recipes in this cookbook, you'll notice that there have been some identifiable labels added to each one. Below is a brief explanation of what these labels represent.

- **Allergy-Free:** Contains none of the top eight allergens: wheat, eggs, dairy, fish, shellfish, soy, peanuts, and tree nuts.

- **Dairy-Free:** Contains no dairy or dairy-containing products.

- **Gluten-Free:** Contains no gluten products: wheat, barley, and rye. Make sure you always double-check labels on items like oats to make sure they are certified gluten-free and/or processed in a gluten-free facility.

- **Nut-Free:** Contains no nuts of any kind, including tree nuts.

- **One Pot:** This meal can be made entirely in one pot with no extra dishes.

- **Vegan:** Contains no meat, dairy, eggs, or other animal products.

- **Vegetarian:** Contains no meat or seafood products, but includes egg and dairy products.

- **30 Minutes or Less:** The recipe's total time for prep and cook is 30 minutes or less. Cook times may vary depending on variables such as the size of pot, number of ingredients, and temperature of the ingredients. I have tried to estimate the pressure-building time required the best I can, but please allow for a few extra minutes.

14-Day Meal Plan

I'm excited to share this simple 14-day meal plan to help you get started on your weight loss journey. It is filled with easy-to-make recipes that are modified versions of some of our favorite meals. This general meal plan has been designed with no specific diet or restrictions in mind. If there are some meals or ingredients that you are not sure of, feel free to substitute them with something equally healthy that you enjoy. With this plan I'd like you to commit to cooking and eating healthy for the first two weeks. Afterward, you'll notice a difference and want to continue to do so on your own.

I know you're excited to get going, but before you start, I want you to take a moment and review the plan and all the recipes for the first week. Make a list of what you may need to buy and go shopping before the week starts. You may be required to do some meal prepping over the weekends before you start, but having everything prepped will make following through with this plan so much easier.

ADJUSTMENTS

The recipes shared in this cookbook are made to serve four to six people. Please make any necessary adjustments for the number of servings you may require. If you end up having leftovers, that's great—you can repeat the same meal with leftovers the next day, making for even easier meal prep.

WEEK 1

It's here! It's the first week of your new weight loss journey, and I am so excited to share this meal plan to help get you started. The goal of this plan is to assist you in making healthier food choices and to watch portion sizes. If you feel hungry after a meal or throughout the day, reach for some raw vegetables to snack on or add a side salad to your meals. These are low-calorie foods that can help fill you up.

Day	Breakfast	Lunch	Snack	Dinner
Monday	Very Berry Cauli-Oats (page 22)	Avocado Egg Salad (page 79) with lettuce wraps	Beet Hummus (page 46) with grain and seed crackers	Veggie and Lentil Bolognese (page 112) on spaghetti squash
Tuesday	Sprouted grain toast with avocado and boiled egg	Mexican Black Bean and Quinoa Bowl (page 73)	Leftover Avocado Egg Salad on celery sticks	Cashew Chicken (page 147) with Cauliflower Fried Rice (page 58)
Wednesday	Spinach and Feta Egg Muffins (page 27)	Thai Lentil Soup (page 89)	Fresh blueberries	Orange-Ginger Salmon Dinner (page 133)
Thursday	Maple-Blueberry Pancake Bites (page 31)	Steak Fajita Wraps (page 69)	Celery sticks and almond butter	Quinoa and Lentil Stuffed Peppers (page 116) with a side salad
Friday	Perfect Poached Eggs (page 24) on sprouted grain toast	Tzatziki Lamb Meatballs (page 172) on a large salad	Cucumber slices with leftover Beet Hummus	Spicy Mexican Chicken (page 146) with Chili-Lime Brown Rice (page 57)
Saturday	Eggy Ratatouille (page 28)	Mushroom and Wild Rice Soup (page 96)	Apple slices and almond butter	Hearty Lentil Stew (page 121) with side salad
Sunday	Breakfast Casserole (page 38)	Spicy Black Bean and Rice Salad (page 76)	Cucumber and red bell pepper slices	Mediterranean Lamb Chops (page 174)

WEEK 2

You did it! You finished the first week of this meal plan. I hope you enjoyed the meals and are feeling lighter and more energized. Now we're on to the second week. Continue this week as you did week 1, and if you would like to make any adjustments or substitutes to your personal taste, feel free to do so as long as they're healthy.

Day	Breakfast	Lunch	Snack	Dinner
Monday	Creamy Coconut Yogurt (page 25) with Maple-Almond Granola (page 40) and fruit	Vegetable Barley Soup (page 93)	Celery sticks and almond butter	Cauliflower-Potato Curry (page 113) with brown rice
Tuesday	Perfectly Boiled Eggs (page 37) and sprouted grain toast	Sweet Potato Quinoa Salad (page 80)	Carrot and cucumber sticks	Lemon-Cilantro Chicken (page 137) and Root Vegetable Medley (page 51)
Wednesday	Turmeric Latte Quinoa Oats (page 23)	Mediterranean Chickpea Bowl (page 74)	1 boiled egg and grain and seed crackers	Garlic-Lime Shrimp Scampi (page 142) and Parmesan Spaghetti Squash (page 52)
Thursday	Tex-Mex Breakfast Scramble (page 30)	Greek Chicken Salad Lettuce Wraps (page 72)	Fresh strawberries	Vegetable Pad Thai (page 119)
Friday	Fajitas Fiesta Eggs (page 35)	Turmeric Lentil Soup (page 91)	Coconut yogurt and blueberries	Mediterranean Chicken Shawarma (page 77) on brown rice
Saturday	Maple-Blueberry Pancake Bites (page 31)	Shredded Beef Lettuce Cups (page 82)	Red bell pepper and cucumber slices	Vegetable Risotto (page 115)
Sunday	Egg and Sweet Potato Hash (page 33)	Two-Bean Rice Bowl (page 67)	Apple slices and almond butter	Cuban Beef Picadillo (page 164) with quinoa and salad

Spinach and Feta Egg Muffins, page 27

CHAPTER THREE

Breakfast

Very Berry Cauli-Oats 22

Turmeric Latte Quinoa Oats 23

Perfect Poached Eggs 24

Creamy Coconut Yogurt 25

Spinach and Feta Egg Muffins 27

Eggy Ratatouille 28

Tex-Mex Breakfast Scramble 30

Maple-Blueberry Pancake Bites 31

Egg and Sweet Potato Hash 33

Maple-Pecan French Toast 34

Fajitas Fiesta Eggs 35

Perfectly Boiled Eggs 37

Breakfast Casserole 38

Blueberry Chia Jam 39

Maple-Almond Granola 40

DAIRY-FREE, GLUTEN-FREE, VEGAN

Very Berry Cauli-Oats

Serves: 6 / **Prep Time:** 10 minutes / **Pressure Cook:** 5 minutes / **Release:** Natural for 10 minutes, then quick, plus 5 minutes / **Total Time:** 35 minutes

I usually make a large batch of oats so they're prepped for a week of grab-and-go breakfasts. Adding the riced cauliflower in this recipe is completely optional; however, the cauliflower reduces the carbohydrate content and provides an added nutritional boost.

4 cups water, divided

1½ cups steel-cut oats

¼ cup frozen riced cauliflower

1 teaspoon pure vanilla extract

½ teaspoon ground cinnamon

Pinch sea salt

1 cup unsweetened or vanilla almond milk or nut milk of choice

½ cup frozen mixed berries

2 tablespoons chia seeds

Sliced fresh fruit, nuts, or seeds, for serving

1. In a 6-cup oven-safe bowl, combine 3 cups of water, the oats, riced cauliflower, vanilla, cinnamon, and salt.

2. Pour the remaining 1 cup of water into the pressure cooker pot and place the trivet in the pot. Place the bowl on the trivet.

3. Lock the lid in place and seal the steam valve. Select Pressure/Manual and adjust the time to 5 minutes on high pressure.

4. After cooking, let the pressure release naturally for 10 minutes, then quick release any remaining pressure. Carefully remove the lid and set aside.

5. Add the almond milk, berries, and chia seeds into the oat mixture and mix well. Replace the lid and let sit for 5 minutes to allow the berries to defrost and soften.

6. Carefully remove the bowl from the pot and set on a heat-resistant surface. Check the consistency of the oats and add some extra almond milk, if necessary. Serve, topped with fresh fruit.

SHORTCUT: To have these oats ready faster, use rolled oats instead of steel-cut oats and reduce the cook time to 3 minutes and reduce the water in the bowl to 2 cups.

PER SERVING (¾ cup) Calories: 208; Total Fat: 5g; Fiber: 7g; Protein: 8g; Sodium: 53mg; Sugar: 1g

ALLERGY-FREE, ONE POT, VEGAN, 30 MINUTES OR LESS

Turmeric Latte Quinoa Oats

Serves: 6 / **Prep Time:** 10 minutes / **Pressure Cook:** 5 minutes high pressure / **Release:** Natural for 10 minutes, then quick / **Total Time:** 25 minutes

Turmeric lattes are one of my favorite cold-weather drinks, as they're full of immune-boosting ingredients and a savory flavor profile. Since I'm always looking for new ways to enjoy my favorite morning oats, I thought of combining two of my favorite things, and I loved the results.

3 cups water

1 cup unsweetened or vanilla oat milk or nut milk of choice

¾ cup quinoa, rinsed

¾ cup quick oats

2 tablespoons pure maple syrup

2 tablespoons chia seeds

1 teaspoon ground turmeric

1 teaspoon ground cinnamon

1 teaspoon sea salt

½ teaspoon ground ginger

Sliced fresh fruit, nuts, or seeds, for serving

1. In the pressure cooker pot, combine all the ingredients (except for the fruit used as a garnish) and stir well to mix.

2. Lock the lid in place and seal the steam valve. Select Pressure/Manual and adjust the time to 5 minutes on high pressure.

3. After cooking, let the pressure release naturally for 10 minutes, then quick release any remaining pressure. Carefully remove the lid and set aside.

4. Carefully remove the pot and check the consistency of the oats, adding in some extra oat milk if necessary.

5. Serve, topped with fruit.

HEALTH BOOST: Add a pinch of black pepper to the oats to help the body better absorb the health-promoting benefits of the curcumin enzyme found in turmeric.

PER SERVING (¾ cup) Calories: 167; Total Fat: 4g; Fiber: 5g; Protein: 5g; Sodium: 367mg; Sugar: 5g

BREAKFAST

DAIRY-FREE, GLUTEN-FREE, NUT-FREE, VEGETARIAN, 30 MINUTES OR LESS

Perfect Poached Eggs

Serves: 6 / **Prep Time:** 10 minutes / **Pressure Cook:** 7 minutes high pressure / **Release:** Quick / **Total Time:** 20 minutes

I really enjoy poached eggs, and as a treat, my husband learned how to make them for breakfast. Not to mention, he loves the fact that I can never get them just right when I try. But now I have finally found a way to make perfect poached eggs that rival his, but shh, we won't tell him that—I like being treated to a breakfast made especially for me.

1 cup water
Olive oil cooking spray
6 large eggs

1. Pour the water into the pressure cooker pot and place the trivet inside.

2. Spray an egg steamer rack with cooking spray. Crack an egg into each of the egg molds and carefully transfer the egg mold onto the trivet in the pot.

3. Lock the lid in place and seal the steam valve. Select Pressure/Manual and adjust the time to 7 minutes on high pressure.

4. After cooking, quick release the pressure. Carefully remove the lid and set aside.

5. Using oven mitts, remove the egg mold. Gently run a knife around the edges to make sure the eggs are loose and remove them from the mold. Serve.

VARIATION TIP: For this recipe I used a silicone egg bite mold that I purchased as an Instant Pot accessory. If you don't have one of these molds, you can still make perfect poached eggs with small ramekin bowls. If using ramekin bowls, add three to the trivet then place an elevated stand on top and add another three bowls.

PER SERVING (1 egg) Calories: 72; Total Fat: 5g; Fiber: 0g; Protein: 6g; Sodium: 71mg; Sugar: 0g

ALLERGY-FREE, VEGAN

Creamy Coconut Yogurt

Makes about: 1 quart / **Prep Time:** 5 minutes / **Pressure Cook:** 11 hours on Yogurt / **Release:** Quick / **Total Time:** 11+ hours

Here's a recipe that doesn't fall into the quick-and-easy category, but if you have a yogurt-making function on your electric pressure cooker, this will be one you'll love. This creamy yogurt works great for breakfast with some granola and fruit, and it also makes for a great healthy dessert option: add some chopped fruit and sprinkle on some cinnamon—yum!

2 (14-ounce) cans full-fat coconut cream

1½ tablespoons tapioca starch

1 tablespoon pure maple syrup

1 teaspoon probiotic powder (or open 4 capsules and add)

1. Place the coconut cream in the pressure cooker pot, adding only the thick cream and avoiding any thin liquid, if possible. Use a wooden spoon to mix well.

2. Lock the lid in place and seal the steam valve. Press the Yogurt setting and adjust until the display reads Boil. If your pressure cooker doesn't have a Boil setting, use Sauté.

3. After cooking, quick release the pressure. Carefully open the lid, avoiding any excess water from the lid dropping into the pot.

4. Use a candy thermometer to check the temperature. The temperature should read 185°F (if this temperature has not been reached, cover and seal the lid and start the boil process again). Carefully remove the pot and set on a heat-resistant surface. Remove ¼ cup of coconut cream and stir in the tapioca starch. Stir well, add back into the pot, and stir everything together well.

5. Allow the mixture to cool to 110°F to 115°F. Add the maple syrup and probiotic powder and mix well.

CONTINUED ▶

Creamy Coconut Yogurt CONTINUED

6. Return the pot back to the pressure cooker and lock the lid in place. The valve should remain on the release position as there will be no steam buildup required.

7. Press the Yogurt button and adjust to 10 hours (add more time for a tangier flavor option, up to 18 hours).

8. After cooking, open the lid and set aside. Stir the mixture, pour into clean containers, and allow to cool. Place the containers in the refrigerator to cool and thicken.

9. Store the covered containers in the refrigerator for up to 10 days.

VARIATION TIP: For an even thicker consistency, pour the cooked yogurt into a cheesecloth to remove any excess liquid before placing in the containers.

PER SERVING (¾ cup) Calories: 379; Total Fat: 36g; Fiber: 0g; Protein: 0g; Sodium: 60mg; Sugar: 8g

GLUTEN-FREE, NUT-FREE, VEGETARIAN, 30 MINUTES OR LESS

Spinach and Feta Egg Muffins

Serves: 4 / **Prep Time:** 15 minutes / **Pressure Cook:** 6 minutes high pressure / **Release:** Natural for 5 minutes, then quick / **Total Time:** 30 minutes

Mornings are tough, and having healthy foods prepped and ready to go makes it so much easier to make good breakfast choices. These egg muffins can be prepped ahead of time and warmed up when you're ready to enjoy them.

Olive oil cooking spray
½ cup chopped fresh baby spinach
½ cup chopped red bell pepper
¼ cup crumbled feta cheese
6 large eggs
¼ cup low-fat milk
¼ teaspoon sea salt
⅛ teaspoon freshly ground black pepper
1 cup water

1. Spray each of four ramekins well with cooking spray. Evenly distribute the spinach, bell pepper, and feta cheese among the prepared ramekin bowls.

2. In a large bowl, whisk together the eggs, milk, salt, and pepper together. Pour the egg mixture evenly into the ramekins.

3. Pour the water into the pressure cooker pot and place the trivet inside. Arrange three ramekins on the trivet, place the elevated stand on top, and arrange the remaining three ramekins on it.

4. Lock the lid in place and seal the steam valve. Select Pressure/Manual and adjust the time to 6 minutes on high pressure.

5. After cooking, let the pressure release naturally for 5 minutes, then quick release any remaining pressure. Carefully remove the lid, trying not to let any water from the inside of the lid fall onto the eggs.

6. Using oven mitts, remove the ramekin bowls and set on a heat-resistant surface. Gently run a knife around the edges to make sure the eggs are loose before removing them from the bowls. Serve.

PER SERVING (1 egg muffin) Calories: 150; Total Fat: 10g; Fiber: 1g; Protein: 12g; Sodium: 349mg; Sugar: 2g

DAIRY-FREE, GLUTEN-FREE, NUT-FREE, ONE-POT, VEGETARIAN, 30 MINUTES OR LESS

Eggy Ratatouille

Serves: 4 / **Prep Time:** 15 minutes / **Sauté:** 5 minutes / **Pressure Cook:** 5 minutes high pressure / **Release:** Quick / **Total Time:** 25 minutes

Ratatouille is a vegetable stew that originated in France. It's popular in the colder seasons and can include a variety of hearty vegetables in a tomato base. The combination of this stew and eggs makes for a delicious breakfast—or anytime—option that's low in carbs and full of flavor.

1 tablespoon extra-virgin olive oil
1 small onion, chopped
3 garlic cloves, minced
1 teaspoon dried thyme
1 teaspoon dried oregano
1 (28-ounce) can peeled plum tomatoes, drained
1 medium zucchini, cubed
1 medium eggplant, cubed
1 medium red bell pepper, cubed
½ cup halved mushrooms
4 large eggs
2 tablespoons chopped fresh basil
1 tablespoon capers (optional)
Sea salt
Freshly ground black pepper

1. Press the Sauté button and adjust to high. Once hot, heat the olive oil and add the onion. Sauté for about 1 minute, until the onion has softened. Add the garlic, thyme, and oregano and sauté and stir for another 1 minute or so. Add the tomatoes and cook, mixing and gently smashing them as they break apart, for 2 more minutes. Add the zucchini, eggplant, bell pepper, and mushrooms, stirring until everything is combined.

2. Press Cancel, close and seal the lid, and make sure the steam valve is set to steam. Select Pressure/Manual and adjust the time to 3 minutes on high pressure.

3. After cooking, quick release the pressure. Carefully remove the lid and set aside.

4. Give the contents of the pot a gentle stir, then use the back of the spoon to gently press down, making a small well in the pot; repeat this part three more times. Carefully crack an egg into each of the wells.

5. Place the lid back on the cooker, then close and seal it, making sure the steam valve is set to steam. Adjust the time to 2 minutes on high pressure.

6. After cooking, again, quick release the pressure. Carefully remove the lid and set aside. If you would like your eggs cooked slightly more then place the lid back on the pot, leave it unsealed, and allow the eggs to cook in the heat for another minute or so, until desired level is reached.

7. Remove the pot and place it on a heat-resistant surface. Add the basil and capers (if using). Carefully scoop out portions of the ratatouille and eggs on to serving plates. Season with salt and pepper to taste.

VARIATION TIP: If you have leftover ratatouille mix, the next day you can heat up the mixture in a skillet, then make little wells to crack your eggs into. Cover the skillet and allow your eggs to cook.

PER SERVING (1 cup and 1 egg) Calories: 202; Total Fat: 9g; Fiber: 10g; Protein: 11g; Sodium: 191mg; Sugar: 14g

GLUTEN-FREE, NUT-FREE, VEGETARIAN

Tex-Mex Breakfast Scramble

Serves: 6 / **Prep Time:** 15 minutes / **Pressure Cook:** 30 minutes high pressure / **Release:** Natural for 5 minutes, then quick / **Total Time:** 50 minutes

This easy breakfast scramble can be made with whatever vegetables you have on hand. Enjoy as is or wrap the scramble in a gluten-free, low-carb, or multigrain wrap to make a burrito. Try topping your burrito with some fresh avocado and pico de gallo for true Mexican flare.

8 large eggs
½ cup low-fat milk or unsweetened almond milk
½ teaspoon sea salt
½ teaspoon chili powder
½ teaspoon dried oregano
¼ teaspoon freshly ground black pepper
1 small red onion, chopped
1 cup canned black beans, drained and rinsed
½ red bell pepper, chopped
1 small tomato, chopped
1 tablespoon chopped jalapeño (optional)
Olive oil cooking spray
1 cup water

ADD-INS

¼ cup shredded Cheddar cheese
1 to 2 tablespoons chopped fresh cilantro

1. In a large bowl, whisk together the eggs, milk, salt, chili powder, oregano, and black pepper. Stir in the onion, black beans, bell pepper, tomatoes, and jalapeño (if using). Spray an oven-safe dish with cooking spray and pour the egg mixture into the dish.

2. Pour the water into the pressure cooker pot and place a trivet inside. Carefully place the oven-safe dish with the egg mixture onto the trivet.

3. Lock the lid in place and seal the steam valve. Select Pressure/Manual and adjust the time to 30 minutes on high pressure. After cooking, let the pressure naturally release for 5 minutes, then quick release any remaining pressure. Carefully remove the lid, trying not to let any water from the inside of the lid fall onto the eggs.

4. Using oven mitts, remove the dish from the pot and place on a heat-resistant surface.

5. Sprinkle the Cheddar cheese and cilantro on top of the dish, then use a silicone spatula to break up the cooked eggs into scrambled egg pieces and mix in the cilantro and cheese. Serve.

PER SERVING (1 cup egg mixture) Calories: 154; Total Fat: 7g; Fiber: 3g; Protein: 12g; Sodium: 321mg; Sugar: 2g

DAIRY-FREE, GLUTEN-FREE, VEGETARIAN, 30 MINUTES OR LESS

Maple-Blueberry Pancake Bites

Serves: 3 to 4 / **Prep Time:** 10 minutes / **Pressure Cook:** 5 minutes on low / **Release:** Natural for 3 minutes, then quick / **Total Time:** 20 minutes

When I say that you can make just about anything in an electric pressure cooker, I mean it. Yes, pancakes are easy to make in a skillet, but with an electric pressure cooker, you can put all the ingredients in it and be done with it. These pancake bites may not look like traditional pancakes, but they have the same great flavor packed in a more compact grab-and-go shape.

1 cup brown rice flour

1 teaspoon baking powder

½ teaspoon ground cinnamon

⅛ teaspoon sea salt

⅔ cup unsweetened almond milk

1 large egg

2 tablespoons pure maple syrup, plus more for serving

1 tablespoon coconut oil, melted and cooled to room temperature

¼ cup fresh blueberries, plus more for serving

Olive oil cooking spray

1 cup water

1. In a large bowl, combine the rice flour, baking powder, cinnamon, and salt and mix together. Add the milk, egg, maple syrup, and coconut oil and stir until everything is just combined. The mixture will be a little lumpy. Gently fold in the blueberries.

2. Spray a silicone egg mold with cooking spray. Place the pancake mixture in the egg mold in equal amounts, filling each about three-quarters full.

3. Cover the egg mold with a paper towel followed by the silicone mat cover (or a piece of aluminum foil wrapped around the tray) to ensure no extra moisture seeps in.

4. Pour the water into the pressure cooker pot and place a trivet inside. Carefully place the covered egg mold onto the trivet.

5. Lock the lid in place and seal the steam valve. Select Pressure/Manual and adjust the time to 5 minutes on low.

CONTINUED ▶

Maple-Blueberry Pancake Bites CONTINUED

6. After cooking, let the pressure release naturally for 3 minutes, then quick release any remaining pressure. Carefully remove the lid, trying to avoid letting any extra water from the lid to drip in.

7. Using oven mitts, remove the egg mold and turn upside down onto a flat plate. If the pancake bites seem stuck, gently push down on the back of the molds.

8. Enjoy warm with additional maple syrup and fresh blueberries.

SUBSTITUTION TIP: You can use a ready-made whole-grain pancake mix. Follow the directions on the package and then follow the steps as listed.

PER SERVING (2 pancake bites) Calories: 309; Total Fat: 8g; Fiber: 3g; Protein: 6g; Sodium: 288mg; Sugar: 11g

DAIRY-FREE, GLUTEN-FREE, NUT-FREE, VEGETARIAN, 30 MINUTES OR LESS

Egg and Sweet Potato Hash

Serves: 5 / **Prep Time:** 10 minutes / **Sauté:** 2 minutes / **Pressure Cook:** 2 minutes high pressure / **Release:** Quick / **Total Time:** 20 minutes

When it came to incorporating more sweet potatoes into my diet, I felt like I was cheating on regular potatoes. However, their unique, slightly sweet flavor is winning me over.

Olive oil cooking spray

1 tablespoon ghee or unsalted butter

2 scallions, both white and green parts, chopped

2 garlic cloves, minced

5 cups shredded sweet potato (about 2 large)

3 cups fresh baby spinach

1 teaspoon sea salt

¼ teaspoon freshly ground black pepper

1 cup water

5 large eggs

1 tablespoon dried parsley

4 or 5 green olives, pitted and sliced

1. Spray an oven-safe dish with cooking spray and set aside. Press the Sauté button and adjust to normal. Add the ghee. Once melted, add the scallions and garlic and sauté and stir for about 1 minute, until the scallions have softened. Add the sweet potato and spinach. Sauté and stir for 1 minute, then add the salt and pepper.

2. Press the Cancel/Off button. Remove the pressure cooker pot, scoop the sweet potato mixture into the prepared dish, and return the pot to the cooker.

3. Pour the water into the pot and place a trivet on the bottom. Place the dish with the sweet potato hash on top of the trivet. Use the back of a spoon to make five wells in the hash. Crack an egg into each well.

4. Lock the lid in place and seal the steam valve. Select Pressure/Manual and adjust the time to 2 minutes on high pressure. After cooking, quick release the pressure. Carefully open the lid, trying to avoid letting any extra water from the lid to drip in.

5. Using oven mitts, remove the dish and sprinkle on the parsley and olives. Scoop out the cooked eggs with the sweet potato hash and serve.

PER SERVING (1 cup hash and 1 egg) Calories: 148; Total Fat: 8g; Fiber: 2g; Protein: 8g; Sodium: 632mg; Sugar: 3g

VEGETARIAN

Maple-Pecan French Toast

Serves: 8 / **Prep Time:** 15 minutes / **Pressure Cook:** 30 minutes high pressure / **Release:** Quick / **Total Time:** 50 minutes

I have an overnight French toast recipe that a friend shared with me that is always a hit whenever we entertain. I decided to adapt the recipe to make it a little healthier and pressure cooker friendly.

FOR THE FRENCH TOAST

6 large eggs
1¼ cups milk
2 tablespoons pure maple syrup
1 teaspoon vanilla extract
1 teaspoon ground cinnamon
¼ teaspoon sea salt
1 (14-ounce) challah bread loaf, cut into 1-inch cubes, not including end pieces

FOR THE MAPLE PECAN BASE

Olive oil cooking spray
4 tablespoons unsalted butter
¼ cup coconut sugar
½ cup chopped pecans
1 tablespoon pure maple syrup
1 cup water

1. **To make the French toast:** In a large bowl, whisk together the eggs, milk, syrup, vanilla, cinnamon, and salt. Add the bread and toss until covered in the egg mixture, then set aside.

2. **To make the maple pecan base:** In a small pot, melt the butter over medium heat, then add the coconut sugar and mix until the sugar has dissolved. Add the pecans and maple syrup and stir well.

3. Spray a baking dish with cooking spray. Transfer the maple-pecan mixture to the prepared dish. Add the egg and bread mixture on top of maple-pecan base and squeeze the bread in tightly. Cover the dish tightly with aluminum foil.

4. Pour the water into the pressure cooker pot, place trivet inside, and carefully place the covered dish on top. Lock the lid in place and seal the steam valve. Select Pressure/Manual and adjust the time to 30 minutes on high pressure.

5. After cooking, quick release the pressure. Carefully remove the lid and set aside. Using oven mitts, remove the pot and set it aside to rest for 10 minutes. Serve warm.

PER SERVING (½ cup) Calories: 339; Total Fat: 16g; Fiber: 2g; Protein: 12g; Sodium: 487mg; Sugar: 12g

DAIRY-FREE, GLUTEN-FREE, NUT-FREE, VEGETARIAN, 30 MINUTES OR LESS

Fajitas Fiesta Eggs

Serves: 5 / **Prep Time:** 10 minutes / **Sauté:** 5 minutes / **Pressure Cook:** 2 minutes high pressure / **Release:** Quick / **Total Time:** 20 minutes

Here's another breakfast recipe based on my love for Mexican flavors—it's something about the combination of cilantro, lime, and jalapeños that gets me every time. This recipe is in the breakfast section, but it's a great option for breakfast, lunch, or dinner.

Olive oil cooking spray
1 tablespoon extra-virgin olive oil
1 cup sliced red onion
½ green bell pepper, sliced
½ yellow bell pepper, sliced
1 red bell pepper, sliced
2 garlic cloves, minced
1 teaspoon chili powder
½ teaspoon dried oregano
½ teaspoon sea salt
1 cup water
5 large eggs

ADD-INS
1 tablespoon chopped fresh cilantro
1 to 2 tablespoons chopped jalapeño
½ lime
1 avocado, sliced

1. Spray an oven-safe dish with cooking spray and set aside.

2. Press the Sauté button and adjust to normal. Pour in the olive oil. Once hot, add the onion, bell peppers, and garlic and sauté until the edges start to brown, about 5 minutes. Add the chili powder, oregano, and salt and mix well. Press the Cancel/Off button.

3. Remove the pressure cooker pot and scoop the vegetable mixture into the prepared dish. Return the pot to the cooker.

4. Pour the water into the pressure cooker pot and place a trivet inside. Place the dish with the fajita mixture on top of the trivet. Gently crack the eggs into the dish as evenly spaced out as possible.

5. Lock the lid in place and seal the steam valve. Select Pressure/Manual and adjust the time to 2 minutes on high pressure.

6. After cooking, quick release the pressure. Carefully remove the lid and set aside.

CONTINUED ▶

Fajitas Fiesta Eggs CONTINUED

7. Using oven mitts, remove the dish. Before serving, sprinkle on the cilantro and jalapeño and squeeze lime juice all around the dish. Serve with the avocado.

HEALTH BOOST: Red bell peppers have a high amount of immune-boosting vitamin C and vitamin A, more so than the other peppers. Add an extra serving in this recipe for an extra boost.

PER SERVING (1 cup fajita mix and 1 egg) Calories: 201; Total Fat: 14g; Fiber: 5g; Protein: 9g; Sodium: 323mg; Sugar: 4g

DAIRY-FREE, GLUTEN-FREE, NUT-FREE, VEGETARIAN, 30 MINUTES OR LESS

Perfectly Boiled Eggs

Serves: 6 / **Prep Time:** 2 minutes / **Pressure Cook:** 7 minutes high pressure / **Release:** Quick / **Total Time:** 15 minutes

I love making boiled eggs in my electric pressure cooker. They're so quick and easy to make and turn out just the way I like them. Cooking them in the steam seems to make them easier to peel as well. Research has now shown that yolks contain essential nutrients for our overall health, so keep eating those yolks, too.

1 cup water

8 to 12 large eggs

1. Pour the water into the pressure cooker pot and place an egg stand, trivet, or steamer basket inside. If using the egg stand, carefully place the eggs in it. If using a trivet or steamer basket, try to leave space between the eggs for even cooking.

2. Lock the lid in place and seal the steam valve. Select Pressure/Manual and adjust the time to 7 minutes on high pressure.

3. After cooking, quick release the pressure. Carefully remove the lid and set aside.

4. Carefully remove the eggs and gently place them into a bowl of cold water with four or five ice cubes. Let the eggs rest for about 1 minute, then remove them from the water. Peel the eggs and serve.

VARIATION TIP: The cook time suggested above is for hard-boiled eggs. For soft-boiled eggs, adjust the time to 4 minutes; for medium-boiled eggs, adjust the time to 5 minutes. Please note that there are many variables involved with cooking boiled eggs—size, freshness, spacing between eggs, and altitude—so give the above timings a try and adjust to meet your preference.

PER SERVING (2 eggs) Calories: 143; Total Fat: 10g; Fiber: 0g; Protein: 13g; Sodium: 142mg; Sugar: 0g

GLUTEN-FREE, NUT-FREE, VEGETARIAN

Breakfast Casserole

Serves: 6 to 8 / **Prep Time:** 15 minutes / **Pressure Cook:** 25 minutes high pressure / **Release:** Natural for 10 minutes, then quick / **Total Time:** 55 minutes

Looking for something *wow* to serve at your next brunch? This breakfast casserole is packed with eggs, vegetables, and hash browns, and is full of healthy nutrients, making it a welcome addition to any table.

Olive oil cooking spray
2 cups frozen shredded hash browns
1 red bell pepper, chopped
1 yellow bell pepper, chopped
1 cup chopped fresh spinach
½ cup chopped red onion
½ cup sliced mushrooms
8 large eggs
¼ cup low-fat milk
1 teaspoon hot sauce (optional)
½ teaspoon sea salt
½ teaspoon freshly ground black pepper
1 cup shredded cheese
1 cup water
1 tablespoon chopped fresh chives

1. Spray a baking dish well with cooking spray.

2. Place the hash browns in the base of the prepared dish and press down lightly. Add the bell peppers, spinach, onion, and mushrooms on top.

3. In a large bowl, whisk together the eggs, milk, hot sauce (if using), salt, and black pepper and pour into the baking dish, stirring gently to combine. Sprinkle the cheese on top. Cover tightly with aluminum foil.

4. Pour the water into the pressure cooker pot, place a trivet inside, and carefully set the baking dish on it.

5. Lock the lid in place and seal the steam valve. Select Pressure/Manual and adjust the time to 25 minutes on high pressure.

6. After cooking, let the pressure release naturally for 10 minutes, then quick release any remaining pressure. Carefully remove the lid and set aside.

7. Using oven mitts, remove the dish. Sprinkle the chives on top and let the dish cool for 10 minutes. Cut into slices and enjoy.

VARIATION TIP: Chopped meats, like bacon, ham, or sausage, can also be added in for an even heartier meal.

PER SERVING (1 cup) Calories: 254; Total Fat: 13g; Fiber: 2g; Protein: 15g; Sodium: 436mg; Sugar: 2g

ALLERGY-FREE, ONE POT, VEGAN, 30 MINUTES OR LESS

Blueberry Chia Jam

Makes: 2 cups / **Prep Time:** 5 minutes / **Pressure Cook:** 6 minutes high pressure / **Release:** Natural for 10 minutes, then quick / **Sauté:** 2 minutes / **Total Time:** 25 minutes

It's amazing how much sugar is packed into jars of store-bought jams, but with a little experimenting, I was able to find a combination of ingredients to make a healthy version of a childhood staple. This jam is naturally sweetened with maple syrup and there's just four ingredients.

4 cups frozen blueberries or berries of choice
¼ cup pure maple syrup
1 tablespoon freshly squeezed lemon juice
¼ cup chia seeds

1. In the pressure cooker pot, combine the blueberries, maple syrup, and lemon juice and stir.

2. Lock the lid in place and seal the steam valve. Select Pressure/Manual and adjust the time to 6 minutes on high pressure.

3. After cooking, let the pressure release naturally for 10 minutes, then quick release any remaining pressure. Carefully remove the lid and set aside.

4. Press the Sauté button and adjust to low. Stir in the chia seeds. Simmer, constantly stirring and breaking up any large pieces of blueberries, for 1 to 2 minutes, until the jam starts to thicken.

5. When the desired consistency has been reached, press the Cancel/Off button. Remove the pot. Allow the jam to cool, then transfer to clean jars.

6. Store sealed jars in the refrigerator for up to 2 weeks or in the freezer for 2 months.

VARIATION TIP: All berries are a great source of antioxidants and are low on the glycemic index. You can use this same recipe with any berry. I love using fresh strawberries when they're in season.

PER SERVING (2 tablespoons) Calories: 51; Total Fat: 1g; Fiber: 2g; Protein: 1g; Sodium: 2mg; Sugar: 7g

DAIRY-FREE, GLUTEN-FREE, VEGAN

Maple-Almond Granola

Serves: 12 / **Prep Time:** 10 minutes / **Slow Cook:** 3 hours / **Total Time:** 3 hours 10 minutes

Nothing beats the taste of homemade granola, especially when you can control what ingredients you add and the amount of sugar. This granola recipe uses the slow cooker function of your pressure cooker and takes more time to make, but the results are worth it.

½ cup coconut oil
½ cup pure maple syrup
1 teaspoon pure vanilla extract
Olive oil cooking spray
4 cups steel-cut oats
1 cup coarsely chopped almonds
½ cup pumpkin seeds
2 tablespoons packed coconut sugar or raw date sugar
1 teaspoon ground cinnamon
¼ teaspoon sea salt
½ cup dried cranberries
¼ cup hemp hearts

1. In a small saucepan, heat the coconut oil, maple syrup, and vanilla over low heat, stirring until melted and combined. Remove from the heat and let cool.

2. Spray the pressure cooker pot with cooking spray. Place the oats, almonds, pumpkin seeds, coconut sugar, cinnamon, and salt in it and mix well.

3. Pour the maple syrup mixture into the pot, mixing until everything is coated.

4. Place the glass lid over the pot to partially cover it, leaving a 3- to 4-inch gap so steam can release during the cook time. This allows the granola to crisp.

5. Press the Slow Cooker button and adjust the time to 3 hours (180 minutes). Allow the granola to slow cook, giving the mixture a quick stir every 30 to 40 minutes.

6. After cooking, press the Cancel/Off button, remove the lid, and stir in the cranberries and hemp hearts. Transfer the granola to a baking sheet and allow to cool completely.

7. Once cooled, store in an airtight container at room temperature for up to 2 weeks.

PER SERVING (½ cup) Calories: 264; Total Fat: 12g; Fiber: 5g; Protein: 7g; Sodium: 36mg; Sugar: 8g

Honey-Garlic Brussels Sprouts, page 50

CHAPTER FOUR

Sides and Snacks

Baba Ganoush **44**

Beet Hummus **46**

Saucy Garden-Fresh Salsa **48**

Cauli-Queso Dip **49**

Honey-Garlic Brussels Sprouts **50**

Root Vegetable Medley **51**

Parmesan Spaghetti Squash **52**

Lemony Green Beans **53**

Buttery Mashed Potatoes **54**

Coconut-Lime Quinoa **55**

Baked Sweet Potatoes **56**

Chili-Lime Brown Rice **57**

Cauliflower Fried Rice **58**

Creamy Mashed Cauliflower **59**

Spiced Roasted Cauliflower Head **60**

ALLERGY-FREE, VEGAN

Baba Ganoush

Serves: 8 / **Prep Time:** 5 minutes / **Steam:** 16 minutes / **Release:** Natural for 10 minutes, then quick / **Total Time:** 35 minutes

Baba ganoush is a Middle Eastern dip that has always been a favorite of mine. I used to love dipping warm naan pieces into it, but since going gluten-free, I have been enjoying it with crunchy gluten-free crackers and raw vegetables, which is just as delicious and satisfying.

1 medium eggplant

1 cup water

⅓ cup freshly squeezed lemon juice

¼ cup extra-virgin olive oil

¼ cup tahini (100-percent sesame)

2 garlic cloves, minced

½ teaspoon sea salt

1. Poke a hole lengthwise through the eggplant. This will allow the steam to be released from inside.

2. Pour the water into the pressure cooker pot and place a trivet inside. Place the whole eggplant on the trivet.

3. Lock the lid in place and seal the steam valve. Press the Steam button and adjust the time to 16 minutes.

4. After cooking, let the pressure release naturally for 10 minutes, then quick release any remaining pressure. Carefully remove the lid and set aside.

5. Remove the trivet and eggplant and carefully transfer the cooked eggplant to a cutting board. Let rest while you rinse out the pot and place it on the counter.

6. Cut the eggplant lengthwise and scoop out the insides, leaving the skin layer, and add the flesh back into the pot along with the lemon juice, olive oil, tahini, garlic, and salt.

7. Using a hand blender, blend until smooth. Taste for seasonings and add more as needed. Transfer to a serving dish and let cool.

8. Cover the baba ganoush and store in the refrigerator for up to 1 week. The flavors deepen over time. Let the baba ganoush to sit at least 2 hours at room temperature before serving.

HEALTH BOOST: For more fiber, potassium, and a nutrient boost, leave the skin of the eggplant on before blending. The result will be a darker version, but it will still be full of delicious flavor.

PER SERVING (¼ cup) Calories: 125; Total Fat: 11g; Fiber: 3g; Protein: 2g; Sodium: 10mg; Sugar: 3g

ALLERGY-FREE, VEGAN

Beet Hummus

Serves: 8 / **Prep Time:** 10 minutes, plus 10 hours to soak the chickpeas / **Pressure Cook:** 18 minutes high pressure / **Release:** Natural for 10 minutes, then quick / **Total Time:** 10 hours 40 minutes

Hummus is a popular Middle Eastern dip and a great addition to any weight loss plan. It contains a variety of vitamins and nutrients and is a good source of plant-based protein, a great option for anyone following a vegan diet. There are a lot of ready-made varieties on the market, which is beneficial if you are rushed for time, but by taking the time to make your own at home, you have control of what's being included.

½ cup dried chickpeas

1 teaspoon sea salt, divided

1 cup water

2 medium beets, peeled and quartered

¼ cup tahini (100-percent sesame)

¼ cup extra-virgin olive oil

¼ cup freshly squeezed lemon juice

1 or 2 garlic cloves, minced

1. In a large bowl, soak the chickpeas in enough water to cover them with ½ teaspoon of salt for 8 to 10 hours.

2. Drain and rinse the soaked chickpeas well and transfer them to the pressure cooker pot. Pour the 1 cup of water into the pressure cooker pot, place a trivet in the pot around the chickpeas, and place a steamer basket on the trivet. (If your steamer basket has a built-in stand, skip the trivet.)

3. Place the beets into the steamer basket.

4. Lock the lid in place and seal the steam valve. Select Pressure/Manual and adjust the time to 18 minutes on high pressure.

5. After cooking, let the pressure release naturally for 10 minutes, then quick release any remaining pressure. Carefully remove the lid and set aside.

6. Remove the steamer basket and set aside. Place a strainer in the sink, remove the pot, and drain the chickpeas in the strainer. Rinse well with cool water.

7. Transfer the beets and chickpeas back to the pot, along with the tahini, olive oil, lemon juice, garlic, and the remaining ½ teaspoon of salt. Using a hand blender, blend until well combined and smooth.

8. Taste the hummus for seasonings and add more as needed. Transfer to a glass dish and let cool.

9. Cover the hummus and store in the refrigerator for up to 1 week. The flavors deepen over time. Let the hummus sit at least 2 hours at room temperature before serving.

VARIATION TIP: For a basic hummus recipe, skip the addition of beets and follow the above recipe and directions.

PER SERVING (¼ cup) Calories: 163; Total Fat: 12g; Fiber: 3g; Protein: 4g; Sodium: 173mg; Sugar: 3g

ALLERGY-FREE, ONE POT, VEGAN

Saucy Garden-Fresh Salsa

Makes: 4 cups / **Prep Time:** 15 minutes / **Pressure Cook:** 10 minutes high pressure / **Release:** Natural for 10 minutes, then quick / **Total Time:** 40 minutes

Move over store-bought salsa, here is a quick-and-easy recipe that's full of vegetables and flavor. One of the issues with ready-made foods is that some of the ingredients that are added are not good for us. Sometimes we need the convenience of grabbing something quick, and there are some good options available—just be sure to read the labels of anything you buy.

2 cups chopped peeled and seeded tomatoes
½ green bell pepper, chopped
½ red bell pepper, chopped
1 medium onion, chopped
6 tablespoons tomato paste
2 or 3 jalapeño peppers, chopped (leave seeds in for more heat)
2 garlic cloves, minced
1 tablespoon apple cider vinegar or white vinegar
1 teaspoon sea salt
½ teaspoon ground cumin
½ teaspoon freshly ground black pepper

ADD-INS
¼ cup chopped fresh cilantro
Juice of 1 lime

1. In the pressure cooker pot, combine all the ingredients except for the add-ins.

2. Lock the lid in place and seal the steam valve. Select Pressure/Manual and adjust the time to 10 minutes on high pressure.

3. After cooking, let the pressure release naturally for 10 minutes, then quick release any remaining pressure. Carefully remove the lid and set aside.

4. Stir in the cilantro and lime. Allow the salsa to cool before transferring into jars. Once cooled, seal tightly. Extra salsa can be stored in the refrigerator for up to 7 days or in the freezer for up to 2 months.

VARIATION TIP: This recipe makes a mild/medium spice salsa. If you prefer a spicier version, increase the number of jalapeños and amount of cayenne pepper.

PER SERVING (¼ cup) Calories: 16; Total Fat: 0g; Fiber: 1g; Protein: 1g; Sodium: 156mg; Sugar: 2g

GLUTEN-FREE, ONE POT, VEGETARIAN, 30 MINUTES OR LESS

Cauli-Queso Dip

Serves: 6 / **Prep Time:** 10 minutes / **Pressure Cook:** 5 minutes high pressure / **Release:** Quick / **Total Time:** 20 minutes

Following a healthy weight loss meal plan does not mean you have to give up on your favorite foods. You just need to get a little creative and know what ingredients make a healthy substitute. Finding healthier alternatives for your favorite foods—like creamy queso—is helpful for staying on track of your long-term health goals. Serve this dip with tortilla chips or raw vegetables.

2 cups cauliflower florets
1 cup low-sodium vegetable broth
½ cup chopped carrots
¼ cup raw cashews
½ cup shredded Parmesan cheese
1 or 2 jalapeños, chopped (leave seeds in for more heat)
3 garlic cloves, minced
½ tablespoon apple cider vinegar
1 teaspoon sea salt
1 teaspoon smoked paprika
½ teaspoon ground turmeric

ADD-INS
½ small red onion, chopped (optional)
¼ cup chopped fresh cilantro leaves (optional)

1. In the pressure cooker pot, combine the cauliflower, broth, carrots, and cashews.
2. Lock the lid in place and seal the steam valve. Select Pressure/Manual and adjust the time to 5 minutes on high pressure.
3. After cooking, quick release the pressure. Carefully remove the lid and set aside. Remove the pot and place on a heat-resistant surface.
4. Add the Parmesan cheese, jalapeños, garlic, vinegar, salt, paprika, and turmeric. Using a hand blender, pulse the ingredients until smooth and creamy.
5. Stir in the red onion, and cilantro (if using) for a chunky queso or leave as is for a creamy option. Serve warm.

HEALTH BOOST: For a vegan and more nutritious option, substitute nutritional yeast for Parmesan cheese, and reduce the amount added to ¼ cup.

PER SERVING (¼ cup) Calories: 90; Total Fat: 5g; Fiber: 2g; Protein: 5g; Sodium: 557mg; Sugar: 2g

ALLERGY-FREE, VEGETARIAN, 30 MINUTES OR LESS

Honey-Garlic Brussels Sprouts

Serves: 6 / **Prep Time:** 5 minutes / **Sauté:** 2 minutes / **Pressure Cook:** 1 minute high pressure/ **Release:** Quick / **Total Time:** 10 minutes

When my kids were little, they used to refer to Brussels sprouts as shrunken alien heads. As much as I wanted to get my kids to love eating this nutritious vegetable, they always gave me a hard time. That is, until I added a magic ingredient—honey.

1 tablespoon avocado oil or oil of choice
3 cups halved Brussels sprouts
½ cup low-sodium vegetable broth
3 to 4 garlic cloves, minced
2 tablespoons honey
½ teaspoon sea salt
½ teaspoon freshly ground black pepper

ADD-INS
2 tablespoons freshly squeezed lemon juice

1. Press the Sauté button and adjust to normal. Pour in the avocado oil. Once hot, add the Brussels sprouts and sear for about 1 minute, until browned. Gently stir and turn the Brussels sprouts over to sear on the other side, about 1 minute.

2. In a medium bowl, whisk together the broth, garlic, honey, salt, and pepper. Pour the broth mixture into the pot, and stir to deglaze the pot, scraping up any brown bits. Press the Cancel/Off button.

3. Lock the lid in place and seal the steam valve. Select Pressure/Manual and adjust the time to 1 minute on high pressure.

4. After cooking, quick release the pressure. Carefully remove the lid and set aside.

5. Remove the pot and transfer to a heat-resistant surface. Drizzle the lemon juice over the Brussels sprouts and serve.

VARIATION TIP: Try lemon garlic Brussels sprouts by skipping the honey and increasing the lemon juice to 2 tablespoons. Then follow the steps as listed.

PER SERVING (½ cup) Calories: 78; Total Fat: 3g; Fiber: 2g; Protein: 3g; Sodium: 212mg; Sugar: 7g

ALLERGY-FREE, ONE POT, VEGAN

Root Vegetable Medley

Serves: 6 / **Prep Time:** 10 minutes / **Sauté:** 5 minutes / **Pressure Cook:** 5 minutes high pressure / **Release:** Natural for 10 minutes, then quick / **Total Time:** 35 minutes

I love prepping a big pot of vegetables at the beginning of the week for my meal prep. Then, depending on what we're having for dinner, I always have some vegetables ready to add as a side. Remember that when you're trying to eat healthier your plate should be at least half-filled with vegetables. With a little prep, it's easy to do.

- 2 tablespoons extra-virgin olive oil
- 1 small red onion, chopped
- 3 garlic cloves, minced
- 1 cup ½-inch peeled carrot rounds
- 1 cup ½-inch peeled parsnips rounds
- 2 cups quartered Yukon gold potatoes
- 2 cups sweet potato pieces (cut to match the potato quarters)
- 1 cup low-sodium vegetable broth
- 1 teaspoon dried rosemary
- 1 teaspoon dried thyme
- 1 teaspoon sea salt
- ½ teaspoon freshly ground black pepper

ADD-INS

- ½ cup chopped fresh parsley
- Juice of ½ lemon

1. Press the Sauté button and adjust to normal. Pour in the olive oil. Once hot, add the onion and garlic and sauté for 1 minute, until the onion starts to soften. Add the carrots and parsnips and sauté for another 1 to 2 minutes. Add the potatoes and sweet potatoes and sauté for 2 minutes. Add the vegetable broth, rosemary, thyme, salt, and pepper. Stir the vegetables together. Press the Cancel/Off button.

2. Lock the lid in place and seal the steam valve. Select Pressure/Manual and adjust the time to 5 minutes on high pressure.

3. After cooking, let the pressure release naturally for 10 minutes, then quick release any remaining pressure. Carefully remove the lid and set aside.

4. Gently stir the root vegetables together and sprinkle the parsley and lemon juice on top before serving.

SUBSTITUTION TIP: This recipe can be made with just potatoes and carrots to keep it simple but just as satisfying.

PER SERVING (1 cup) Calories: 180; Total Fat: 6g; Fiber: 5g; Protein: 5g; Sodium: 450mg; Sugar: 5g

GLUTEN-FREE, NUT-FREE, ONE POT, VEGETARIAN, 30 MINUTES OR LESS

Parmesan Spaghetti Squash

Serves: 6 / **Prep Time:** 10 minutes / **Pressure Cook:** 7 minutes high pressure / **Release:** Quick / **Sauté:** 2 minutes / **Total Time:** 25 minutes

Spaghetti squash is a great low-carbohydrate, low-calorie substitute for regular spaghetti. With its mild flavor, it can be used in a variety of recipes, and it can be ready in about 25 minutes with an electric pressure cooker.

1 cup water
1 large spaghetti squash, halved lengthwise and seeded
3 tablespoons unsalted butter
3 garlic cloves, minced
½ teaspoon sea salt
¼ teaspoon freshly ground black pepper

ADD-INS
½ cup shaved Parmesan cheese
¼ cup chopped fresh basil

1. Pour the water into the pressure cooker pot. Place a trivet inside and arrange the spaghetti squash, cut-side up, inside.

2. Lock the lid in place and seal the steam valve. Select Pressure/Manual and adjust the time to 7 minutes on high pressure.

3. After cooking, quick release any remaining pressure. Carefully remove the lid and set aside.

4. Remove the spaghetti squash halves and place on a flat surface. Using a fork, gently scrape the sides of the squash to make spaghetti-like strands. Once the shell has been scraped clean, set the halves aside.

5. Remove the pot and rinse and dry it before placing it back into the base.

6. Press the Sauté button and adjust to normal. Stir in the butter. Once melted, add the garlic and sauté for 1 to 2 minutes, then add salt and pepper to taste. Add the cooked spaghetti squash and gently toss until coated with butter. Press the Cancel/Off button.

7. Add the Parmesan cheese and basil, toss lightly, and serve warm.

PER SERVING (½ cup) Calories: 119; Total Fat: 9g; Fiber: 2g; Protein: 3g; Sodium: 407mg; Sugar: 3g

ALLERGY-FREE, ONE POT, VEGAN, 30 MINUTES OR LESS

Lemony Green Beans

Serves: 6 / **Prep Time:** 5 minutes / **Pressure Cook:** 0 minutes high pressure / **Release:** Quick / **Total Time:** 10 minutes

I love adding vegetable sides to our meals, and I'm always on the lookout for something that's quick and easy to make. These greens beans are it. As a bonus, they can be seasoned in a variety of ways, making them a great side to any meal.

1 cup water

2 cups green beans, trimmed

ADD-INS

Juice of ½ lemon

1 teaspoon extra-virgin olive oil

½ teaspoon sea salt

¼ teaspoon freshly ground black pepper

1. Pour the water into the pressure cooker pot. Place the green beans in a steamer basket and set the steamer basket in the pot.

2. Lock the lid in place and seal the steam valve. Select Pressure/Manual and adjust the time to 0 minutes on high pressure.

3. After cooking, quick release the pressure. Carefully remove the lid and set aside. Remove the steamer basket and transfer the green beans to a serving dish. Add the lemon juice, olive oil, salt, and pepper, tossing to coat. Serve warm.

VARIATION TIP: A cook time of 0 minutes results in tender-crisp green beans. Set the cook time to 1 minute for softer beans.

PER SERVING (¼ cup) Calories: 18; Total Fat: 1g; Fiber: 1g; Protein: 1g; Sodium: 196mg; Sugar: 1g

GLUTEN-FREE, NUT-FREE, ONE POT, VEGETARIAN, 30 MINUTES OR LESS

Buttery Mashed Potatoes

Serves: 6 / **Prep Time:** 10 minutes / **Pressure Cook:** 10 minutes high pressure / **Release:** Quick / **Total Time:** 25 minutes

Mashed potatoes may be my least favorite way to enjoy potatoes, but when slathered in butter, who wouldn't enjoy this comforting side dish? This version of mashed potatoes may not be the healthiest side dish recipe in this cookbook, but it may be the most comforting. And we all need some good comfort food every now and then.

5 to 6 russet potatoes, peeled and quartered

½ cup water

1 teaspoon sea salt, plus more as needed

½ cup milk, plus more as needed

4 tablespoons unsalted butter

1 teaspoon garlic powder

½ teaspoon freshly ground black pepper

ADD-INS

1 tablespoon chopped fresh chives

1. In the pressure cooker pot, combine the potatoes, water, and salt.

2. Lock the lid in place and seal the steam valve. Select Pressure/Manual and adjust the time to 10 minutes on high pressure.

3. After cooking, quick release the pressure. Carefully remove the lid and set aside.

4. Remove the pot and place it on a heat-resistant surface. Add the milk, butter, garlic powder, and pepper. Use a silicone or plastic potato masher to mash the potatoes. Add more milk as needed, 1 tablespoon at a time. Taste the potatoes and add more salt as needed.

5. Sprinkle with the chives and serve warm.

HEALTH BOOST: For a healthier option that's higher in antioxidants and nutrients, use sweet potatoes in place of russet potatoes.

PER SERVING (½ cup) Calories: 319; Total Fat: 9g; Fiber: 7g; Protein: 7g; Sodium: 476mg; Sugar: 3g

ALLERGY-FREE, ONE POT, VEGAN, 30 MINUTES OR LESS

Coconut-Lime Quinoa

Serves: 6 / **Prep Time:** 5 minutes / **Pressure Cook:** 2 minutes high pressure / **Release:** Natural for 10 minutes, then quick / **Total Time:** 20 minutes

This recipe has become one of my favorites recently. The flavor combination is so tasty, and it's so easy to make. This is a great recipe to double up and use for meal prep, and it freezes well. I usually make it as a side dish, add some to my lettuce wraps, or use it as a grain base for my salad bowls.

1 (13.5-ounce) can full-fat coconut milk
1 cup quinoa, rinsed
¼ cup water
1 teaspoon sea salt

ADD-INS
¼ cup chopped fresh cilantro leaves
¼ cup finely chopped jalapeños (optional)
Grated zest and juice of 1 small lime

1. In the pressure cooker pot, combine the coconut milk, quinoa, water, and salt.

2. Lock the lid in place and seal the steam valve. Select Pressure/Manual and adjust the time to 2 minutes on high pressure.

3. After cooking, let the pressure release naturally for 10 minutes, then quick release any remaining pressure. Carefully remove the lid and set aside.

4. Add the cilantro, jalapeños (if using), lime zest, and lime juice to the pot and use a fork to gently fluff the quinoa and mix ingredients. Serve warm.

VARIATION TIP: Enjoy this quinoa recipe warm as a side dish or cool the cooked quinoa and add it to a salad bowl as a meal of its own.

PER SERVING (½ cup) Calories: 231; Total Fat: 15g; Fiber: 2g; Protein: 5g; Sodium: 398mg; Sugar: 0g

ALLERGY-FREE, VEGAN

Baked Sweet Potatoes

Serves: 8 / **Prep Time:** 5 minutes / **Pressure Cook:** 15 minutes high pressure / **Release:** Natural for 10 minutes, then quick / **Total Time:** 35 minutes

Sweet potatoes are a starchy root vegetable that have a sweet flavor profile and are high in fiber and antioxidants, making them good for gut health. Sweet potatoes come in a variety of sizes and colors and can be a beneficial part of any weight loss plan—I know I have loved adding it into my own.

1 cup water

4 medium sweet potatoes

1. Pour the water into the pressure cooker pot. Place a steamer basket inside the pot and arrange the sweet potatoes inside.
2. Lock the lid in place and seal the steam valve. Select Pressure/Manual and adjust the time to 15 minutes on high pressure.
3. After cooking, let the pressure release naturally for 10 minutes, then quick release any remaining pressure. Carefully remove the lid and set aside.
4. Carefully remove the sweet potatoes and slice open lengthwise. Enjoy as a side or add your favorite toppings and make them into a meal.

VARIATION TIP: You can use this recipe to make regular baked potatoes: substitute four medium russet potatoes for the sweet potatoes.

PER SERVING (½ sweet potato) Calories: 56; Total Fat: 0g; Fiber: 2g; Protein: 1g; Sodium: 36mg; Sugar: 3g

ALLERGY-FREE, ONE POT, VEGAN

Chili-Lime Brown Rice

Serves: 12 / **Prep Time:** 5 minutes / **Pressure Cook:** 22 minutes high pressure / **Release:** Natural for 10 minutes, then quick / **Total Time:** 40 minutes

Brown rice has become a staple in our house, and everyone seems to enjoy eating it. In fact, when I first introduced it to the family, my daughter would refer to it as the "yummy, nutty rice," which was a description I loved hearing. There are a few brown rice varieties available, but I find that the basmati or long-grain versions cook and taste the best.

2 cups brown basmati rice, rinsed

2½ cups water

1 tablespoon extra-virgin olive oil

1 teaspoon sea salt

1 teaspoon chili powder

½ teaspoon ground cumin

ADD-INS

¼ cup chopped fresh cilantro leaves

Grated zest and juice of 1 small lime

1. In the pressure cooker pot, combine the rice, water, olive oil, salt, chili powder, and cumin.

2. Lock the lid in place and seal the steam valve. Select Pressure/Manual and adjust the time to 22 minutes on high pressure.

3. After cooking, let the pressure release naturally for 10 minutes, then quick release any remaining pressure. Carefully remove the lid and set aside.

4. Add the cilantro, lime zest, and lime juice to the pot and use a fork to gently stir and fluff the rice.

5. Serve warm as a side dish or use it in burritos or salad bowls.

VARIATION TIP: Adding the olive oil to the rice is optional, but I find that adding a little oil to the rice water before cooking helps keep the rice from clumping together.

PER SERVING (½ cup) Calories: 126; Total Fat: 2g; Fiber: 1g; Protein: 2g; Sodium: 203mg; Sugar: 1g

SIDES AND SNACKS

DAIRY-FREE, GLUTEN-FREE, NUT-FREE, ONE-POT, VEGETARIAN, 30 MINUTES OR LESS

Cauliflower Fried Rice

Serves: 6 / **Prep Time:** 10 minutes / **Sauté:** 8 minutes / **Pressure Cook:** 1 minute high pressure / **Release:** Quick / **Total Time:** 25 minutes

Cauliflower works great as a low-carb substitute for rice. Its mild flavor profile and riced texture makes it hard to tell the difference when used in recipes such as this fried "rice." Next time you start craving fried rice, give this healthy modified version a try.

- 2 tablespoons extra-virgin olive oil, divided
- ¼ cup chopped onion
- 2 garlic cloves, minced
- ½ cup frozen peas and carrots blend
- 2 cups riced cauliflower
- ¼ cup coconut aminos or low-sodium soy sauce
- 1 teaspoon sea salt
- ½ teaspoon freshly ground black pepper
- 2 large eggs, beaten
- 1 teaspoon toasted sesame oil
- Juice of ½ lime
- 1 scallion, both white and green parts, chopped

1. Press the Sauté button and adjust to high. Pour in 1½ tablespoons of olive oil. Once hot, add the onion and garlic and sauté for 1 to 2 minutes. Add the peas and carrots and sauté for 2 minutes, then add the cauliflower and continue to sauté for 1 minute. Stir in the coconut aminos, salt, and pepper. Press the Cancel/Off button.

2. Lock the lid in place and seal the steam valve. Select Pressure/Manual and adjust the time to 1 minute on high pressure. After cooking, quick release the pressure. Carefully remove the lid and set aside.

3. Press the Sauté button and adjust to normal. Gently stir and push the contents to the edges of the pot, leaving the center empty. Add the remaining ½ tablespoon of olive oil to the center, then add the eggs. Let the eggs rest for a few seconds until they start to solidify, then use a spatula to break up the egg into small pieces. Gently mix the eggs into the rest of the cauliflower mixture until combined.

4. Press the Cancel/Off button. Gently stir in the sesame oil and lime juice. Top with the scallion and serve.

PER SERVING (½ cup) Calories: 97; Total Fat: 7g; Fiber: 1g; Protein: 4g; Sodium: 815mg; Sugar: 1g

GLUTEN-FREE, NUT-FREE, VEGETARIAN, 30 MINUTES OR LESS

Creamy Mashed Cauliflower

Serves: 6 / **Prep Time:** 5 minutes / **Pressure Cook:** 3 minutes high pressure / **Release:** 5 minutes, then quick / **Total Time:** 15 minutes

If you're craving mashed potatoes, try this low-carb, low-calorie option—it's so creamy and flavorful, you'll hardly be able to tell the difference. To get my family used to the texture difference, I half the amount of cauliflower and substituted chopped potatoes for the other half. I increased the amount of cauliflower every time I made it.

1 cup water

1 large cauliflower head, cut into florets

1 tablespoon unsalted butter

¼ cup milk, plus more as needed

1 teaspoon sea salt

¼ teaspoon freshly ground black pepper

½ teaspoon garlic powder

ADD-INS

⅓ cup freshly grated Parmesan cheese

1 tablespoon chopped fresh chives or parsley

1. Pour the water into the pressure cooker pot. Place the cauliflower in a steamer basket and place it inside the pot.

2. Lock the lid in place and seal the steam valve. Select Pressure/Manual and adjust the time to 3 minutes on high pressure.

3. After cooking, let the pressure release naturally for 5 minutes, then quick release any remaining pressure. Carefully remove the lid and set aside. Remove the steamer basket and set aside.

4. Remove the pot, rinse, and place on a flat surface. Place the cooked cauliflower, butter, milk, salt, pepper, and garlic powder in the pot and, using a potato masher, mash the cauliflower until smooth, adding more milk, 1 tablespoon at a time, as needed. Once the desired consistency is reached, stir in the Parmesan cheese until melted. Top with the chives and serve.

HEALTH BOOST: To make this vegan, use an unsweetened nut milk; and nutritional yeast instead of Parmesan cheese—reduce amount to 3 tablespoons.

PER SERVING (½ cup) Calories: 75; Total Fat: 3g; Fiber: 3g; Protein: 5g; Sodium: 467mg; Sugar: 3g

SIDES AND SNACKS

ALLERGY-FREE, VEGAN, 30 MINUTES OR LESS

Spiced Roasted Cauliflower Head

Serves: 6 / **Prep Time:** 5 minutes / **Pressure Cook:** 1 minute high pressure/
Release: Quick / **Total Time:** 10 minutes

Move over, roasted chicken, we're serving up a roasted cauliflower head. For vegans, this variation of cauliflower can be a satisfying replacement for roasted chicken or beef. Just add your favorite seasonings and gravy, and you'll be good to go.

½ cup tahini (100-percent sesame)
2 tablespoons extra-virgin olive oil
Juice of ½ lime
2 garlic cloves, minced
1 teaspoon sea salt
1 teaspoon chili powder
½ teaspoon dried oregano
¼ teaspoon ground cumin
1 large cauliflower head, stalk trimmed flat and leaves removed
1 cup water

ADD-INS
Grated zest of ½ lime
2 tablespoons chopped fresh cilantro leaves

1. In a medium bowl, combine the tahini, olive oil, lime juice, garlic, salt, chili powder, oregano, and cumin, mixing well.

2. Place the cauliflower inside a steamer basket. Using a silicone brush or your hands, cover the cauliflower head with the spiced tahini, being sure to get between the florets.

3. Pour the water into the pressure cooker pot. Carefully place the steamer basket with the cauliflower head into the pot. Lock the lid in place and seal the steam valve. Select Pressure/Manual and adjust the time to 1 minute on high pressure (or 2 minutes for a softer texture).

4. After cooking, quick release the pressure. Carefully remove the lid and set aside. Remove the steamer basket.

5. Sprinkle the lime zest and cilantro on top of the cauliflower. Let the cauliflower rest for 2 to 3 minutes, then slice and serve.

VARIATION TIP: If you like your cauliflower head crispy, place the cooked head on a baking sheet and broil it for 2 to 3 minutes before the add-ins.

PER SERVING Calories: 199; Total Fat: 16g; Fiber: 5g; Protein: 6g; Sodium: 435mg; Sugar: 3g

Beet and Feta Salad, page 71

CHAPTER FIVE

Sandwiches and Bowls

Honey-Garlic Chicken Lettuce Wraps **64**

Tangy Potato Salad **65**

Two-Bean Rice Bowl **67**

Steak Fajita Wraps **69**

Beet and Feta Salad **71**

Greek Chicken Salad Lettuce Wraps **72**

Mexican Black Bean and Quinoa Bowl **73**

Mediterranean Chickpea Bowl **74**

Tex-Mex Chicken Salad Bowl **75**

Spicy Black Bean and Rice Salad **76**

Mediterranean Chicken Shawarma **77**

Avocado Egg Salad **79**

Sweet Potato Quinoa Salad **80**

Tex-Mex Lentil Bowl **81**

Shredded Beef Lettuce Cups **82**

ALLERGY-FREE, 30 MINUTES OR LESS

Honey-Garlic Chicken Lettuce Wraps

Serves: 6 / **Prep Time:** 5 minutes / **Pressure Cook:** 10 minutes high pressure /
Release: 10 minutes, then quick / **Sauté:** 2 minutes / **Total Time:** 30 minutes

Since going gluten-free, lettuce wraps have been my favorite substitute for buns and tortilla wraps. Luckily, a lot of restaurants are now offering lettuce wraps as an option, which is great for those of us who enjoy this low-carb, low-calorie option.

2 pounds boneless, skinless chicken breasts

½ cup low-sodium chicken broth

¼ cup low-sodium soy sauce

¼ cup honey

2 tablespoons white vinegar

1 tablespoon minced peeled ginger

2 garlic cloves, minced

1 teaspoon sesame oil

⅛ teaspoon freshly ground black pepper

2 tablespoons water

1 tablespoon cornstarch

12 prepped Bibb lettuce or romaine lettuce leaves

¼ cup chopped scallions

1 tablespoon sesame seeds (optional)

1. In the pressure cooker pot, place the chicken. In a small bowl, whisk together the broth, soy sauce, honey, vinegar, ginger, garlic, sesame oil, and pepper. Pour this mixture over the chicken, using tongs to move chicken around so it is covered with the sauce.

2. Lock the lid in place and seal the steam valve. Select Pressure/Manual and adjust the time to 10 minutes on high pressure. After cooking, let the pressure release naturally for 10 minutes, then quick release any remaining pressure. Carefully remove the lid and set aside. Transfer the cooked chicken to a dish and, using two forks, shred the chicken apart and set aside.

3. Press the Sauté button, adjust to normal, and bring the remaining sauce to a boil. In a small bowl, mix water and cornstarch, then pour this mixture into the pot. Stir until everything is combined and allow to boil for about 1 minute.

4. Press the Cancel/Off button. Add the shredded chicken and mix until the chicken is coated with sauce. Divide the chicken into the lettuce leaves and top with scallions and sesame seeds (if using). Serve.

PER SERVING (¼ cup chicken mixture per lettuce wrap, 2 wraps) Calories: 200; Total Fat: 9g; Fiber: 1g; Protein: 20g; Sodium: 327mg; Sugar: 7g

ALLERGY-FREE, VEGETARIAN

Tangy Potato Salad

Serves: 6 to 8 / **Prep Time:** 20 minutes / **Pressure Cook:** 5 minutes, plus 0 minutes high pressure / **Release:** Quick / **Total Time:** 35 minutes

Whenever I think of potato salad, I think summer and barbecues. They just seem to go hand in hand, probably because creamy potato salads have always been a barbecue staple. Here's a version that's just as delicious but lighter without the creaminess and added fats—and it can be enjoyed year-round.

FOR THE POTATO SALAD

6 to 7 medium potatoes, skins on and scrubbed

3 cups water, divided

1 teaspoon sea salt

1 cup green beans, trimmed and cut into thirds

FOR THE VINAIGRETTE

¼ cup extra-virgin olive oil

¼ cup balsamic vinegar

1 teaspoon whole-grain mustard or Dijon mustard

1 teaspoon honey

1 teaspoon sea salt

1 teaspoon freshly ground black pepper

1. **To make the potato salad:** In the pressure cooker pot, arrange the potatoes, then pour in 2 cups of water and the salt.

2. Lock the lid in place and seal the steam valve. Select Pressure/Manual and adjust the time to 5 minutes on high pressure.

3. After cooking, quick release the pressure. Carefully remove the lid and set aside. Remove the cooked potatoes and set aside to cool. Remove the pot, rinse it clean, then dry it before returning it to the cooker.

4. Pour the remaining 1 cup of water into the pot, add the green beans into the steamer basket, and place the steamer basket in the pot.

5. Lock the lid in place and seal the steam valve. Select Pressure/Manual and adjust the time to 0 minutes on high pressure.

6. After cooking, quick release the pressure. Carefully remove the lid and set aside. Remove the steamer basket with the green beans and set aside to cool.

CONTINUED ▶

Tangy Potato Salad CONTINUED

ADD-INS

1 cup chopped red bell pepper

1 small red onion, chopped

½ cup thawed frozen green peas

⅓ cup chopped dill pickles

⅓ cup chopped fresh parsley

7. **To make the vinaigrette:** In a glass jar, combine all the ingredients, close the lid securely, and shake until combined. Set aside.

8. One the vegetables are cool, cut the potatoes into half rounds, quarters, or cubes.

9. In a large bowl, combine the potatoes, green beans, and all the add-ins. Drizzle the vinaigrette all over and gently toss until all the ingredients are combined. Serve cooled.

VARIATION TIP: Change up the recipe by adding in fresh seasonal vegetables—cucumbers, carrots and grape tomatoes would taste great.

PER SERVING (⅔ cup) Calories: 142; Total Fat: 5g; Fiber: 4g; Protein: 3g; Sodium: 449mg; Sugar: 3g

ALLERGY-FREE, VEGAN

Two-Bean Rice Bowl

Serves: 6 / **Prep Time:** 15 minutes / **Pressure Cook:** 22 minutes high pressure / **Release:** 10 minutes, then quick / **Total Time:** 50 minutes

Canned beans have always been such a convenience. I used to grab a can whenever I had to add them to a recipe, but with an electric pressure cooker, beans are so easy to prepare, now I prep a potful and freeze them until I need to use them. Plus, cooking your own beans is healthier and more economical, and the beans taste better. In this recipe, you can either use precooked beans or canned. You can serve this as is or on a bed of mixed greens.

½ cup dried red kidney beans, optionally soaked 4 to 8 hours and rinsed

½ cup dried chickpeas, optionally soaked 4 to 8 hours and rinsed

4½ cups water, divided

1 cup brown rice, rinsed

1 teaspoon extra-virgin olive oil

½ teaspoon sea salt

ADD-INS

1 cup halved grape tomatoes

1 cup corn kernels, cooked and cooled

½ cup chopped red onion

¼ cups extra-virgin olive oil

¼ cup chopped fresh cilantro leaves

Juice of 2 limes

1. In the pressure cooker pot, combine the beans and chickpeas and 3 cups of water, or enough water to cover them. Place a trivet in the pot and make sure it rests flat on the bottom.

2. In an oven-safe bowl, add the remaining 1½ cups of water, the rice, olive oil, and salt. Cover the dish with aluminum foil or a silicone lid and place it on the trivet.

3. Lock the lid in place and seal the steam valve. Select Pressure/Manual and adjust the time to 22 minutes on high pressure.

4. After cooking, let the pressure release naturally for 10 minutes, then quick release any remaining pressure. Carefully remove the lid and set aside.

5. Using oven mitts, remove the bowl from the pot and fluff the rice with a fork. Remove the pot, drain the beans, then set the cooked rice and beans aside to cool.

CONTINUED ▶

Two-Bean Rice Bowl CONTINUED

2 garlic cloves, minced

1 teaspoon chili powder

1 teaspoon sea salt

½ teaspoon dried oregano

¼ teaspoon ground cumin

6. In a large bowl, combine all the add-ins. Add the cooled beans and rice and stir gently until mixed. Serve cooled.

VARIATION TIP: Soaking the beans is not mandatory when cooking them in an electric pressure cooker, but soaking the beans for at least six hours before cooking can help with digestion, as the indigestible complex sugars that can cause gas are removed.

PER SERVING (¾ cup) Calories: 357; Total Fat: 12g; Fiber: 7g; Protein: 11g; Sodium: 605mg; Sugar: 4g

ALLERGY-FREE, 30 MINUTES OR LESS

Steak Fajita Wraps

Serves: 6 / **Prep Time:** 10 minutes / **Sauté:** 3 minutes / **Pressure Cook:** 5 minutes high pressure / **Release:** 10 minutes, then quick / **Total Time:** 30 minutes

One of my favorite things to prepare in an electric pressure cooker has to be beef. The quality of the beef and/or steak doesn't seem to make a difference; the meat cooks quickly and comes out soft and tender. In fact, the cheaper, fattier cuts of meat cook better under pressure than more expensive cuts. Serve these as is or top with cheese and salsa.

1 (1-pound) flank steak, cut into thin slices
1 tablespoon chili powder
1 teaspoon dried oregano
½ teaspoon ground cumin
1 tablespoon extra-virgin olive oil
1 cup sliced red bell pepper
½ cup sliced green bell pepper
½ cup sliced onion
½ cup low-sodium beef or vegetable broth or water

1. In a large bowl, combine the steak, chili powder, oregano, and cumin. Mix gently until the steak slices are coated.

2. Press the Sauté button and adjust to high. Pour in the olive oil. Once hot, add the steak and sauté until the steak is browned on all sides, about 3 minutes. Press the Cancel/Off button. Add the bell peppers and onion, then pour in the broth.

3. Lock the lid in place and seal the steam valve. Select Pressure/Manual and adjust the time to 5 minutes on high pressure.

4. After cooking, let the pressure release naturally for 10 minutes, then quick release any remaining pressure. Carefully remove the lid and set aside.

CONTINUED ▶

Steak Fajita Wraps CONTINUED

ADD-INS

Juice of 2 limes

2 tablespoons chopped fresh cilantro leaves

12 whole romaine lettuce leaves or whole-grain tortilla wraps

5. Add the lime juice and cilantro, gently stirring to combine.

6. Use a slotted spoon to scoop out the steak mixture and transfer it to the lettuce leaves. Serve.

SUBSTITUTION TIP: To make this recipe even easier, add 1 tablespoon of fajita seasoning blend instead of the chili powder, oregano, garlic, and cumin. Also, a frozen blend of peppers can be used instead of fresh with similar results.

PER SERVING (½ cup per wrap) Calories: 152; Total Fat: 6g; Fiber: 2g; Protein: 18g; Sodium: 133mg; Sugar: 2g

GLUTEN-FREE, NUT-FREE, VEGETARIAN

Beet and Feta Salad

Serves: 6 / **Prep Time:** 10 minutes / **Pressure Cook:** 20 minutes high pressure / **Release:** 5 minutes, then quick / **Total Time:** 40 minutes

Salads don't have to be complicated with a ton of vegetables or boring with the same vegetables. I love the combination of arugula, feta cheese, and balsamic vinegar; they are the base of many of my salads.

FOR THE BEETS

1 cup water

4 medium beets, scrubbed

FOR THE BALSAMIC VINAIGRETTE

3 tablespoons extra-virgin olive oil

3 tablespoons balsamic vinegar

1 tablespoon freshly squeezed lime juice

½ teaspoon Dijon mustard

½ tablespoon honey

¼ teaspoon sea salt

ADD-INS

2 cups fresh baby spinach leaves

2 cups arugula leaves

¼ cup crumbled feta cheese

¼ cup chopped fresh mint leaves

1. **To make the beets:** Pour the water into the pressure cooker pot. Place a steamer basket inside and set the beets in the basket.

2. Lock the lid in place and seal the steam valve. Select Pressure/Manual and adjust the time to 20 minutes on high pressure.

3. After cooking, let the pressure release naturally for 5 minutes, then quick release any remaining pressure. Carefully remove the lid and set aside. Remove the steamer basket and allow the cooked beets to cool for about 10 minutes.

4. **To make the balsamic vinaigrette:** Meanwhile, in a glass jar, combine all the vinaigrette ingredients. Close the lid and shake until combined.

5. When cool enough to handle, gently remove the skin of the beets with a knife. Cut the beets into the desired sizes and set aside to cool.

6. In a large bowl, place the spinach and arugula leaves, then layer on the cooled beets, feta cheese, and mint. Pour the vinaigrette over the salad, tossing gently to combine. Serve.

PER SERVING (1½ cups) Calories: 117; Total Fat: 8g; Fiber: 2g; Protein: 2g; Sodium: 213mg; Sugar: 7g

GLUTEN-FREE, NUT-FREE, 30 MINUTES OR LESS

Greek Chicken Salad Lettuce Wraps

Serves: 6 / **Prep Time:** 10 minutes / **Pressure Cook:** 10 minutes high pressure / **Release:** 5 minutes, then quick / **Total Time:** 30 minutes

Chicken salad sandwiches are a great lunch option and with a few simple modifications, they can still be enjoyed while on a weight loss diet plan. Here is one of my favorite variations of a creamy chicken salad—just add some on top of lettuce leaves for a low-carb, low-calorie sandwich option, or on top of a garden salad and your protein-packed lunch is ready to go.

1 pound boneless, skinless chicken breasts
1 garlic clove, minced
¼ teaspoon sea salt
½ teaspoon dried oregano
½ cup water

ADD-INS
½ cup quartered grape tomatoes
½ cup chopped cucumber
¼ cup sliced pitted Kalamata olives
¼ cup Tzatziki Sauce (page 172)
12 Bibb, Boston, or romaine lettuce leaves
¼ cup crumbled feta cheese (optional)

1. Pat the chicken dry and season with the garlic, salt, and oregano. Transfer the chicken to the pressure cooker pot and add the water.

2. Lock the lid in place and seal the steam valve. Select Pressure/Manual and adjust the time to 10 minutes on high pressure.

3. After cooking, let the pressure release naturally for 5 minutes, then quick release any remaining pressure. Carefully remove the lid and set aside.

4. Transfer the cooked chicken to a plate. Either chop the chicken to bite-size pieces or shred with a fork. Set aside to cool.

5. In a large bowl, toss the tomatoes, cucumbers, olives and cooled chicken. Top with the tzatziki sauce and mix well until combined.

6. Scoop ¼ cup of the salad into each lettuce leaf. Top with the feta cheese (if using) and serve.

PER SERVING (¼ cup per lettuce wrap) Calories: 112; Total Fat: 3g; Fiber: 1g; Protein: 18g; Sodium: 179mg; Sugar: 1g

DAIRY-FREE, GLUTEN-FREE, NUT-FREE, VEGAN, 30 MINUTES OR LESS

Mexican Black Bean and Quinoa Bowl

Serves: 6 to 8 / **Prep Time:** 15 minutes / **Pressure Cook:** 2 minutes high pressure / **Release:** Quick / **Total Time:** 25 minutes

Quinoa salads make a great addition to any healthy eating meal plan, especially a plant-based one. It's a complete source of plant-based protein and rich in fiber, B-vitamins, and other nutrients. By adding beans or lentils to your quinoa salads, you're including more beneficial fiber, which helps stabilize blood sugar levels and keeps you feeling fuller for longer.

2 cups water

1 cup quinoa, rinsed

ADD-INS

1 (15-ounce) can black beans, rinsed

1 red bell pepper, chopped

1 small red onion, chopped

1 cup cooked corn

2 tablespoons chopped fresh cilantro

FOR THE LIME DRESSING

¼ cup freshly squeezed lime juice

2 tablespoons extra-virgin olive oil

½ teaspoon Dijon mustard

1 teaspoon sea salt

1 tablespoon chili powder

½ teaspoon dried oregano

1. In the pressure cooker pot, combine the water and quinoa. Lock the lid in place and seal the steam valve. Select Pressure/Manual and adjust the time to 2 minutes on high pressure.

2. After cooking, quick release the pressure. Carefully remove the lid and set aside. Let the quinoa cool in the pot for about 10 minutes.

3. Remove the pot and place it on a heat-resistant surface. Add all the add-ins to the pot, stirring to combine.

4. **To make the lime dressing:** In a glass jar, combine all the dressing ingredients, close the lid, and shake until combined.

5. Pour the desired amount of dressing in the pot over the other ingredients and toss gently to combine. Serve warm or cold.

VARIATION TIP: This salad is a great meal prep option and can be enjoyed on its own or as a side dish. For a non-vegan option, try serving it with grilled salmon.

PER SERVING (1½ cup) Calories: 275; Total Fat: 8g; Fiber: 9g; Protein: 12g; Sodium: 436mg; Sugar: 4g

GLUTEN-FREE, NUT-FREE, VEGETARIAN

Mediterranean Chickpea Bowl

Serves: 6 / **Prep Time:** 10 minutes, plus 8 hours to soak chickpeas / **Pressure Cook:** 15 minutes high pressure / **Release:** Natural for 10 minutes, then quick / **Total Time:** 8 hours 45 minutes

Of all the various types of beans available, chickpeas are my favorite. They have a mild flavor and can be added into recipes for an extra fiber boost. Adding fiber to meals is important; it helps stabilize blood sugar levels, which helps reduce cravings.

3 cups water
1 cup chickpeas, soaked 6 to 8 hours and rinsed
1 small red onion, chopped
½ cup halved cherry tomatoes
⅔ cup chopped cucumber
⅔ cup chopped red bell pepper
¼ cup quartered black olives
2 tablespoons chopped fresh cilantro leaves
¼ cup feta cheese

LEMON VINAIGRETTE

2 tablespoons extra-virgin olive oil
1 tablespoon apple cider vinegar
Juice of ½ lemon
1 garlic clove, minced
1 teaspoon sea salt
½ teaspoon freshly ground black pepper
½ teaspoon dried oregano

1. In the pressure cooker pot, combine the water and chickpeas.

2. Lock the lid in place and seal the steam valve. Select Pressure/Manual and adjust the time to 15 minutes on high pressure.

3. After cooking, let the pressure release naturally for 10 minutes, then quick release any remaining pressure. Carefully remove the lid and set aside. Remove the pot, drain any remaining water, rinse, and set aside to cool.

4. Meanwhile, in a large bowl, combine all the add-ins and toss gently to combine. Add the cooled chickpeas and toss to combine.

5. **To make the lemon vinaigrette:** In a glass jar, combine all the vinaigrette ingredients, close the lid, and shake until combined. Pour the dressing over the chickpea salad and toss gently until combined. Serve.

SHORTCUT: If you can't soak the chickpeas overnight, rinse the dried chickpeas, add them to the pot with 3 cups of water, and set the cook time to 35 minutes.

PER SERVING (1 cup) Calories: 202; Total Fat: 8g; Fiber: 5g; Protein: 8g; Sodium: 497mg; Sugar: 5g

ALLERGY-FREE, 30 MINUTES OR LESS

Tex-Mex Chicken Salad Bowl

Serves: 6 to 8 / **Prep Time:** 10 minutes / **Pressure Cook:** 10 minutes high pressure / **Release:** Natural for 5 minutes, then quick / **Sauté:** 2 minutes / **Total Time:** 30 minutes

This chicken recipe is a favorite in our household. It's one of our go-to "what's for dinner?" recipes. There are so many ways to incorporate this easy chicken recipe into your favorite Mexican-inspired meals. Serve this as is or top with shredded cheese, plain Greek yogurt, and salsa.

½ cup water

4 boneless, skinless chicken breasts

¼ cup tomato sauce

½ onion, sliced

1 tablespoon chili powder

1 garlic clove, minced

1 teaspoon dried oregano

1 teaspoon sea salt

½ teaspoon ground cumin

1 (15-ounce) can black beans, rinsed

1 cup corn kernels

ADD-INS

Juice of 1 lime

2 tablespoons chopped fresh cilantro

1 to 2 tablespoons chopped jalapeño

4 cups mixed lettuce greens

1 cup chopped raw vegetables of choice

1. Pour the water into the pressure cooker pot. Place the chicken inside the pot, avoiding any overlapping.

2. Add the tomato sauce, onion, chili powder, garlic, oregano, salt, and cumin. Using tongs, move and flip the chicken until all sides are coated.

3. Lock the lid in place and seal the steam valve. Select Pressure/Manual and adjust the time to 10 minutes on high pressure.

4. After cooking, let the pressure release naturally for 5 minutes, then quick release any remaining pressure. Carefully remove the lid and set aside. Using tongs, transfer the chicken to a plate, then shred it with two forks.

5. Press the Sauté button and adjust to normal. Stir in the beans and corn and simmer gently for 2 minutes. Add the shredded chicken back into the pot and stir. Press the Cancel/Off button and stir in the lime juice, cilantro, and jalapeño.

6. Fill serving bowls with the mixed lettuce greens and vegetables. Add ½ cup of the chicken mixture to each bowl and serve.

PER SERVING (½ cup) Calories: 188; Total Fat: 3g; Fiber: 6g; Protein: 23g; Sodium: 420mg; Sugar: 2g

ALLERGY-FREE, VEGETARIAN

Spicy Black Bean and Rice Salad

Serves: 6 to 8 / **Prep Time:** 15 minutes / **Pressure Cook:** 10 minutes high pressure / **Release:** Natural for 5 minutes, then quick / **Total Time:** 35 minutes

I chose white rice for this recipe because I wanted to cook the rice at the same time as the black beans, following a pot-in-pot method. Serve as is or with chopped avocado on a bed of mixed greens for a nutrient boost.

4 cups water, divided
1 cup black beans, soaked 5 hours and rinsed
1 cup white rice, rinsed
1 teaspoon extra-virgin olive oil
½ teaspoon sea salt
1 small red onion, chopped
½ cup chopped grape tomatoes
½ cup corn kernels
½ red bell pepper, chopped

SPICY LIME VINAIGRETTE

⅓ cup extra-virgin olive oil
3 tablespoons lime juice
1 teaspoon lime zest
1 teaspoon minced serrano or jalapeño pepper
1 teaspoon minced red onion or shallot
2 teaspoons chopped fresh cilantro
¼ teaspoon sea salt
1 teaspoon honey

1. In the pressure cooker pot, combine 3 cups of water and the black beans. Place the trivet inside the pot.

2. In an oven-safe bowl, combine the rice, remaining 1 cup of water, the olive oil, and salt and place on the trivet.

3. Lock the lid in place and seal the steam valve. Select Pressure/Manual and adjust the time to 10 minutes on high pressure.

4. After cooking, let the pressure release naturally for 5 minutes, then quick release any remaining pressure. Carefully remove the lid and set aside.

5. Using oven mitts, remove the dish and fluff the rice with a fork. Remove the pot, then drain and rinse the cooked black beans. Allow the rice and beans to cool.

6. **To make the spicy lime vinaigrette:** Meanwhile, in a glass jar, combine all the vinaigrette ingredients, close the lid, and shake the jar until mixed.

7. In a large bowl, toss the onion, tomatoes, corn, bell pepper, and cooled rice and beans. Pour the desired amount of dressing over everything, and toss until well combined. Taste and add more dressing if desired. Serve.

PER SERVING (1 cup) Calories: 293; Total Fat: 13g; Fiber: 4g; Protein: 5g; Sodium: 333mg; Sugar: 3g

GLUTEN-FREE, NUT-FREE

Mediterranean Chicken Shawarma

Serves: 6 / **Prep Time:** 15 minutes, plus 1 hour to marinate / **Sauté:** 2 minutes / **Pressure Cook:** 8 minutes high pressure / **Release:** Natural for 5 minutes, then quick / **Total Time:** 1 hour 35 minutes

Shawarma is a traditional Middle Eastern way of cooking meats by adding slices onto a skewer and roasting them over a slow-turning vertical rotisserie. We won't be using one of those to prep our chicken in this recipe, but we will be including all the tasty ingredients to make this modified electric pressure cooker version.

FOR THE CHICKEN MARINADE

- 2 pounds boneless, skinless chicken breasts, cut into strips
- 4 tablespoons extra-virgin olive oil, divided
- 2 garlic cloves, minced
- 1 teaspoon allspice
- 2 teaspoons paprika
- 1 teaspoons ground cumin
- ¼ teaspoon ground cinnamon
- ½ teaspoon sea salt
- ½ teaspoon freshly ground black pepper
- ½ tablespoon apple cider vinegar
- ½ cup water

1. **To make the chicken marinade:** In a large bowl, combine the chicken, 2 tablespoons of olive oil, the garlic, allspice, paprika, cumin, cinnamon, salt, pepper, and vinegar. Cover and marinate for at least 1 hour or as long as overnight.

2. Press the Sauté button and adjust to high. Pour in the remaining 2 tablespoons of olive oil. Once hot, add the marinated chicken and sear for about 1 minute to brown, then flip and sear on the other side for 1 minute, until brown. Press the Cancel/Off button.

3. Pour the water into the pot and gently scrape the bottom, dislodging any browned chicken. Lock the lid in place and seal the steam valve. Select Pressure/Manual and adjust the time to 8 minutes on high pressure.

4. **To make the garlic sauce:** Meanwhile, in a small bowl, combine all the sauce ingredients and mix well. Set aside to rest and allow the flavors to meld.

5. After cooking, let the pressure release naturally for 5 minutes, then quick release any remaining pressure. Carefully remove the lid and set aside.

CONTINUED ▶

Mediterranean Chicken Shawarma CONTINUED

FOR THE GARLIC SAUCE

1 cup plain yogurt

¼ cup freshly squeezed lemon juice

1 tablespoon extra-virgin olive oil

2 garlic cloves, minced

1 teaspoon sea salt

1 teaspoon minced fresh or dried dill

ADD-INS

12 romaine or Bibb lettuce leaves

½ cup sliced red onion

¼ cup chopped fresh parsley

6. Add ⅓ cup of chicken shawarma to the lettuce leaves. Top with the onion, parsley, and garlic sauce. Serve.

SUBSTITUTION TIP: For a cheaper, moister, and slightly fattier option, boneless chicken thighs can be used in this recipe or you can combine both chicken breasts and thighs together.

PER SERVING (⅓ cup per lettuce wrap, 2 wraps)
Calories: 274; Total Fat: 16g; Fiber: 1g; Protein: 27g; Sodium: 590mg; Sugar: 2g

DAIRY-FREE, GLUTEN-FREE, NUT-FREE, VEGETARIAN, 30 MINUTES OR LESS

Avocado Egg Salad

Serves: 6 to 8 / **Prep Time:** 10 minutes / **Pressure Cook:** 5 minutes high pressure / **Release:** Natural for 5 minutes, then quick / **Total Time:** 25 minutes

This electric pressure hack to make bulk boiled eggs is a game changer! If you have any recipes that call for chopped boiled eggs, this is a hack you have to try. The result is an egg loaf that you can then chop into pieces.

Olive oil cooking spray
5 large eggs
1 cup water

ADD-INS
1 avocado, pitted and peeled
Juice of ½ lime
¼ cup chopped red bell pepper
¼ cup chopped celery
½ teaspoon sea salt
½ teaspoon dried dill
½ teaspoon garlic powder
¼ teaspoon paprika
12 romaine or Bibb lettuce leaves, or sprouted grain bread, for serving

1. Spray the oven-safe dish with cooking spray. Crack all the eggs right into an oven-safe bowl, keeping the yolks intact.

2. Pour the water into the pressure cooker pot, place a trivet inside, and the dish on top of the trivet. Lock the lid in place and seal the steam valve. Select Pressure/Manual and adjust the time to 5 minutes on high pressure.

3. After cooking, let the pressure release naturally for 5 minutes, then quick release any remaining pressure. Carefully remove the lid and set aside.

4. Using oven mitts, lift the bowl out of the pot and turn it over onto a cutting board so the cooked egg loaf releases onto the board. Allow the cooked eggs to cool for 5 minutes, then use a sharp knife to chop it.

5. In a large bowl, put the avocado and mash well. Add the chopped egg and rest of the add-in ingredients (except the lettuce leaves) and mix well. Scoop the egg salad into the lettuce leaves and serve.

SUBSTITUTION TIP: For a less-expensive and longer-lasting option, substitute the avocado for ¼ cup of mayonnaise.

PER SERVING (¼ cup) Calories: 129; Total Fat: 9g; Fiber: 4g; Protein: 7g; Sodium: 261mg; Sugar: 2g

ALLERGY-FREE, VEGAN, 30 MINUTES OR LESS

Sweet Potato Quinoa Salad

Serves: 6 / **Prep Time:** 15 minutes / **Sauté:** 2 minutes / **Pressure Cook:** 8 minutes high pressure / **Release:** Quick / **Total Time:** 30 minutes

This quick-and-easy, nutritiously packed quinoa bowl is full of nutrients, fiber, and protein, making it the perfect addition to any healthy-eating plan.

- 2 tablespoons extra-virgin olive oil
- 1 garlic clove, minced
- 1 large sweet potato, peeled and cut into 1½-inch pieces
- 1 cup quinoa, rinsed
- 4 cups chopped kale
- 2 cups low-sodium vegetable broth
- ½ teaspoon sea salt
- ¼ teaspoon freshly ground black pepper
- 1 (15-ounce) can low-sodium chickpeas, rinsed

ADD-INS
- 2 tablespoons extra-virgin olive oil
- Juice of 1 lime
- 2 teaspoons hot sauce of choice
- 1 tablespoon chopped fresh cilantro
- ¼ cup chopped scallions

1. Press the Sauté button and adjust to normal. Pour in the olive oil. Once hot, add the garlic and sauté, stirring, for about 1 minute, until fragrant. Add the sweet potato and quinoa, and sauté for 1 minute more. Press the Cancel/Off button, then add the kale, broth, salt, and pepper.

2. Lock the lid in place and seal the steam valve. Select Pressure/Manual and adjust the time to 8 minutes on high pressure.

3. After cooking, quick release the pressure. Carefully remove the lid and set aside.

4. Add the chickpeas, stir, and allow the mixture to cool for 5 minutes.

5. Meanwhile, in a small bowl, combine the olive oil, lime juice, and hot sauce and mix well. Add the oil mixture to the pot, gently tossing to combine. Sprinkle with the cilantro and scallions before serving.

HEALTH BOOST: When buying canned beans, always get the no-salt options. Make sure to rinse canned beans well before adding them to recipes to remove the liquid they were in, which will help with digestion.

PER SERVING (1 cup) Calories: 345; Total Fat: 14g; Fiber: 7g; Protein: 13g; Sodium: 402mg; Sugar: 5g

ALLERGY-FREE, ONE POT, VEGAN, 30 MINUTES OR LESS

Tex-Mex Lentil Bowl

Serves: 6 / **Prep Time:** 5 minutes / **Sauté:** 2 minutes / **Pressure Cook:** 10 minutes high pressure / **Release:** Natural for 10 minutes, then quick / **Total Time:** 30 minutes

My goal is to start following a more flexitarian way of eating, which is a vegetarian diet that has the occasional addition of meat and meat products. Remember, it takes only a few sustainable changes that work for you to achieve long-term success. This Tex-Mex lentil recipe has been a great way for me to continue eating my favorite Mexican dishes while trying to maintain a more plant-based way of eating.

2 tablespoons extra-virgin olive oil
1 small red onion, chopped
2 garlic cloves, minced
1 cup dried green lentils, rinsed
2½ cups low-sodium vegetable broth
1 tablespoon chili powder
1 teaspoon ground cumin
1 teaspoon dried oregano
½ teaspoon sea salt

ADD-INS
Juice of 1 lime
1 tablespoon chopped fresh cilantro leaves
2 cups mixed greens
½ avocado
2 tablespoons salsa
1 tablespoon chopped jalapeño (optional)

1. Press the Sauté button and adjust to normal. Pour in the olive oil. Once hot, add the onion and garlic and sauté for 1 minute, until the onions have softened. Add the lentils and sauté for about 1 minute. Press the Cancel/Off button.

2. Add the broth, chili powder, cumin, oregano, and salt, mixing to combine.

3. Lock the lid in place and seal the steam valve. Select Pressure/Manual and adjust the time to 10 minutes on high pressure.

4. After cooking, let the pressure release naturally for 10 minutes, then quick release any remaining pressure. Carefully remove the lid and set aside.

5. Add the lime juice and cilantro, stirring to combine.

6. Fill bowls with the mixed greens, then add the lentil filling, avocado, salsa, and jalapeño (if using). Serve.

SUBSTITUTION TIP: If you are able to find a Tex-Mex seasoning blend, you can use 2 tablespoons of that in place of the chili powder, cumin, and oregano.

PER SERVING (½ cup) Calories: 270; Total Fat: 10g; Fiber: 6g; Protein: 14g; Sodium: 314mg; Sugar: 4g

ALLERGY-FREE

Shredded Beef Lettuce Cups

Serves: 6 / **Prep Time:** 10 minutes / **Sauté:** 10 minutes / **Pressure Cook:** 12 minutes high pressure / **Release:** Natural for 5 minutes, then quick / **Total Time:** 40 minutes

Growing up, I was always a sandwich girl. When I changed over to being gluten-free, I missed my easy meals. But no more. Give me some fresh, crisp lettuce for my usual sandwich fillings and I'm now a happy girl.

1 tablespoon extra-virgin olive oil
2 pounds flank steak, sliced thin about ½ inch
¼ cup honey
¼ cup coconut aminos or low-sodium soy sauce
¼ cup low-sodium beef broth or water
2 garlic cloves, minced
½ tablespoon peeled minced ginger
½ teaspoon sea salt
½ red pepper flakes (optional)
¼ teaspoon freshly ground black pepper
2 teaspoons arrowroot powder or cornstarch
2 tablespoons water
12 romaine or Bibb lettuce leaves, for serving
½ cup shredded carrots

1. Press the Sauté button and adjust to high. Pour in the olive oil. Once hot, working in batches, add the steak and sauté until browned. Remove from the pot and set aside while browning the next batch.

2. In a small bowl, mix honey, coconut aminos, broth, garlic, ginger, salt, red pepper flakes and black pepper.

3. Once the steak slices are browned and set aside, pour the sauce into the pot. Use a silicone spatula to deglaze the pot, scraping up any brown bits. Add the steak pieces. Press the Cancel/Off button, lock the lid in place, and seal the steam valve.

4. Select Pressure/Manual and adjust to 12 minutes on high pressure. After, let the pressure release naturally for 5 minutes, then quick release the remaining pressure. Remove the lid and set aside.

5. Press the Sauté button, adjust to normal, and bring the mixture to simmer. In a small bowl, combine the arrowroot powder and water, then pour this into the pot and stir for 1 to 2 minutes, until sauce thickens. Spoon ¼ cup of the steak mixture onto each lettuce leaf, then top with the carrots.

PER SERVING (¼ cup) Calories: 295; Total Fat: 10g; Fiber: 1g; Protein: 34g; Sodium: 696mg; Sugar: 13g

Carrot-Ginger Soup, page 92

CHAPTER SIX

Chilis, Soups, and Sauces

Healing Bone Broth 86

Tex-Mex Butternut Squash Soup 87

Thai Lentil Soup 89

Sweet Potato and Corn Soup 90

Turmeric Lentil Soup 91

Carrot-Ginger Soup 92

Vegetable Barley Soup 93

Creamy Root Vegetable Soup 94

Chicken Tortilla Soup 95

Mushroom and Wild Rice Soup 96

Beef and Bean Chili 97

White Chicken Chili 98

Vegan Lentil Chili 99

Mushroom-Turkey Chili 100

Sweet Potato and Quinoa Chili 101

Easy Homemade Ketchup 102

Creamy Vegan Alfredo Sauce 103

Garlic-Basil Marinara Sauce 104

Cinnamon Applesauce 105

Spicy Cranberry Sauce 106

ALLERGY-FREE, ONE POT

Healing Bone Broth

Serves: 10 / **Prep Time:** 10 minutes, plus 1 hour to rest / **Pressure Cook:** 4 hours on high / **Release:** Natural for 25 minutes / **Total Time:** 5 hours 35 minutes

This broth is so easy to make and provides a multitude of healing benefits. Bone broth is said to help heal the gut lining, protect joints, support immune function, and support hair, nail, and skin health.

- 2 pounds beef bones
- 2 celery stalks, cut into 1-inch pieces
- 2 carrots, cut into 1-inch pieces
- 1 red onion, unpeeled and quartered
- 1 lemon, unpeeled and quartered
- 1-inch fresh ginger piece, peeled and quartered
- 4 or 5 garlic cloves, lightly smashed
- 1-inch turmeric root piece, peeled and quartered
- 4 bay leaves
- 1 or 2 thyme sprigs
- 1 teaspoon whole black peppercorns
- 2 teaspoons sea salt
- 2 tablespoons apple cider vinegar

1. In the pressure cooker pot, combine all the ingredients and cover with water until the pot is two-thirds full.

2. Lock the lid in place and seal the steam valve. Select Pressure/Manual and adjust the time to 4 hours on high pressure.

3. After cooking, let the pressure release naturally, which can take about 25 minutes. Carefully remove the lid and set aside.

4. Remove the pot from the pressure cooker and let sit for 1 hour. Using a large spoon, scoop off any fat that may have settled on top. Using a strainer, strain the liquid and pour it into jars. Discard the cooked bones and vegetables.

5. Let the broth cool completely in the jars, then skim off any fat that may have accumulated on top, seal the jars, and store them in the refrigerator for up to five days or in the freezer up to three months.

VARIATION TIP: This broth can be enjoyed warm as is or added into any soup, sauce, or recipe that calls for broth.

PER SERVING (½ cup) Calories: 43; Total Fat: 2g; Fiber: 0g; Protein: 4g; Sodium: 349mg; Sugar: 0g

ALLERGY-FREE, ONE POT, VEGAN, 30 MINUTES OR LESS

Tex-Mex Butternut Squash Soup

Serves: 6 / **Prep Time:** 10 minutes / **Sauté:** 5 minutes / **Pressure Cook:** 8 minutes high pressure / **Release:** Natural for 5 minutes, then quick / **Total Time:** 30 minutes

While searching for a soup to share with some friends, I decided to mix one of my favorite flavor combinations with one of my favorite winter vegetables, and this soup was the result. Originally, I made this soup by roasting the squash in the oven first, but this version is just as delicious and ready much faster. Serve this with a bit of shredded cheese and Greek yogurt on top for even more flavor.

1 tablespoon extra-virgin olive oil

2 scallions, both white and green parts, minced

2 garlic cloves, minced

1 medium butternut squash, peeled, seeded, and cut into cubes

2 cups low-sodium vegetable broth

1 cup water

1 teaspoon chili powder

½ teaspoon dried oregano

½ teaspoon sea salt

¼ teaspoon ground cumin

1 cup cooked black beans

1 cup frozen corn kernels

1. Press the Sauté button and adjust to normal. Pour in the olive oil. Once hot, add the scallions and garlic and sauté for 1 to 2 minutes, until the scallions begin to soften. Add the squash and sauté for about 1 minute. Stir in the broth, water, chili powder, oregano, salt, and cumin, stirring to combine. Press the Cancel/Off button.

2. Lock the lid in place and seal the steam valve. Select Pressure/Manual and adjust the time to 8 minutes on high pressure.

3. After cooking, let the pressure release naturally for 5 minutes, then quick release any remaining pressure. Carefully remove the lid and set aside.

CONTINUED ▸

Tex-Mex Butternut Squash Soup CONTINUED

ADD-INS

Juice of ½ lime

2 tablespoons chopped fresh cilantro leaves

1 tablespoon chopped jalapeño

4. Remove the pot and place it on a heat-resistant surface. Using a hand blender, blend until smooth. Place the pot back into the cooker, press the Sauté button, and adjust to low. Stir in the black beans and corn and simmer for 2 minutes, until warmed through. Press the Cancel/Off button.

5. Stir in the lime juice, cilantro, and jalapeño and serve.

SHORTCUT: To save a little time, pick up some butternut squash that has already been peeled, seeded, and cubed; this can be found in the produce section at most grocery stores.

PER SERVING (1 cup) Calories: 171; Total Fat: 3g; Fiber: 7g; Protein: 6g; Sodium: 281mg; Sugar: 6g

ALLERGY-FREE, ONE POT, VEGAN, 30 MINUTES OR LESS

Thai Lentil Soup

Serves: 6 to 8 / **Prep Time:** 10 minutes / **Sauté:** 6 minutes / **Pressure Cook:** 5 minutes high pressure / **Release:** Quick / **Total Time:** 25 minutes

My husband and I went to Thailand a few years ago. I found that we enjoyed the foods available at street vendors more than those available in many of the restaurants! It was on this trip that I fell in love with all the Thai flavors.

- 2 tablespoons extra-virgin olive oil
- ½ small red onion, minced
- 2 garlic cloves, minced
- ½ cup dried red lentils, rinsed
- ⅓ cup dried mung beans, rinsed
- ¼ cup quinoa, rinsed
- 2 stalks lemongrass, halved
- 4 or 5 lime leaves
- 4 cups low-sodium vegetable broth
- 2 tablespoons tom yum paste
- 2 bay leaves
- 1 teaspoon sea salt
- 2 cups frozen vegetable blend of choice

ADD-INS
- Juice of ½ lemon
- 1 tablespoon chopped fresh cilantro

1. Press the Sauté button and adjust to normal. Pour in the olive oil. Once hot, add the onion and garlic and sauté for 1 to 2 minutes, until the onions have softened. Add the lentils, mung beans, quinoa, lemongrass, and lime leaves and sauté for 1 minute. Add the broth, tom yum paste, bay leaves, and salt, stirring well. Press the Cancel/Off button.

2. Lock the lid in place and seal the steam valve. Select Pressure/Manual and adjust the time to 5 minutes on high pressure.

3. After cooking, quick release the pressure. Carefully remove the lid and set aside.

4. Press the Sauté button, adjust to normal, and stir in the frozen vegetables. Simmer for 2 to 3 minutes, until the vegetables are cooked. Press the Cancel/Off button.

5. Remove the bay leaves, stir in the lemon juice and cilantro, and serve.

SUBSTITUTION TIP: If you cannot find lemongrass, lime leaves or tom yum paste, use 2 tablespoons of red curry paste for a similar flavor.

PER SERVING (1 cup) Calories: 258; Total Fat: 6g; Fiber: 8g; Protein: 11g; Sodium: 614mg; Sugar: 5g

ALLERGY-FREE, ONE POT, VEGAN, 30 MINUTES OR LESS

Sweet Potato and Corn Soup

Serves: 6 to 8 / **Prep Time:** 10 minutes / **Sauté:** 3 minutes / **Pressure Cook:** 6 minutes high pressure / **Release:** Natural for 5 minutes, then quick / **Total Time:** 30 minutes

When I was younger, my family went to vegetable stands and chose our corn cobs, husks and all, from barrels. We would peel back the husks to see what the kernels looked like, trying to find the best ones. Cutting the corn from the cobs always bring back those childhood memories.

2 tablespoons extra-virgin olive oil
1 small red onion, minced
3 garlic cloves, minced
2 medium sweet potatoes, cut into cubes
4 corn cobs, kernels cut off (about 2½ cups)
2 medium carrots, chopped
1 red bell pepper, chopped
4 cups low-sodium vegetable broth
1 teaspoon sea salt
1 teaspoon smoked paprika
1 teaspoon ground cumin
½ teaspoon freshly ground black pepper

ADD-INS

1 cup full-fat coconut milk
Juice of ½ lime
1 tablespoon chopped fresh cilantro

1. Press the Sauté button and adjust to normal. Pour in the olive oil. Once hot, add the onion and garlic and sauté for 1 to 2 minutes, until the onions have softened. Add the sweet potatoes, corn, carrots, and bell pepper and sauté for 1 minute. Add the broth, salt, paprika, cumin, and black pepper, stirring until combined. Press the Cancel/Off button.

2. Lock the lid in place and seal the steam valve. Select Pressure/Manual and adjust the time to 6 minutes on high pressure.

3. After cooking, let the pressure release naturally for 5 minutes, then quick release any remaining pressure. Carefully remove the lid and set aside.

4. Add the coconut milk and lime juice, stirring to combine. Serve warm topped with the cilantro.

SHORTCUT: For a quicker prep, use 2½ cups frozen corn kernels instead of cutting the corn fresh from the cob.

PER SERVING (1 cup) Calories: 292; Total Fat: 14g; Fiber: 7g; Protein: 6g; Sodium: 762mg; Sugar: 14g

ALLERGY-FREE, ONE POT, VEGAN, 30 MINUTES OR LESS

Turmeric Lentil Soup

Serves: 6 / **Prep Time:** 5 minutes / **Sauté:** 6 minutes / **Pressure Cook:** 4 minutes high pressure / **Release:** Natural for 5 minutes, then quick / **Total Time:** 25 minutes

When someone in the house gets sick, this quick-and-easy lentil soup is what we have. It has great immune-boosting ingredients like turmeric, ginger, and garlic, and the lentils are soothing. Bookmark this page for the next time someone gets a cold.

- 2 tablespoons extra-virgin olive oil
- 1 small onion, chopped
- 3 garlic cloves, minced
- ¼ cup red lentils, rinsed
- ¼ cup mung beans, rinsed
- ¼ cup quinoa, rinsed
- 2 cups low-sodium vegetable broth
- 2 cups water
- 1 teaspoon minced ginger
- 2 bay leaves
- 1 teaspoon ground turmeric
- 1 teaspoon sea salt
- ½ teaspoon freshly ground black pepper
- 2 cups frozen vegetable mix of choice
- 1 cup chopped fresh spinach
- Juice of ½ lemon
- 2 tablespoons cilantro

1. Press the Sauté button and adjust to normal. Pour in the olive oil. Once hot, and the onion and garlic and sauté for 1 to 2 minutes, until the onion has softened. Add the lentils, mung beans, and quinoa and sauté for about 1 minute. Add the broth, water, ginger, bay leaves, turmeric, salt, and pepper, stirring to combine. Press the Cancel/Off button.

2. Lock the lid in place and seal the steam valve. Select Pressure/Manual and adjust the time to 4 minutes on high pressure.

3. After cooking, let the pressure release naturally for 5 minutes, then quick release any remaining pressure. Carefully remove the lid and set aside.

4. Press the Sauté button, adjust to normal, stir in the frozen vegetables and fresh spinach, and simmer for 2 to 3 minutes, until the vegetables are cooked. Press the Cancel/Off button.

5. Remove and discard the bay leaves, then stir in the lemon juice and cilantro before serving.

PER SERVING (1½ cups) Calories: 170; Total Fat: 6g; Fiber: 5g; Protein: 7g; Sodium: 417mg; Sugar: 1g

ALLERGY-FREE, ONE POT, VEGAN, 30 MINUTES OR LESS

Carrot-Ginger Soup

Serves: 6 / **Prep Time:** 10 minutes / **Sauté:** 3 minutes / **Pressure Cook:** 8 minutes high pressure / **Release:** Natural for 5 minutes, then quick / **Total Time:** 30 minutes

"Eat more carrots, they're good for your eyes," is something I recall hearing repeatedly as a child, and yes, they are! Being high in beta-carotene, carrots are very beneficial to good eye health. This creamy, delicious soup is a great way to ensure you're getting enough of this orange veggie into your diet.

- 1 tablespoon extra-virgin olive oil
- 1 medium onion, chopped
- 2 garlic cloves, minced
- 3 cups chopped carrots
- 2 celery stalks, chopped
- 1 small apple, chopped
- 2 cups low-sodium vegetable broth
- 1 cup water
- 1½ tablespoons minced fresh ginger
- 1 teaspoon sea salt
- ½ teaspoon ground turmeric

ADD-INS
- 1 cup full-fat coconut milk
- Juice of ½ lime
- 1 tablespoon chopped fresh parsley

1. Press the Sauté button and adjust to normal. Pour in the olive oil. Once hot, add the onion and garlic and sauté for 1 to 2 minutes, until the onion has softened. Add the carrots, celery, and apple and sauté for 1 minute. Add the broth, water, ginger, salt, and turmeric, stirring to combine. Press the Cancel/Off button.

2. Lock the lid in place and seal the steam valve. Select Pressure/Manual and adjust the time to 8 minutes on high pressure.

3. After cooking, let the pressure release naturally for 5 minutes, then quick release any remaining pressure. Carefully remove the lid and set aside.

4. Remove the pot and place it on a heat-resistant surface. Add the coconut milk and, using a hand blender, blend the soup to the desired consistency. Add the lime juice and stir to combine. Top with the parsley and serve.

SUBSTITUTE TIP: If you don't have a can of coconut milk, use 1 cup of unsweetened milk alternative for a vegan option or 1 cup of milk for a non-vegan option.

PER SERVING (1 cup) Calories: 142; Total Fat: 11g; Fiber: 3g; Protein: 2g; Sodium: 437mg; Sugar: 6g

DAIRY-FREE, NUT-FREE, ONE POT, VEGAN

Vegetable Barley Soup

Serves: 6 / **Prep Time:** 15 minutes, plus 8 hours to soak the barley / **Sauté:** 6 minutes / **Pressure Cook:** 15 minutes high pressure / **Release:** Natural for 10 minutes, then quick / **Total Time:** 8 hours 50 minutes

This hearty soup contains barley, which is a grain that's low in calories and low on the glycemic index. Although it's not a whole grain, it's full of dietary fiber that helps keep you feeling fuller for longer. Pearl barley is not a whole grain nor is it gluten-free, but it's still a highly nutritious addition to any healthy meal plan.

- 2 tablespoons extra-virgin olive oil
- 1 medium onion, chopped
- 3 garlic cloves, minced
- 2 cups chopped carrots
- 2 cups quartered cremini mushrooms
- 1 cup chopped celery
- ½ cup pearl barley, soaked 6 to 8 hours and rinsed
- 2 cups low-sodium vegetable broth
- 2 cups water
- 1 (14.5-ounce) can diced tomatoes, drained
- 2 bay leaves
- 1 teaspoon sea salt
- ½ teaspoon freshly ground black pepper
- 1 cup frozen peas

1. Press the Sauté button and adjust to normal. Pour in the olive oil. Once hot, add the onion and garlic and sauté for 1 to 2 minutes, until the onion has softened. Add the carrots, mushrooms, celery, and barley and sauté for 1 minute. Add the broth, water, tomatoes, bay leaves, salt, and pepper, stirring to combine. Press the Cancel/Off button.

2. Lock the lid in place and seal the steam valve. Select Pressure/Manual and adjust the time to 15 minutes on high pressure.

3. After cooking, let the pressure release naturally for 10 minutes, then quick release any remaining pressure. Carefully remove the lid and set aside.

4. Press the Sauté button, adjust to normal, stir in the peas, and simmer for 2 to 3 minutes, until the peas are cooked. Press the Cancel/Off button.

5. Remove and discard the bay leaves, and serve.

HEALTH BOOST: For a whole-grain, gluten-free option, substitute brown rice for pearl barley and increase the cook time to 20 minutes.

PER SERVING (1 cup) Calories: 155; Total Fat: 5g; Fiber: 7g; Protein: 5g; Sodium: 515mg; Sugar: 5g

ALLERGY-FREE, ONE POT, VEGAN

Creamy Root Vegetable Soup

Serves: 6 to 8 / **Prep Time:** 10 minutes / **Pressure Cook:** 10 minutes high pressure / **Release:** Natural for 10 minutes, then quick / **Total Time:** 35 minutes

I grew up with turmeric being a staple in all our meals, and now that I fully understand all the amazing health benefits turmeric offers, I have been including it into more of our meals, too. Turmeric has anti-inflammatory, antibacterial, and immune-boosting benefits, and I love adding it into my winter soups and recipes.

2 cups chopped carrots

2 cups chopped peeled butternut squash

2 cups low-sodium vegetable broth

2 cups water

1 medium sweet potato, peeled and chopped

1 medium onion, chopped

4 garlic cloves, minced

1 teaspoon minced ginger

1 teaspoon dried thyme leaves

½ teaspoon ground turmeric

1 teaspoon sea salt

¼ teaspoon freshly ground black pepper

ADD-IN

1 tablespoon chopped fresh parsley

1. In the pressure cooker pot, combine all the ingredients except the add-ins.

2. Lock the lid in place and seal the steam valve. Select Pressure/Manual and adjust the time to 10 minutes on high pressure.

3. After cooking, let the pressure release naturally for 10 minutes, then quick release any remaining pressure. Carefully remove the lid and set aside.

4. Remove the pot and place on a heat-resistant surface. Using a hand blender, blend the soup to the desired consistency, adding more water if necessary. Serve warm topped with parsley.

VARIATION TIP: To make a creamier version of this soup, add ½ cup of canned full-fat coconut milk, ¾ cup of unsweetened milk alternative, or ¾ cup of dairy milk to the pot before blending.

PER SERVING (1 cup) Calories: 69; Total Fat: 0g; Fiber: 3g; Protein: 2g; Sodium: 432mg; Sugar: 5g

NUT-FREE

Chicken Tortilla Soup

Serves: 6 / **Prep Time:** 10 minutes / **Sauté:** 1 minute / **Pressure Cook:** 10 minutes high pressure / **Release:** Natural for 10 minutes, then quick / **Total Time:** 35 minutes

Mexican cuisine is a staple at our house! We usually have all the ingredients for this flavorful soup in the house, and it often ends up being one of our quick weekend meals. We like it topped with broken tortilla chips and plain Greek yogurt

- 1 tablespoon extra-virgin olive oil
- 3 scallions, chopped
- 3 garlic cloves, minced
- 2 cups low-sodium vegetable broth
- 2 cups water
- 1 (18-ounce) can diced tomatoes with chili seasonings
- 1 cup tomato sauce
- 3 tablespoons Tex-Mex seasoning
- 1 teaspoon sea salt
- ½ teaspoon freshly ground black pepper
- 1 pound boneless, skinless chicken breasts
- 1 (15-ounce) can black beans, rinsed
- 1 cup frozen corn kernels
- Juice of 1 lime

1. Press the Sauté button and adjust to normal. Pour in the olive oil. Once hot, add the scallions and garlic and sauté for 1 minute. Add the broth, water, tomatoes and their juices, tomato sauce, Tex-Mex seasoning, salt, and pepper, stirring to combine. Place the chicken in the pot. Press the Cancel/Off button.

2. Lock the lid in place and seal the steam valve. Select Pressure/Manual and adjust the time to 10 minutes on high pressure.

3. After cooking, let the pressure release naturally for 10 minutes, then quick release any remaining pressure. Carefully remove the lid and set aside.

4. Keep the pot on the Keep Warm setting and transfer the chicken breasts to a plate. Add the beans and corn into the pot and let cook while you shred the chicken with two forks. Add the shredded chicken back to the pot along with the lime juice.

5. Serve the soup warm.

PER SERVING (1 cup) Calories: 240; Total Fat: 8g; Fiber: 7g; Protein: 19g; Sodium: 684mg; Sugar: 3g

ALLERGY-FREE, VEGAN

Mushroom and Wild Rice Soup

Serves: 6 / **Prep Time:** 15 minutes / **Sauté:** 7 minutes / **Pressure Cook:** 30 minutes high pressure / **Release:** Natural for 10 minutes, then quick / **Total Time:** 1 hour 5 minutes

For this soup, you want to use real wild rice and avoid any mixed blends. Wild rice should be easy to find at most grocery stores, but you only need a little less than a cup of it, so try your local bulk store to get the exact amount needed for this recipe to prevent any waste.

- 2 tablespoons extra-virgin olive oil
- 1 medium onion, chopped
- 4 garlic cloves, minced
- 2 cups chopped carrots
- 2 cups quartered mushrooms
- ¾ cup wild rice, rinsed
- ½ cup dried Northern white beans, rinsed
- 3 cups low-sodium vegetable broth
- 2 cups water
- 1 tablespoon Italian seasoning
- 1½ teaspoons sea salt
- 1 teaspoon freshly ground black pepper
- ½ teaspoon ground turmeric

ADD-INS

- 2 tablespoons cornstarch
- 2 tablespoons water
- 1 cup full-fat coconut milk

1. Press the Sauté button and adjust to normal. Pour in the olive oil. Once hot, add the onion and garlic and sauté for 1 minute. Add the carrots, mushrooms, rice, and beans and sauté for 1 minute. Add the broth, water, Italian seasoning, salt, pepper, and turmeric, stirring to combine. Press the Cancel/Off button.

2. Lock the lid in place and seal the steam valve. Select Pressure/Manual and adjust the time to 30 minutes on high pressure. After cooking, let the pressure release naturally for 10 minutes, then quick release any remaining pressure. Carefully remove the lid and set aside.

3. Meanwhile, in a small bowl, mix the cornstarch and water until a thick mixture forms.

4. Press the Sauté button, adjust to normal, and pour in the coconut milk and cornstarch mixture, and simmer for about 5 minutes, until thickened. Serve warm.

HEALTH BOOST: Use a variety of mushrooms for the added health benefits they provide.

PER SERVING (1 cup) Calories: 288; Total Fat: 13g; Fiber: 6g; Protein: 9g; Sodium: 438mg; Sugar: 4g

DIARY-FREE, NUT-FREE, ONE POT

Beef and Bean Chili

Serves: 6 to 8 / **Prep Time:** 10 minutes / **Sauté:** 7 minutes / **Pressure Cook:** 20 minutes high pressure / **Release:** Natural for 10 minutes, then quick / **Total Time:** 50 minutes

My son loves tomatoes and my daughter refuses to eat them. For this recipe, I have omitted diced tomatoes for my daughter so she can fully enjoy this favored chili, but if you like, a can of diced tomatoes can be added along with the tomato sauce.

- ½ tablespoon extra-virgin olive oil
- 1½ pounds lean ground beef
- 1 medium onion, chopped
- 1 (15-ounce) can red kidney beans, rinsed
- 1 (15-ounce) can black beans, rinsed
- 2 cups tomato sauce
- 1 cup chopped carrots
- 1 cup water
- 1 cup frozen corn kernels
- 2 tablespoons chili powder
- 3 garlic cloves, minced
- ½ tablespoon dried oregano
- 1 teaspoon ground cumin
- 1 teaspoon sea salt
- 1 tablespoon Worcestershire sauce
- Juice of ½ lime

1. Press the Sauté button and adjust to high. Pour in the olive oil. Once hot, add the beef and cook, stirring and breaking into pieces, for about 5 minutes, until browned. Drain the fat, if needed. Add the onion and sauté for another 2 minutes, until the onion has softened.

2. Add the beans, tomato sauce, carrots, water, corn, chili powder, garlic, oregano, cumin, salt, and Worcestershire sauce, stirring to combine. Press the Cancel/Off button.

3. Lock the lid in place and seal the steam valve. Select Chili/Bean (or Pressure/Manual) and adjust the time to 20 minutes on high pressure.

4. After cooking, let the pressure release naturally for 10 minutes, then quick release any remaining pressure. Carefully remove the lid and set aside.

5. Stir in the lime juice before serving.

VARIATION TIP: Enjoy this easy chili on its own, on top of cooked brown rice, or on top of baked potatoes—top all options with shredded cheese and plain Greek yogurt for extra flavor.

PER SERVING (1 cup) Calories: 260; Total Fat: 6g; Fiber: 8g; Protein: 26g; Sodium: 430mg; Sugar: 4g

GLUTEN-FREE, NUT-FREE, ONE POT

White Chicken Chili

Serves: 6 / **Prep Time:** 15 minutes / **Sauté:** 6 minutes / **Pressure Cook:** 10 minutes high pressure / **Release:** Natural for 5 minutes, then quick / **Total Time:** 40 minutes

This chili recipe is a little different. Rather than ground beef or ground chicken, it's made with diced chicken and there are no tomatoes of any kind, which makes my daughter happy.

- 2 tablespoons extra-virgin olive oil
- 1 medium onion, chopped
- 2 boneless, skinless chicken breasts, cubed
- 3 garlic cloves, minced
- 2 cups low-sodium chicken broth
- 1 (15-ounce) can low-sodium cannellini beans, rinsed
- 1 (15-ounce) can low-sodium black beans, rinsed
- 1 cup chopped carrots
- 1 cup frozen corn kernels
- 2 tablespoons chili powder
- 1 tablespoon dried oregano
- 1 teaspoon sea salt
- ½ teaspoon freshly ground black pepper

ADD-INS

- ¼ cup plain whole-milk Greek yogurt
- 2 tablespoons chopped fresh cilantro leaves

1. Press the Sauté button and adjust to high. Pour in olive oil. Once hot, add the onion and sauté for 1 minute. Add the chicken and garlic and sauté for 2 to 3 minutes, until the chicken is no longer pink. Add the broth and use a silicone spatula to deglaze the pot, scraping up any brown bits. Add the beans, carrots, corn, chili powder, oregano, salt, and pepper, stirring to combine. Press the Cancel/Off button.

2. Lock the lid in place and seal the steam valve. Select Pressure/Manual and adjust the time to 10 minutes on high pressure.

3. After cooking, let the pressure release naturally for 5 minutes, then quick release any remaining pressure. Carefully remove the lid and set aside.

4. Press the Sauté button and adjust to low. Use a silicone spatula to mash the beans to help thicken the chili, then add the yogurt and simmer for 1 to 2 minutes. Serve warm, topped with cilantro.

SUBSTITUTION TIP: For a creamier version of this chili, use ½ cup of sour cream or ½ cup of cream cheese instead of yogurt. But just a warning: these additions will also increase calories and fat per serving.

PER SERVING (1 cup) Calories: 252; Total Fat: 9g; Fiber: 9g; Protein: 16g; Sodium: 401mg; Sugar: 3g

ALLERGY-FREE, ONE POT, VEGAN

Vegan Lentil Chili

Serves: 6 / **Prep Time:** 10 minutes / **Sauté:** 2 minute / **Pressure Cook:** 12 minutes high pressure / **Release:** Natural for 10 minutes, then quick / **Total Time:** 40 minutes

Lentils make a wonderful substitute for meat in many vegetarian meals, and that's just what they do in this recipe. Lentils are low in calories, packed full of fiber, and when eaten with whole grains, they can provide a complete source of protein.

- 2 tablespoons extra-virgin olive oil
- 1 medium onion, chopped
- 4 garlic cloves, minced
- 1 (18-ounce) can diced tomatoes with chili seasonings, drained
- 1 (15-ounce) can red kidney beans, rinsed
- 1½ cups tomato sauce
- 1½ cups dried green lentils, rinsed
- ½ cup dried red lentils, rinsed
- 2 tablespoons chili powder
- 1 tablespoon tomato paste
- 1 tablespoon pure maple syrup
- ½ tablespoon dried oregano
- 1 teaspoon ground cumin
- 1 teaspoon sea salt
- Juice of 1 lime

1. Press the Sauté button and adjust to normal. Pour in the olive oil. Once hot, add the onion and sauté for 1 minute. Add the garlic and sauté for 1 minute. Add the tomatoes, beans, tomato sauce, lentils, chili powder, tomato paste, maple syrup, oregano, cumin, and salt, stirring to combine. Press the Cancel/Off button.

2. Lock the lid in place and seal the steam valve. Select Chili/Bean (or Pressure/Manual) and adjust the time to 12 minutes on high pressure.

3. After cooking, let the pressure release naturally for 10 minutes, then quick release any remaining pressure. Carefully remove the lid and set aside.

4. Stir in the lime juice and serve warm.

VARIATION TIP: This lentil chili freezes well and can be enjoyed on its own, in a bowl with field greens, or on top of a baked potato.

PER SERVING (1 cup) Calories: 293; Total Fat: 5g; Fiber: 10g; Protein: 17g; Sodium: 632mg; Sugar: 5g

GLUTEN-FREE, NUT-FREE, ONE POT

Mushroom-Turkey Chili

Serves: 6 / **Prep Time:** 10 minutes / **Sauté:** 7 minutes / **Pressure Cook:** 20 minutes high pressure / **Release:** Natural for 5 minutes, then quick / **Total Time:** 45 minutes

The base of this chili is like others I have shared in this cookbook, but this version is leaner and more nutritious with the turkey and mushrooms. Mushrooms are a great addition to your healthy-eating plan. They are high in protein, fiber, B vitamins, and antioxidants, and may help improve immune function.

2 tablespoons extra-virgin olive oil
1 medium onion, chopped
3 garlic cloves, minced
1½ pounds ground turkey
2 cups sliced mushrooms
1 (18-ounce) can diced tomatoes with chili seasonings, drained
1 (15-ounce) can low-sodium red kidney beans, rinsed
1 (15-ounce) can low sodium black beans, rinsed
1 cup tomato sauce
1 cup frozen corn kernels
½ cup low-sodium chicken broth
2 tablespoons chili powder
1 teaspoon sea salt
1 teaspoon ground cumin
½ tablespoon oregano

1. Press the Sauté button and adjust to high. Pour in the olive oil. Once hot, add the onion, and garlic and sauté for 1 to 2 minutes, until the onion has softened. Add the turkey and cook, stirring and breaking up the meat, for about 5 minutes, until the turkey is no longer pink. Add the mushrooms, tomatoes, beans, tomato sauce, corn, broth, chili powder, salt, cumin, and oregano, stirring to combine. Press the Cancel/Off button.

2. Lock the lid in place and seal the steam valve. Select Chili/Bean (or Pressure/Manual) and adjust the time to 20 minutes on high pressure.

3. After cooking, let the pressure release naturally for 5 minutes, then quick release any remaining pressure. Carefully remove the lid and set aside. Serve warm.

SUBSTITUTION TIP: Not everyone is a fan of ground turkey. In this recipe, the ground turkey can easily be replaced with lean ground chicken.

PER SERVING (1 cup) Calories: 310; Total Fat: 12g; Fiber: 8g; Protein: 25g; Sodium: 547mg; Sugar: 5g

ALLERGY-FREE, ONE POT, VEGAN, 30 MINUTES OR LESS

Sweet Potato and Quinoa Chili

Serves: 6 / **Prep Time:** 10 minutes / **Sauté:** 3 minutes / **Pressure Cook:** 5 minutes high pressure / **Release:** Natural for 5 minutes, then quick / **Total Time:** 25 minutes

Of all the chili recipes I have tried over the years, this one may be my favorite. It's packed full of protein, nutrients, and fiber, plus the combination of sweetness from the sweet potatoes, the spiciness from the jalapeños, and the tang from the lime is oh so yum!

2 tablespoons extra-virgin olive oil

1 medium onion, chopped

3 garlic cloves, minced

2 medium sweet potatoes, cut into 1-inch cubes

½ cup quinoa, rinsed

2 cups tomato sauce

1 (15-ounce) can low-sodium black beans, rinsed

1 cup low-sodium vegetable broth

1 cup frozen corn kernels

1 cup chopped carrots

1 tablespoon chopped jalapeño

ADD-INS

Juice of 1 lime

1 to 2 tablespoons chopped fresh cilantro

1. Press the Sauté button and adjust to normal. Pour in the olive oil. Once hot, add the onion and garlic and sauté for 1 to 2 minutes, until the onion has softened. Add the sweet potato and quinoa and sauté for 1 minute. Add the tomato sauce, beans, broth, corn, carrots, and jalapeño, stirring to combine. Press the Cancel/Off button.

2. Lock the lid in place and seal the steam valve. Select Pressure/Manual and adjust the time to 5 minutes on high pressure.

3. After cooking, let the pressure release naturally for 5 minutes, then quick release any remaining pressure. Carefully remove the lid and set aside.

4. Add the lime juice and cilantro and serve.

SHORTCUT: To reduce prep time, purchase precut sweet potato cubes from the produce area of most grocery stores.

PER SERVING (¾ cup) Calories: 256; Total Fat: 6g; Fiber: 9g; Protein: 9g; Sodium: 157mg; Sugar: 8g

ALLERGY-FREE, ONE POT, VEGAN, 30 MINUTES OR LESS

Easy Homemade Ketchup

Makes: 4 cups / **Prep Time:** 5 minutes / **Pressure Cook:** 8 minutes high pressure / **Release:** Quick / **Sauté:** 10 minutes / **Total Time:** 25 minutes

I love French fries and enjoying them with ketchup is just a given. But have you ever read the back of a ketchup bottle? The amount of sugar added in is outrageous, so I ended up cutting out ketchup altogether and my fry obsession has never been the same... until now. This easy-to-make ketchup is life changing, and I have been happy indulging in my occasional French fry cravings again.

- 1 (28-ounce) can crushed tomatoes
- 2 tablespoons tomato paste
- ¼ cup apple cider vinegar
- ¼ cup water
- ¼ cup pure maple syrup
- 2 teaspoons onion powder
- 2 teaspoons garlic powder
- 1 teaspoon Italian seasoning
- ½ teaspoon sea salt

1. In the pressure cooker pot, combine all the ingredients and stir to combine.
2. Lock the lid in place and seal the steam valve. Select Pressure/Manual and adjust the time to 8 minutes on high pressure.
3. After cooking, quick release the pressure. Carefully remove the lid and set aside.
4. Remove the pot and place it on a heat-resistant surface. Using a hand blender, blend the contents until smooth and creamy.
5. Place the pot back into the cooker, press the Sauté button, and adjust to low. Simmer for 10 minutes, until thickened. Remove from the heat and allow to cool.
6. Transfer the ketchup to an airtight container and store in the refrigerator for up to three weeks.

VARIATION TIP: To add a little kick to your homemade ketchup, add ½ teaspoon of cayenne pepper (or more).

PER SERVING (2 tablespoons) Calories: 26; Total Fat: 1g; Fiber: 1g; Protein: 1g; Sodium: 87mg; Sugar: 2g

DAIRY-FREE, GLUTEN-FREE, ONE POT, VEGAN, 30 MINUTES OR LESS

Creamy Vegan Alfredo Sauce

Serves: 8 / **Prep Time:** 10 minutes / **Sauté:** 1 minute / **Pressure Cook:** 3 minutes high pressure / **Release:** Quick / **Total Time:** 20 minutes

Cauliflower and cashews are two very common ingredients to add to vegan dishes to produce a creamy texture. In certain recipes, cashews are soaked first for a few hours to help soften them up for easy blending. This step is not necessary when using an electric pressure cooker, as the steam from the pressure softens the cashews the same as soaking would. Toss this sauce warm with the pasta of your choice.

- 2 tablespoons extra-virgin olive oil
- 4 garlic cloves, minced
- 4 cups fresh or frozen cauliflower florets
- 2 cups low-sodium vegetable broth
- ½ cup raw cashews
- 2 tablespoons nutritional yeast
- ½ teaspoon onion powder
- ½ teaspoon Italian seasoning
- 1 teaspoon sea salt
- ¼ teaspoon freshly ground black pepper

1. Press the Sauté button and adjust to normal. Pour in the olive oil. Once hot, add the garlic and sauté for about 1 minute, until fragrant. Add the cauliflower, broth, cashews, nutritional yeast, onion powder, Italian seasoning, salt, and pepper, stirring to combine. Press the Cancel/Off button.

2. Lock the lid in place and seal the steam valve. Select Pressure/Manual and adjust the time to 3 minutes on high pressure.

3. After cooking, quick release the pressure. Carefully remove the lid and set aside. Remove the pot and place on a heat-resistant surface. Using a hand blender, blend to a smooth, creamy consistency.

4. Serve right away or store in airtight containers in the refrigerator for up to three days or in the freezer for up to two months.

HEALTH BOOST: For a lower calorie, more nutritious meal, toss the warm sauce with spiralized zucchini noodles or spaghetti squash.

PER SERVING (½ cup) Calories: 101; Total Fat: 8g; Fiber: 1g; Protein: 3g; Sodium: 443mg; Sugar: 2g

ALLERGY-FREE, ONE POT, VEGAN, 30 MINUTES OR LESS

Garlic-Basil Marinara Sauce

Serves: 12 / **Prep Time:** 5 minutes / **Sauté:** 2 minutes / **Pressure Cook:** 10 minutes high pressure / **Release:** Natural for 5 minutes, then quick / **Total Time:** 25 minutes

If you read the ingredients on the back of most marinara or pasta sauces, you'll notice that sugar is a common ingredient. The reason is that tomatoes can be a bit acidic and the addition of something sweet can help balance the flavors. In this recipe I add a little maple syrup as a natural sweetener option.

- 2 tablespoons extra-virgin olive oil
- 4 garlic cloves, minced
- 2 (28-ounce) cans whole, peeled tomatoes, drained
- 1 tablespoon dried oregano
- 1 tablespoon dried basil
- ½ tablespoon pure maple syrup (optional)
- ¾ teaspoon sea salt
- ¼ teaspoon red pepper flakes (optional)

ADD-INS
- ½ cup chopped fresh basil leaves
- ½ teaspoon grated lemon zest

1. Press the Sauté button and adjust to normal. Pour in the olive oil. Once hot, add the garlic and sauté for about 1 minute, until fragrant. Add the tomatoes, oregano, basil, maple syrup (if using), salt, and red pepper flakes (if using), stirring to combine. Simmer for 1 minute. Press the Cancel/Off button.

2. Lock the lid in place and seal the steam valve. Select Pressure/Manual and adjust the time to 10 minutes on high pressure.

3. After cooking, let the pressure release naturally for 5 minutes, then quick release any remaining pressure. Carefully remove the lid and set aside.

4. Remove the pot and place it on a heat-resistant surface. Using a hand blender, blend until smooth or to your preferred consistency. Stir in the basil and lemon zest and allow the sauce to sit for a few minutes to combine flavors.

5. Serve warm. Store in an airtight container in the refrigerator for up to one week or in the freezer for up to one month.

PER SERVING (½ cup) Calories: 45; Total Fat: 3g; Fiber: 3g; Protein: 1g; Sodium: 160mg; Sugar: 4g

ALLERGY-FREE, ONE POT, VEGAN, 30 MINUTES OR LESS

Cinnamon Applesauce

Serves: 8 / **Prep Time:** 5 minutes / **Pressure Cook:** 8 minutes high pressure / **Release:** Natural for 5 minutes, then quick / **Total Time:** 20 minutes

One of my favorite things about the fall season are the apples—all the varieties available, their freshness, and their reasonable price. And the flavor of these fresh-off-the-tree apples can be enjoyed for months by making them into an applesauce. This version is spiced but can also be enjoyed without that.

3 pounds Gala, Golden Delicious, Fuji, and/or Honeycrisp apples, cored and chopped (9 cups)

1 cup water

1 tablespoon freshly squeezed lemon juice

2 cinnamon sticks

½ teaspoon ground cinnamon

1. In the pressure cooker pot, combine the apples, water, lemon juice, and cinnamon sticks, stirring to combine.

2. Lock the lid in place and seal the steam valve. Select Pressure/Manual and adjust the time to 8 minutes on high pressure.

3. After cooking, let the pressure release naturally for 5 minutes, then quick release any remaining pressure. Carefully remove the lid and set aside.

4. Remove the pot and place on a heat-resistant surface. Remove the cinnamon sticks and apple peels, if desired. (I like to leave them for a fiber boost.) Using a hand blender, blend the apples until smooth or your preferred consistency. Stir in the ground cinnamon and allow to cool.

5. Store in an airtight container in the refrigerator for up to 7 days and the freezer up to 4 months.

VARIATION TIP: This sauce can be used as a natural sweetener in baked goods like the Fudgy Chocolate Brownies recipe (see page 186) in this book.

PER SERVING (½ cup) Calories: 89; Total Fat: 0g; Fiber: 2g; Protein: 0g; Sodium: 2mg; Sugar: 17g

ALLERGY-FREE, ONE POT, VEGAN, 30 MINUTES OR LESS

Spicy Cranberry Sauce

Serves: 8 to 10 / **Prep Time:** 5 minutes / **Pressure Cook:** 1 minute high pressure/
Release: Natural for 8 minutes, then quick / **Sauté:** 2 minutes / **Total Time:** 20 minutes

I'm not sure why cranberry sauce is just for the holidays. Yes, it tastes great with turkey, but it is just as delicious with chicken or vegetables, and added into oats or parfaits. Cranberries are small but are packed full of nutrients, antioxidants, and can help prevent urinary tract infections. With this easy, naturally sweetened version, we can include more cranberries in our meals and reap the benefits.

- 1 (12-ounce) bag cranberries, fresh or frozen, rinsed
- ¼ cup freshly squeezed orange juice or water
- ¼ cup pure maple syrup
- ½ teaspoon ground cinnamon
- ½ teaspoon ground allspice
- ¼ teaspoon sea salt
- ⅛ teaspoon ground ginger

1. In the pressure cooker pot, combine all the ingredients and mix well.

2. Lock the lid in place and seal the steam valve. Select Pressure/Manual and adjust the time to 1 minute on high pressure.

3. After cooking, let the pressure release naturally for 8 minutes, then quick release any remaining pressure. Carefully remove the lid and set aside.

4. Using a silicone potato masher, mash the cranberry sauce to the desired texture. Press the Sauté button, adjust to low, and simmer for 2 minutes. Remove the sauce from the heat to thicken as it cools. Taste and add more maple syrup or spices as needed.

5. Store in an airtight container in the refrigerator for up to seven days or in the freezer for up to two months.

HEALTH BOOST: Add one grated apple to the above recipe for added natural sweetness, nutrients, and a fiber boost.

PER SERVING (⅓ cup) Calories: 49; Total Fat: 0g; Fiber: 2g; Protein: 0g; Sodium: 75mg; Sugar: 8g

Quinoa and Lentil Stuffed Peppers, page 116

CHAPTER SEVEN

Meatless Mains

Chana Masala 110

Veggie and Lentil Bolognese 112

Cauliflower-Potato Curry 113

One-Pot Mexican Rice and Beans 114

Vegetable Risotto 115

Quinoa and Lentil Stuffed Peppers 116

Coconut-Lentil Curry 117

Vegetable Pad Thai 119

Hearty Lentil Stew 121

Meatless Shepherd's Pie 122

Creamy Mushroom Penne 124

Sweet and Savory Wild Rice 126

Coconut-Quinoa Curry 127

Veggie Rice Pilaf 128

Spinach-and-Tofu Curry 129

ALLERGY-FREE, VEGAN

Chana Masala

Serves: 6 / **Prep Time:** 10 minutes, plus 6 hours to soak / **Sauté:** 9 minutes / **Pressure Cook:** 22 minutes high pressure / **Release:** Natural for 10 minutes, then quick / **Total Time:** 6 hours 55 minutes

Chana masala is a popular East Indian curry that's packed full of chickpeas, which are naturally high in iron, protein, and fiber. Since the cook time for the chickpeas in this recipe is close to the cook time for brown rice, I've included a one-pot option to help make dinner even easier.

FOR THE BROWN RICE

- 1½ cups brown basmati rice, rinsed
- 1½ cups water
- 1 teaspoon sea salt
- 1 teaspoon extra-virgin olive oil

FOR THE CHANA MASALA

- 1 tablespoon extra-virgin olive oil
- 1 medium onion, chopped
- 1 teaspoon cumin seeds
- 1 medium tomato, chopped
- 1 cup tomato sauce
- 2 garlic cloves, minced
- 1 teaspoon minced ginger
- 1 teaspoon sea salt
- ½ teaspoon turmeric
- ½ teaspoon ground cumin
- ½ teaspoon ground coriander

1. **To make the brown rice:** In an oven-safe bowl, combine the rice, water, salt, and olive oil and set aside.

2. **To make the chana masala:** Press the Sauté button and adjust to normal. Pour in the olive oil. Once hot, add the onion and cumin and sauté for about 2 minutes, until the onion has softened. Add the tomato and sauté for 3 minutes, until the tomatoes have softened and start to mash. Add the tomato sauce, garlic, ginger, salt, turmeric, cumin, coriander, garam masala, and red chili powder, stirring to combine. Simmer for 2 minutes, until the flavors combine. Add the chickpeas and water, stirring well to combine. Press the Cancel/Off button.

3. Place a trivet in the pot and arrange so the legs are flat on the bottom of the pot. Place the bowl with rice and water on top of the trivet.

4. Lock the lid in place and seal the steam valve. Select Pressure/Manual and adjust the time to 22 minutes on high pressure.

1 teaspoon garam masala

¼ teaspoon red chili powder or cayenne pepper

1 cup dried chickpeas, soaked at least 6 hours and rinsed

2 cups water

ADD-INS

2 cups chopped fresh spinach

Juice of 1 lemon

½ cup chopped fresh cilantro leaves

5. After cooking, let the pressure release naturally for 10 minutes, then quick release any remaining pressure. Carefully remove the lid and set aside. Using oven mitts, remove the bowl with cooked rice, cover it, and set aside.

6. Press the Sauté button and adjust to low. Stir in the spinach and simmer for 1 to 2 minutes, until the spinach is cooked. Use a silicone spatula to mash some of the cooked chickpeas against the side of the pot. This will naturally thicken the curry.

7. Remove the pot and place it on a heat-resistant surface. Stir in the lemon juice and sprinkle with the cilantro just before serving with the rice.

SHORTCUT: To get this tasty meal on the table faster, use two (15-ounce) cans of low-sodium chickpeas (rinsed well) and reduce the cook time to 5 minutes with a natural steam release of 10 minutes and skip the brown rice option. Also, use 1 tablespoon of ready-made curry powder in place of the turmeric, ground cumin, ground coriander, and garam masala. The resulting taste will be a little different but still delicious.

PER SERVING (½ cup) Calories: 265; Total Fat: 5g; Fiber: 5g; Protein: 9g; Sodium: 378mg; Sugar: 5g

MEATLESS MAINS

ALLERGY-FREE, ONE POT, VEGAN

Veggie and Lentil Bolognese

Serves: 6 / **Prep Time:** 10 minutes / **Sauté:** 5 minutes / **Pressure Cook:** 15 minutes high pressure / **Release:** Natural for 10 minutes, then quick / **Total Time:** 45 minutes

Here's a lentil bolognese sauce that's so full of flavor and texture you won't even miss the meat. Green and brown lentils hold their shape a little better than red lentils. In this recipe, I used green lentils for texture and red lentils to help thicken the sauce.

1 tablespoon extra-virgin olive oil

1 medium onion, chopped

1 cup chopped carrots

1 cup chopped mushrooms

3 garlic cloves, minced

3 cups low-sodium vegetable broth

1 (15-ounce) can diced tomatoes, drained

1 (15-ounce) can low-sodium tomato sauce

1½ teaspoons Italian seasoning

1 teaspoon sea salt

½ teaspoon freshly ground black pepper

1 cup green lentils, rinsed

¼ cup red lentils, rinsed

½ cup chopped fresh basil

1 teaspoon lemon zest

1. Press the Sauté button and adjust to normal. Pour in the olive oil. Once hot, add the onion and carrots, sauté for 2 to 3 minutes, until the onion has softened. Add the mushrooms and garlic, stirring to combine, and sauté for 2 minutes. Add the broth, tomatoes, and tomato sauce, stirring to combine. Add the Italian seasoning, salt, and pepper, stirring to combine. Mix in the green and red lentils, stirring to combine. Press the Cancel/Off button.

2. Lock the lid in place and seal the steam valve. Select Pressure/Manual and adjust the time to 15 minutes on high pressure.

3. After cooking, allow the team to naturally release for 10 minutes, then quick release any remaining pressure. Carefully remove the lid and set aside.

4. Remove the pot and place it on a heat-resistant surface. Stir in the basil and lemon zest. Taste, add additional seasonings if desired, and serve.

HEALTH BOOST: For a low-calorie and low-carbohydrate option, serve over cooked spaghetti squash or sautéed spiralized zucchini.

PER SERVING (½ cup) Calories: 214; Total Fat: 3g; Fiber: 8g; Protein: 12g; Sodium: 506mg; Sugar: 7g

ALLERGY-FREE, ONE POT, VEGAN, 30 MINUTES OR LESS

Cauliflower-Potato Curry

Serves: 6 / **Prep Time:** 10 minutes / **Sauté:** 10 minutes / **Pressure Cook:** 1 minute high pressure / **Release:** Quick / **Total Time:** 25 minutes

The proper Indian name for this popular vegetarian curry is *aloo gobi*. It's full of flavors I grew up on and love. As an adult, I am more appreciative of these childhood favorites, and making them for my children brings me so much warmth and comfort. It's like sharing a piece of my childhood with them.

- 1 tablespoon extra-virgin olive oil
- 1 teaspoon cumin seeds
- 3 Yukon gold potatoes, cut into 1-inch cubes (about 2 cups)
- 1 small onion, chopped
- 1 small tomato, chopped
- 2 garlic cloves, minced
- 1 teaspoon peeled and minced ginger
- 1 teaspoon sea salt
- 1 teaspoon ground cumin
- 1 teaspoon ground coriander
- ¾ teaspoon turmeric
- ¼ cup water
- 1 large cauliflower, cut into large florets

ADD-INS
- Juice of ½ lemon
- 2 tablespoons chopped fresh cilantro

1. Press the Sauté button and adjust to normal. Pour in the olive oil. Once hot, add the cumin seeds and heat for about 30 seconds, or until they start to pop. Add the potatoes and onion and sauté for about 3 minutes, until the onion has softened. Add the tomato and sauté for 2 minutes. Add the garlic, ginger, salt, ground cumin, coriander, and turmeric, stirring well until combined. Add the water and use a silicone spatula to scrape up any brown bits on the base of the pot. Simmer for 2 minutes. Add the cauliflower and gently stir to combine. Press the Cancel/Off button.

2. Lock the lid in place and seal the steam valve. Select Pressure/Manual and adjust the time to 1 minute on high pressure.

3. After cooking, quick release the pressure. Carefully removed the lid and set aside.

4. Remove the pot and place it on a heat-resistant surface. Gently stir in the lemon juice. Serve warm with a sprinkle of the cilantro.

PER SERVING (¾ cup) Calories: 211; Total Fat: 3g; Fiber: 8g; Protein: 7g; Sodium: 444mg; Sugar: 5g

ALLERGY-FREE, ONE POT, VEGAN

One-Pot Mexican Rice and Beans

Serves: 6 / **Prep Time:** 7 minutes / **Pressure Cook:** 22 minutes high pressure / **Release:** Natural for 5 minutes, then quick / **Total Time:** 40 minutes

This simple recipe is a busy weeknight lifesaver. Everything is combined and cooked in one pot for a complete meal that's full of some of my favorite flavors. The combination of brown rice and black beans provides a good source of fiber and protein to this delicious meatless meal.

1 large onion, chopped

2 cups brown rice, rinsed

1 cup dried black beans, rinsed

2 cups low-sodium vegetable broth

2 cups water

2 bay leaves

2 tablespoons chili powder

2 teaspoons dried oregano leaves

1 teaspoon ground cumin

1½ teaspoons sea salt

1 (28-ounce) can diced tomatoes, drained

ADD-INS

½ cup chopped fresh cilantro leaves

Juice of ½ lime

1 tablespoon chopped jalapeño (leave seeds in for more heat)

1. In the pressure cooker, evenly place the onion, rice, beans, broth, water, bay leaves, chili powder, oregano, cumin, salt, and diced tomatoes. Do not stir.

2. Lock the lid in place and seal the steam valve. Select Pressure/Manual and adjust the time to 22 minutes on high pressure.

3. After cooking, let the pressure release naturally for 5 minutes, then quick release any remaining pressure. Carefully remove the lid and set aside.

4. Remove the pot and place it on a heat-resistant surface. Gently stir in the cilantro, lime juice, and jalapeño. Remove the bay leaves and serve.

HEALTH BOOST: Serve the rice and beans with a fresh garden salad to add a nutritional boost to this meal. Remember to fill half your plate with vegetables to help promote optimal health.

PER SERVING (1 cup) Calories: 256; Total Fat: 2g; Fiber: 8g; Protein: 9g; Sodium: 550mg; Sugar: 4g

GLUTEN-FREE, NUT-FREE, ONE POT, VEGETARIAN, 30 MINUTES OR LESS

Vegetable Risotto

Serves: 6 / **Prep Time:** 15 minutes / **Sauté:** 3 minutes / **Pressure Cook:** 5 minutes high pressure / **Release:** Natural for 5 minutes, then quick / **Total Time:** 30 minutes

I used to make risottos all the time and then I just stopped; I have no idea why. When I started looking into recipes to try in my electric pressure cooker, risottos were ones that kept popping up, so I thought I would give it a try and I'm back in love with them again. This light vegetable-packed risotto is so easy to make, I'm sure you'll love it, too.

- **1 tablespoon extra-virgin olive oil**
- **1 small onion, chopped**
- **½ cup chopped celery**
- **2 garlic cloves, minced**
- **3 cups Arborio rice**
- **1 cup packed chopped kale leaves**
- **1 cup frozen peas**
- **½ cup chopped zucchini**
- **½ cup chopped mushrooms**
- **4 cups low-sodium vegetable broth**
- **1 teaspoon sea salt**
- **1 teaspoon dried basil**
- **¼ teaspoon freshly ground black pepper**

ADD-INS
- **¼ cup shredded Parmesan cheese**
- **Juice of ½ lemon**
- **4 tablespoons chopped fresh parsley**

1. Press the Sauté button and adjust to normal. Pour in the olive oil. Once hot, add the onion, celery, and garlic and sauté for 2 minutes, until the onion has softened. Add the rice, kale, peas, zucchini, and mushrooms, stirring to combine, and sauté for 1 minute. Add the broth, salt, basil, and pepper, stirring to combine. Press the Cancel/Off button.

2. Lock the lid in place and seal the steam valve. Select Pressure/Manual and adjust the time to 5 minutes on high pressure.

3. After cooking, let the pressure release naturally for 5 minutes, then quick release any remaining pressure. Carefully remove the lid and set aside.

4. Stir in Parmesan cheese, lemon juice, and parsley. Serve warm.

SUBSTITUTION TIP: For a dairy-free, vegan version, substitute 2 tablespoons of nutritional yeast for the Parmesan cheese.

PER SERVING (¾ cup) Calories: 344; Total Fat: 3g; Fiber: 3g; Protein: 8g; Sodium: 411mg; Sugar: 1g

GLUTEN-FREE, NUT-FREE, VEGETARIAN, 30 MINUTES OR LESS

Quinoa and Lentil Stuffed Peppers

Serves: 4 to 5 / **Prep Time:** 10 minutes / **Pressure Cook:** 5 minutes high pressure / **Release:** Natural for 5 minutes, then quick / **Total Time:** 25 minutes

Try to prepare large batches of quinoa and freeze leftover portions to add to simple recipes like this or into salads for an added protein boost. Don't have any leftover quinoa? That's okay, this easy recipe works great with any leftover cooked grains you may have—try it with leftover brown or white rice. Enjoy these with a side salad for a complete meal.

2 cups cooked quinoa

1 (15-ounce) can low-sodium black beans, rinsed

1 (15-ounce) can diced tomatoes, drained

1 cup canned corn kernels or thawed frozen corn

½ small red onion, chopped

Juice of ½ lime

1 tablespoon chili powder

1 tablespoon chopped jalapeño

1 teaspoon dried oregano

½ teaspoon sea salt

2 red bell peppers, tops cut off and seeded

2 yellow bell peppers, tops cut off and seeded

1 cup water

ADD-INS

¼ cup shredded mozzarella cheese

1. In a large bowl, combine the quinoa, beans, tomatoes, corn, onion, lime juice, chili powder, jalapeño, oregano, and salt, mixing to combine. Fill the bell peppers with the quinoa mixture.

2. Pour the water into the pressure cooker pot and place a trivet inside. Carefully arrange the stuffed peppers on the trivet.

3. Lock the lid in place and seal the steam valve. Select Pressure/Manual and adjust the time to 5 minutes on high pressure.

4. After cooking, let the pressure release naturally for 5 minutes, then quick release any remaining pressure. Carefully remove the lid and set aside.

5. Sprinkle the mozzarella cheese on top of the peppers while they are still hot. Carefully remove the peppers from the pot and serve warm.

HEALTH BOOST: Use a combination of yellow and red bell peppers for an added vitamin A and vitamin C boost.

PER SERVING (1 pepper) Calories: 423; Total Fat: 13g; Fiber: 19g; Protein: 17g; Sodium: 537mg; Sugar: 9g

ALLERGY-FREE, VEGAN

Coconut-Lentil Curry

Serves: 6 / **Prep Time:** 15 minutes / **Sauté:** 8 minutes / **Pressure Cook:** 6 minutes high pressure / **Release:** Natural for 5 minutes, then quick / **Total Time:** 40 minutes

Growing up, lentil curries were our ultimate comfort meal, and this version with the coconut milk is a favorite. I've increased the nutrients in this classic recipe by adding in some fresh vegetables and spinach. To make dinner even easier, I have included a method in which you can cook the rice right along with the curry.

FOR THE BASMATI RICE

- 1½ cups white basmati rice
- 1½ cups water
- 1½ teaspoons sea salt
- 1 teaspoon extra-virgin olive oil

FOR THE LENTIL CURRY

- 1 tablespoon extra-virgin olive oil
- 1 small onion, minced
- 1 tomato, finely chopped
- ½ cup chopped mushrooms
- ½ cup chopped zucchini
- 2 garlic cloves, minced
- 1 teaspoon minced ginger
- 1 teaspoon sea salt
- ½ teaspoon turmeric
- ½ teaspoon ground coriander
- ½ teaspoon ground cumin

1. **To start the basmati rice:** Before cooking, rinse the rice and place in the oven-safe bowl with the water, salt, and olive oil for at least 10 minutes. This will reduce the cooking time.

2. **To make the lentil curry:** Press the Sauté button and adjust to normal. Pour in the olive oil. Once hot, add the onion and sauté for 2 to 3 minutes, until the onion has softened. Add the tomato and sauté for 2 minutes, until the tomato is softened. Add the mushrooms, zucchini, garlic, ginger, salt, turmeric, coriander, and cumin, stirring to combine. Pour in the water and lentils. Press the Cancel/Off button.

3. Place a trivet into the pot, making sure it's resting flat on the bottom. Place the dish with rice on the trivet.

4. Lock the lid in place and seal the steam valve. Select Pressure/Manual and adjust the time to 6 minutes on high pressure.

CONTINUED ▶

Coconut-Lentil Curry CONTINUED

3 cups water

¾ cup dried red lentils, rinsed

ADD-INS

1 cup coconut milk

½ cup chopped fresh spinach

Juice of ½ to 1 lemon

2 tablespoons chopped fresh cilantro

5. After cooking, let the pressure release naturally for 5 minutes, then quick release any remaining pressure. Carefully remove the lid and set aside. Using oven mitts, remove the dish and fluff the rice with a fork. If the rice seems a little undercooked, cover the dish to allow rice to continue to soften. Carefully remove trivet and set aside.

6. Press the Sauté button and adjust to low. Pour in the coconut milk and stir to combine. Add the spinach and simmer for 2 to 3 minutes, until the spinach wilts. Press the Cancel/Off button. Remove the pot and place it on a heat-resistant surface. Add the lemon juice and cilantro, stir and taste for seasoning, then serve with the rice.

SHORTCUT: For a simpler prep time, use 1 tablespoon of curry powder instead of the turmeric, cumin, and coriander. You can also reduce the amount of vegetables you add.

PER SERVING (½ cup) Calories: 377; Total Fat: 12g; Fiber: 4g; Protein: 11g; Sodium: 787mg; Sugar: 1g

DAIRY-FREE, GLUTEN-FREE, VEGAN, 30 MINUTES OR LESS

Vegetable Pad Thai

Serves: 6 / **Prep Time:** 15 minutes / **Sauté:** 2 minutes / **Pressure Cook:** 3 minutes high pressure / **Release:** Quick / **Total Time:** 25 minutes

Pad Thai is another favorite dish at our house; we love the Asian-inspired peanut flavor... *yum*! This vegetarian version is quick and easy to make, and you can pile in the vegetables for extra nutrients and bulk.

- ¼ cup coconut aminos or low-sodium soy sauce
- 3 tablespoons smooth natural peanut butter
- 2 tablespoons apple cider vinegar or rice vinegar
- 2 tablespoons pure maple syrup
- 2 tablespoons freshly squeezed lime juice
- ¼ teaspoon red pepper flakes
- 1 tablespoon sesame oil
- 3 garlic cloves, minced
- 2 teaspoons minced ginger
- 3 cups thinly sliced red cabbage
- 1 cup halved sugar snap peas
- ½ cup thinly sliced carrots
- 1½ cups low-sodium vegetable broth or water
- 8 ounces rice noodles

1. In a medium glass bowl, whisk together the coconut aminos, peanut butter, vinegar, maple syrup, lime juice, and red pepper flakes until the sauce is smooth. Set aside.

2. Press the Sauté button and adjust to normal. Pour in the sesame oil. Once hot, add the garlic and ginger and sauté for 1 minute. Add the cabbage, peas, and carrots and sauté for 1 minute. Pour in the prepared sauce and stir well. Add the broth. Break the rice noodles in half and add to the pot, spreading out in alternating directions. Press the noodles down to submerge the noodles in the liquid as much as possible.

3. Lock the lid in place and seal the steam valve. Select Pressure/Manual and adjust the time to 3 minutes on high pressure.

4. After cooking, quick release the pressure. Carefully remove the lid and set aside.

CONTINUED ▶

Vegetable Pad Thai CONTINUED

ADD-INS

2 tablespoons chopped fresh cilantro

2 tablespoons chopped scallions

1 tablespoon crushed peanuts

½ lime

5. Use silicone tongs to gently mix the noodles and other ingredients together. If the noodles seem undercooked, place the lid back on the pot and let sit for 5 minutes. Remove the pot and place it on a heat-resistant surface. Taste and adjust the seasoning if necessary.

6. Serve immediately topped with the cilantro, scallions, peanuts, and a squeeze of lime juice.

SUBSTITUTION TIP: This recipe can be made with whole-wheat spaghetti instead of rice noodles. If using spaghetti, break the noodles in half and add them into the pot in crisscross layers, add enough water or broth to cover the spaghetti, and increase the cook time to 4 minutes.

PER SERVING (1¼ cup) Calories: 276; Total Fat: 8g; Fiber: 3g; Protein: 8g; Sodium: 525mg; Sugar: 8g

ALLERGY-FREE, ONE POT, VEGAN

Hearty Lentil Stew

Serves: 6 / **Prep Time:** 15 minutes / **Pressure Cook:** 16 minutes high pressure / **Release:** Natural for 5 minutes, then quick / **Sauté:** 2 minutes / **Total Time:** 40 minutes

I've always wondered what the difference was between a soup and a stew. Essentially both are a combination of liquids, vegetables, and proteins, but the difference is in the consistency. Stews are thicker, heartier, and cooked at lower temperatures for longer periods of time, whereas soups are a little thinner in consistency.

4 cups halved baby potatoes, red or yellow
4 cups low-sodium vegetable broth
2 cups water
2 cups carrots, cut into ½-inch slices
1 (15-ounce) can diced tomatoes, drained
1 medium onion, chopped
3 garlic cloves, minced
1 teaspoon sea salt
½ teaspoon freshly ground black pepper
½ tablespoon Italian seasoning
1¾ cups dried green lentils, rinsed

ADD-INS
2 cups chopped kale or chard
1 cup frozen peas
Juice of ½ lemon

1. In the pressure cooker pot, combine all the stew ingredients.
2. Lock the lid in place and seal the steam valve. Select Pressure/Manual and adjust the time to 16 minutes on high pressure.
3. After cooking, let the pressure release naturally for 5 minutes, then quick release any remaining pressure. Carefully remove the lid and set aside.
4. Press the Sauté button and adjust to low. Stir in the kale and peas, stirring to combine, and simmer for 2 minutes. Press the Cancel/Off button. Stir in the lemon juice and serve warm.

HEALTH BOOST: Add a variety of hearty dark greens with the kale, like Swiss chard, collard greens, or arugula, for added vitamin K and antioxidant benefits.

PER SERVING (1¼ cups) Calories: 320; Total Fat: 1g; Fiber: 12g; Protein: 18g; Sodium: 592mg; Sugar: 8g

GLUTEN-FREE, NUT-FREE, VEGETARIAN, 30 MINUTES OR LESS

Meatless Shepherd's Pie

Serves: 4 / **Prep Time:** 10 minutes / **Pressure Cook:** 6 minutes high pressure / **Release:** Natural for 5 minutes, then quick / **Sauté:** 3 minutes / **Total Time:** 30 minutes

There is often some confusion between shepherd's pie and cottage pie, as both originated in the United Kingdom. The main difference is in the meats used. Shepherd's pie is made with lamb, and cottage pie is made with beef. Not sure what this meatless version should be named, but we'll just borrow the shepherd's pie name for now and hope no one notices.

FOR THE PIE FILLING

- 2 cups chopped carrots
- 2 cups chopped mushrooms
- 1 (15-ounce) can low-sodium chickpeas, rinsed
- 1 (15-ounce) can diced tomatoes, drained
- 1½ cups low-sodium vegetable broth
- 1 medium onion, chopped
- ½ cup dried red lentils, rinsed
- 2 tablespoons coconut aminos or low-sodium soy sauce
- 2 garlic cloves, minced
- 1 teaspoon sea salt
- 1 teaspoon dried oregano
- ¼ teaspoon freshly ground black pepper
- ½ cup frozen peas
- ½ cup frozen corn
- 1 cup chopped fresh spinach

1. **To make the pie filling:** In the pressure cooker pot, combine the carrots, mushrooms, chickpeas, tomatoes, broth, onion, lentils, coconut aminos, garlic, salt, oregano, and pepper, stirring to combine. Place a trivet into the pot, making sure it is resting flat on the bottom.

2. **To make the mashed cauliflower:** Place the cauliflower into a steaming basket and set the basket on top of the trivet.

3. Lock the lid in place and seal the steam valve. Select Pressure/Manual and adjust the time to 6 minutes on high pressure.

4. After cooking, let the pressure release naturally for 5 minutes, then quick release any remaining pressure. Carefully remove the lid and set aside.

5. Remove the steamer basket and set aside, and remove the trivet and set aside. Press the Sauté button and adjust to low. Stir in the peas, corn, and spinach and simmer for 2 to 3 minutes. Press the Cancel/Off button and let the mixture rest.

FOR THE MASHED CAULIFLOWER

1 large cauliflower head, cut into florets

1 tablespoon unsalted butter

½ teaspoon sea salt

¼ teaspoon freshly ground black pepper

1 tablespoon chopped fresh parsley

6. Transfer the steamed cauliflower to a large bowl and add the butter, salt, and pepper and mash with a fork.

7. Transfer the lentil mixture into a greased 11-by-8-inch baking dish. Add the cauliflower mash on top, sprinkle with the parsley, and serve.

VARIATION TIP: If you'd like a crispy brown finish on the cauliflower, place the baking dish in a preheated oven and bake at 375°F for 5 to 10 minutes, until the cauliflower mash begins to brown. Sprinkle with parsley before serving.

PER SERVING (¾ cup vegetable and lentil base, ¼ cup mashed cauliflower) Calories: 163; Total Fat: 3g; Fiber: 9g; Protein: 9g; Sodium: 608mg; Sugar: 6g

GLUTEN-FREE, NUT-FREE, ONE POT, VEGETARIAN, 30 MINUTES OR LESS

Creamy Mushroom Penne

Serves: 6 / **Prep Time:** 8 minutes / **Sauté:** 6 minutes / **Pressure Cook:** 1 minute high pressure/
Release: Natural for 8 minutes, then quick / **Total Time:** 25 minutes

Over the years, I have been trying to include more mushrooms in my meals for all the benefits they offer, and I finally decided to try a mushroom cream sauce—and I'm so glad I did. The delicious flavors in this sauce are nothing like the creamy mushroom soup from my childhood.

- 2 tablespoons extra-virgin olive oil
- 1 medium onion, chopped
- 1 red bell pepper, chopped
- 4 garlic cloves, minced
- 3 cups sliced mushrooms
- 2 cups low-sodium vegetable broth, plus more as needed
- 1 (13.5-ounce) can light coconut milk
- 2 tablespoons coconut aminos or low-sodium soy sauce
- 1 teaspoon dried thyme
- ½ teaspoon sea salt
- ½ teaspoon freshly ground black pepper
- 1 (12-ounce) box brown rice penne

1. Press the Sauté button and adjust to normal. Pour in the olive oil. Once hot, add the onion, bell pepper, and garlic and sauté for 2 minutes, until the onion has softened. Add the mushrooms and sauté for 2 minutes, until the mushrooms begin to brown. Pour in half the broth and use a silicone spatula to scrape any brown bits from the bottom of the pot. Add the remaining broth, as well as the coconut milk, coconut aminos, thyme, salt, and black pepper, stirring to combine. Add the pasta and press it down below the liquid line, adding more broth if necessary. Press the Cancel/Off button.

2. Lock the lid in place and seal the steam valve. Select Pressure/Manual and adjust the time to 1 minute on high pressure.

3. After cooking, let the pressure release naturally for 8 minutes, then quick release any remaining pressure. Carefully remove the lid and set aside.

4. Gently stir in the pasta, press the Sauté button, adjust to low, and bring to a simmer. Add the spinach and peas, stir to combine, and simmer for 2 minutes, until the spinach wilts. Press the Cancel/Off button. The sauce will thicken as it cools.

ADD-INS

2 cups chopped fresh baby spinach

1½ cups frozen peas

½ cup shredded fresh Parmesan cheese

5. Remove the pot and place it on a heat-resistant surface. Stir in the Parmesan cheese before serving.

SUBSTITUTION TIP: In order to use whole-wheat pasta instead of brown rice pasta, adjust the time to half the amount listed on the pasta packaging and reduce that by another minute; additionally, release the steam right after cook time ends.

PER SERVING (1⅓ cup) Calories: 435; Total Fat: 22g; Fiber: 5g; Protein: 11g; Sodium: 536mg; Sugar: 2g

GLUTEN-FREE, NUT-FREE, ONE POT, VEGETARIAN

Sweet and Savory Wild Rice

Serves: 6 / **Prep Time:** 15 minutes / **Sauté:** 3 minutes / **Pressure Cook:** 15 minutes high pressure / **Release:** Natural for 10 minutes, then quick / **Total Time:** 45 minutes

I love combining balsamic vinegar and feta cheese in my salads; it adds a delicious combination of sweet and salty. This hearty recipe has an amazing combination of flavors and textures, making this a great side dish or a filling meal. Enjoy with a side salad for an additional nutrition boost.

1 tablespoon extra-virgin olive oil
1 red onion, chopped
1 red bell pepper, chopped
1½ cups chopped mushrooms
4 garlic cloves, minced
1 (15-ounce) can low-sodium chickpeas, rinsed
1½ cups wild rice, rinsed
1½ teaspoons Italian seasoning
½ teaspoon sea salt
2½ cups low-sodium vegetable broth
2 tablespoons low-sodium soy sauce

ADD-INS

½ cup raw pumpkin seeds
⅓ cup balsamic vinegar
¼ cup dried cranberries
2 tablespoons crumbled feta cheese

1. Press the Sauté button and adjust to normal. Pour in the olive oil. Once hot, add the onion and sauté for 2 minutes, until it has softened. Add the bell pepper, mushrooms, and garlic and sauté for 1 minute. Add the chickpeas, rice, Italian seasoning, and salt, stirring to combine. Add the broth and soy sauce. Press the Cancel/Off button.

2. Lock the lid in place and seal the steam valve. Select Pressure/Manual and adjust the time to 15 minutes on high pressure.

3. After cooking, let the pressure release naturally for 10 minutes, then quick release any remaining pressure. Carefully remove the lid and set aside.

4. Remove the pot and place on a heat-resistant surface. Stir in the pumpkin seeds, vinegar, and cranberries. Serve warm with a sprinkle of the feta cheese.

SUBSTITUTION TIP: Get creative with add-ins; instead of cranberries, try dried raisins or dates, and instead of pumpkin seeds, add your favorite nuts or seeds.

PER SERVING (1 cup) Calories: 331; Total Fat: 8g; Fiber: 8g; Protein: 14g; Sodium: 427mg; Sugar: 11g

ALLERGY-FREE, ONE POT, VEGAN

Coconut-Quinoa Curry

Serves: 6 / **Prep Time:** 10 minutes / **Sauté:** 7 minutes / **Pressure Cook:** 2 minutes high pressure / **Release:** Natural for 10 minutes, then quick / **Total Time:** 35 minutes

Quinoa is a popular gluten-free grain that is often used to replace higher carbohydrate options. It offers a complete source of protein, making it beneficial for those following a vegetarian or vegan lifestyle. Quinoa is also high in fiber, iron, magnesium, B vitamins, and antioxidants, making it a great addition to any healthy-eating plan.

1 tablespoon extra-virgin olive oil
3 cups cubed sweet potato
1 red onion, chopped
1 (15-ounce) can diced tomatoes, drained
3 garlic cloves, minced
1 teaspoon minced ginger
1 teaspoon ground cumin
1 teaspoon ground coriander
1 teaspoon sea salt
½ teaspoon turmeric
1 (15-ounce) can low-sodium chickpeas, rinsed
1½ cups water
½ cup quinoa, rinsed
1 (13.5-ounce) can full-fat coconut milk
1 cup chopped fresh spinach
Juice of 1 lemon
2 tablespoons chopped fresh cilantro

1. Press the Sauté button and adjust to normal. Pour in the olive oil. Once hot, add the sweet potatoes and onion and sauté for 2 minutes, until the onion has softened. Add the tomatoes, garlic, ginger, cumin, coriander, salt, and turmeric, stirring to combine. Simmer for 2 minutes. Add the chickpeas, water, and quinoa, and press the Cancel/Off button.

2. Lock the lid in place and seal the steam valve. Select Pressure/Manual and adjust the time to 2 minutes on high pressure.

3. After cooking, let the pressure release naturally for 10 minutes, then quick release any remaining pressure. Carefully remove the lid and set aside.

4. Press the Sauté button and adjust to low. Stir in the coconut milk and spinach and simmer for 2 to 3 minutes, until the spinach cooks. Press the Cancel/Off button. Remove the pot and place it on a heat-resistant surface. Add the lemon juice and cilantro before serving.

VARIATION TIP: This curry can be enjoyed on its own as a stew, or on top of brown rice or cauliflower rice.

PER SERVING (¾ cup) Calories: 349 Total Fat: 18g; Fiber: 8g; Protein: 9g; Sodium: 528mg; Sugar: 8g

ALLERGY-FREE, ONE POT, VEGAN

Veggie Rice Pilaf

Serves: 6 / **Prep Time:** 10 minutes / **Sauté:** 4 minutes / **Pressure Cook:** 22 minutes high pressure / **Release:** Natural for 10 minutes, then quick / **Keep Warm:** 5 minutes / Total Time: 55 minutes

Vegetables provide us with a ton of nutrients and fiber, and the more colors of vegetables we include, the more antioxidant benefits we receive. With this recipe, you can use the vegetables listed below or change them up for some of your favorites.

2 tablespoons extra-virgin olive oil
1 teaspoon cumin seeds
1 cinnamon stick
1 bay leaf
1 medium onion, chopped
3 garlic cloves, minced
1 teaspoon minced ginger
1 tomato, chopped
1 teaspoon sea salt
½ teaspoon ground turmeric
1½ cups water
1½ cups long-grain brown rice, rinsed

ADD-INS
½ cup frozen peas
½ cup frozen corn
½ cup sliced red bell pepper
1 cup chopped fresh spinach
2 tablespoons chopped fresh cilantro

1. Press the Sauté button and adjust to normal. Pour in the olive oil. Once hot, add the cumin seeds, cinnamon stick, and bay leaf and simmer for about 30 seconds, until the cumin seeds start to sizzle. Add the onion, garlic, and ginger and sauté for 2 minutes, until the onion has softened. Add the tomato, salt, and turmeric and sauté for 1 minute. Add the water and rice. Press the Cancel/Off button.

2. Lock the lid in place and seal the steam valve. Select Pressure/Manual and adjust the time to 22 minutes on high pressure.

3. After cooking, let the pressure release naturally for 10 minutes, then quick release any remaining pressure. Carefully remove the lid and set aside.

4. Press the Keep Warm button. Add the peas, corn, bell pepper, and spinach, stirring to combine. Cover the pot and allow the pilaf to rest for 5 minutes.

5. Uncover the pot, remove and discard the cinnamon stick and bay leaf, and sprinkle on the cilantro before serving.

PER SERVING (1 cup) Calories: 254; Total Fat: 6g; Fiber: 3g; Protein: 5g; Sodium: 411mg; Sugar: 3g

DAIRY-FREE, GLUTEN-FREE, NUT-FREE, ONE POT, VEGAN

Spinach-and-Tofu Curry

Serves: 6 / **Prep Time:** 10 minutes / **Sauté:** 10 minutes / **Pressure Cook:** 5 minutes high pressure / **Release:** Natural for 5 minutes, then quick / **Total Time:** 35 minutes

Spinach and other dark green leafy vegetables contain a high source of plant-based iron, which is beneficial to our overall health. Here's a quick tip: Whenever preparing foods that are high in iron, add some citrus fruit or any other food that is high in vitamin C. Studies have shown that vitamin C can help our bodies better absorb iron.

- 4 tablespoons extra-virgin olive oil, divided
- 1 pound extra-firm tofu, patted dry and cut into cubes
- 1 medium onion, chopped
- 3 garlic cloves, minced
- 1 teaspoon minced ginger
- 1 tomato, chopped
- 1 teaspoon sea salt
- ½ teaspoon turmeric
- ½ teaspoon ground cumin
- 16 ounces chopped frozen spinach, thawed
- 8 ounces frozen kale
- ¼ cup water

ADD-INS
- ⅓ cup full-fat coconut milk
- Juice of 1 lemon

1. Press the Sauté button and adjust to normal. Pour in 2 tablespoons of olive oil. Once hot, add the tofu and sear on all sides for 4 to 6 minutes, until browned. Use a silicone spoon to remove the tofu and set aside. Scrape away any seared bits from the base of the pot.

2. Heat the remaining 2 tablespoons of olive oil. Add the onion, garlic, and ginger and sauté for 2 minutes, until the onion has softened. Add the tomato, salt, turmeric, and cumin, and sauté for 1 minute. Add the spinach, kale, seared tofu, and water, stirring to combine. Press the Cancel/Off button.

3. Lock the lid in place and seal the steam valve. Select Pressure/Manual and adjust the time to 5 minutes on high pressure.

4. After cooking, let the pressure release naturally for 5 minutes, then quick release any remaining pressure. Carefully remove the lid and set aside.

5. Stir in the coconut milk and lemon juice. Serve warm.

SUBSTITUTION TIP: For a non-vegan option, try paneer cheese instead of tofu.

PER SERVING (½ cup) Calories: 222; Total Fat: 17g; Fiber: 4g; Protein: 12g; Sodium: 460mg; Sugar: 2g

Orange-Ginger Salmon Dinner, page 133

CHAPTER EIGHT

Poultry and Seafood

Chili-Lime Chicken and Rice **132**

Orange-Ginger Salmon Dinner **133**

Roasted Chicken and Veggies **135**

Lemon-Cilantro Chicken **137**

Light 'n' Easy Butter Chicken **139**

Creamy Chicken and Broccoli Rice **141**

Garlic-Lime Shrimp Scampi **142**

Lemon-Dill Salmon **143**

Thai Red Chicken Curry **145**

Spicy Mexican Chicken **146**

Cashew Chicken **147**

Mediterranean Turkey-Quinoa Bowl **149**

Saucy Italian Fish and Quinoa **150**

Parmesan Turkey Meatballs **152**

Orange Shrimp Stir-Fry **153**

ALLERGY-FREE, 30 MINUTES OR LESS

Chili-Lime Chicken and Rice

Serves: 6 / **Prep Time:** 10 minutes / **Sauté:** 3 minutes / **Pressure Cook:** 8 minutes high pressure / **Release:** Natural for 5 minutes, then quick / **Total Time:** 30 minutes

Personally, I'm a sucker for the chili-lime flavor combination. Just thinking about it makes my mouth water! Is it any wonder we're starting off this chapter with a recipe that's full of this flavor combination and ridiculously easy to make?

2 boneless, skinless chicken breasts, cubed
1 tablespoon chili powder
1 teaspoon sea salt
½ teaspoon ground cumin
½ teaspoon garlic powder
½ teaspoon onion powder
1 tablespoon extra-virgin olive oil
1 (15-ounce) can diced tomatoes, drained
2 garlic cloves, minced
1 (15-ounce) can low-sodium black beans, rinsed
1½ cups white basmati rice, rinsed
1½ cups low-sodium chicken broth
1 cup frozen corn kernels

ADD-INS
¼ cup chopped fresh cilantro leaves
Juice of ½ lime

1. In a medium bowl, combine the chicken, chili powder, salt, cumin, garlic powder, and onion powder and mix until the chicken is coated.

2. Press the Sauté button and adjust to high. Pour in the olive oil. Once hot, add the chicken and sauté for 2 minutes, until the chicken is no longer pink. Add the tomatoes, and using a silicone spatula, scrape any brown bits from the base of the pot. Add the garlic and sauté 1 minute. Add the beans, rice, broth, and corn, stirring to combine. Press the Cancel/Off button.

3. Lock the lid in place and seal the steam valve. Select Pressure/Manual and adjust the time to 8 minutes on high pressure.

4. After cooking, let the pressure release naturally for 5 minutes, then quick release any remaining pressure. Carefully remove the lid and set aside.

5. Stir in the cilantro and lime juice, and serve.

HEALTH BOOST: Top with fresh avocado, chopped tomatoes, and plain Greek yogurt for an added healthy fat and protein source.

PER SERVING (1 cup) Calories: 294; Total Fat: 3g; Fiber: 6g; Protein: 15g; Sodium: 376mg; Sugar: 3g

DAIRY-FREE, GLUTEN-FREE, NUT-FREE, 30 MINUTES OR LESS

Orange-Ginger Salmon Dinner

Serves: 6 / **Prep Time:** 15 minutes / **Pressure Cook:** 3 minutes high pressure / **Release:** Quick / **Total Time:** 20 minutes

Salmon is one of the easiest foods to prepare in an electric pressure cooker, which is great for me as I'm the only one who enjoys seafood in my house. Since I still want to enjoy salmon but don't want to spend all my time in the kitchen, I'm always looking for easy recipes that allow me to enjoy it while making something different for the family.

FOR THE VEGETABLE QUINOA

1½ cups water
¾ cup quinoa, rinsed
½ cup chopped carrots
½ cup chopped celery
½ cup frozen peas
1 teaspoon sea salt
1 teaspoon dried oregano

FOR THE ORANGE-GINGER SALMON

2 pounds salmon fillet
¼ teaspoon sea salt
¼ teaspoon freshly ground black pepper
¼ cup honey
2 tablespoons freshly squeezed orange juice
1 tablespoon coconut aminos or low-sodium soy sauce
1 tablespoon grated orange zest
2 garlic cloves, minced
½ orange, sliced

1. **To make the vegetable quinoa:** In the pressure cooker pot, combine all the vegetable quinoa ingredients and stir to combine.

2. **To make the orange-ginger salmon:** Place a trivet in the pot, making sure it's resting flat on the bottom. Cut a piece of aluminum foil that's a little larger than the size of the salmon and place on top of the trivet.

3. Dry the salmon fillet and place it on the prepared trivet. Sprinkle with the salt and pepper. In a small bowl, whisk together the honey, orange juice, coconut aminos, orange zest, and garlic. Pour the honey mixture over the salmon and spread evenly. Place the orange slices on top.

4. Lock the lid in place and seal the steam valve. Select Pressure/Manual and adjust the time to 3 minutes on high pressure.

5. After cooking, quick release the pressure. Carefully remove the lid and set aside. Carefully remove the trivet/stand with the salmon and set aside.

CONTINUED ▶

Orange-Ginger Salmon Dinner CONTINUED

6. Using a silicone spatula, fluff and mix the quinoa, taste, and add additional seasoning if necessary.

7. Serve the quinoa and salmon together.

SUBSTITUTION TIP: You can also use frozen salmon fillets; just increase the cook time to 5 minutes and arrange the fillets so they are not overlapping.

PER SERVING (⅓ pound salmon fillet and ½ cup quinoa) Calories: 357; Total Fat: 11g; Fiber: 3g; Protein: 34g; Sodium: 664mg; Sugar: 13g

ALLERGY-FREE

Roasted Chicken and Veggies

Serves: 4 to 6 / **Prep Time:** 10 minutes / **Sauté:** 9 minutes / **Pressure Cook:** 25 minutes high pressure / **Release:** Natural for 10 minutes, then quick / **Total Time:** 1 hour

All the comfort of roasted chicken and vegetables ready from start to finish in about an hour? Count me in. With this recipe, you can enjoy a roasted chicken dinner any day of the week instead of waiting for the weekend. Roasted chicken is also great for meal prep; you can use the cooked chicken in various meals throughout the week.

1 (4-pound) whole chicken

1 lemon, quartered

3 to 4 garlic cloves, flattened with the side of a knife

3 rosemary sprigs, divided

3 thyme sprigs, divided

2 teaspoons sea salt

2 teaspoons dried thyme

1 teaspoon dried oregano

½ teaspoon freshly ground black pepper

3 tablespoons extra-virgin olive oil, divided

1 cup low-sodium chicken broth, divided

5 potatoes, cut into 2-inch cubes

3 carrots, cut into 2-inch pieces

1 red onion, cut into 1-inch pieces

1. Make sure inside the chicken is clean and clear of giblets. Rinse and pat the chicken dry and place the lemon, garlic, two rosemary sprigs, and two thyme sprigs in the chicken cavity.

2. In a small bowl, mix together the salt, thyme, oregano, and pepper and set aside. Rub 1 tablespoon of olive oil all over the chicken and sprinkle the spice blend all over, patting it down gently to get it to stick to the chicken skin.

3. Press the Sauté button and adjust to high. Pour in the remaining 2 tablespoons of olive oil. Once hot, carefully place the chicken, breast-side down, inside and sear for 5 minutes, until browned. Use silicone tongs to gently turn the chicken over and sear the other side for 4 minutes, until browned. Use the tongs to carefully remove chicken from the pot and set aside.

CONTINUED ▶

Roasted Chicken and Veggies CONTINUED

4. Add ¼ cup of broth. Use a silicone spatula to deglaze the pot, scraping up any brown bits. Add the potatoes, carrots, and onion and place the chicken on top of the vegetables. Pour the remaining ¾ cup of broth around the chicken. Press the Cancel/Off button.

5. Lock the lid in place and seal the steam valve. Select Pressure/Manual and adjust the time to 25 minutes on high pressure.

6. After cooking, let the pressure release naturally for 10 minutes, then quick release any remaining pressure. Carefully remove the lid and set aside.

7. Remove the chicken from the pot and set aside. Carve and slice the chicken, discard the contents from inside the chicken, and serve with a portion of potatoes and vegetables.

VARIATION TIP: For a crispy skin option, place the cooked chicken in an oven-safe dish and broil at 425°F for 10 to 15 minutes, until the skin has browned.

PER SERVING (½ cup chicken, 1 cup vegetable mix) Calories: 274; Total Fat: 9g; Fiber: 6g; Protein: 9g; Sodium: 341mg; Sugar: 4g

ALLERGY-FREE

Lemon-Cilantro Chicken

Serves: 6 / **Prep Time:** 10 minutes / **Sauté:** 14 minutes / **Pressure Cook:** 8 minutes high pressure / **Release:** Natural for 5 minutes, then quick / **Total Time:** 40 minutes

Here's a fun fact about cilantro: Some people really enjoy the taste of cilantro, and some people claim it has a distinct soapy taste. The reason behind this has more to do with our genetic makeup than personal taste. If you don't like the flavor of cilantro, replace it with parsley for a different flavor profile. This is great served with cauliflower rice.

3 boneless, skinless chicken breasts, halved horizontally, or 6 to 8 chicken thighs

½ teaspoon sea salt

½ teaspoon paprika

½ teaspoon garlic powder

¼ teaspoon freshly ground black pepper

3 tablespoons extra-virgin olive oil, divided

1 small onion, chopped

4 garlic cloves, minced

1 teaspoon dried oregano

1 teaspoon dried thyme

Juice of 1 lemon

½ cup low-sodium chicken broth

1. In a medium bowl, season the chicken with the salt, paprika, garlic powder, and pepper and set aside.

2. Press the Sauté button and adjust to high. Pour in 2 tablespoons of olive oil. Once hot, add the chicken breasts and sear on one side for about 4 minutes, until brown. Use silicone tongs to gently turn the chicken over and sear the other side for 4 minutes, until browned. Use silicone tongs to remove the chicken from the pot and set aside.

3. Add the remaining 1 tablespoon of olive oil. Add the onion and sauté for 2 minutes, until the onion is translucent. Add the garlic, oregano, and thyme and sauté for 2 minutes. Add the lemon juice and stir to deglaze the pot, scraping up any brown bits. Add the broth and press the Cancel/Off button.

4. Lock the lid in place and seal the steam valve. Select Pressure/Manual and adjust the time to 8 minutes on high pressure.

CONTINUED ▶

Lemon-Cilantro Chicken CONTINUED

ADD-INS

1 tablespoon lemon zest

¼ cup chopped fresh cilantro leaves or parsley

5. After cooking, let the pressure release naturally for 5 minutes, then quick release any remaining pressure. Carefully remove the lid and set aside.

6. Press the Sauté button, adjust to normal, and bring to a boil for 2 minutes, until the sauce is reduced. Press the Cancel/Off button and stir in the lemon zest and cilantro. Serve warm, spooning the sauce over the chicken.

VARIATION TIP: For a thicker sauce, mix together 1 tablespoon of cornstarch and 2 tablespoons of water. After cooking, open the lid and press the Sauté button, pour the cornstarch mix into the pot, mix, and simmer until the desired consistency is reached.

PER SERVING (1 piece of chicken) Calories: 209; Total Fat: 11g; Fiber: 1g; Protein: 23g; Sodium: 303mg; Sugar: 1g

GLUTEN-FREE, NUT-FREE

Light 'n' Easy Butter Chicken

Serves: 6 / **Prep Time:** 10 minutes, plus 1 hour to marinate / **Sauté:** 8 minutes /
Pressure Cook: 8 minutes high pressure / **Release:** Natural for 10 minutes, then quick /
Total Time: 1 hour 40 minutes

Butter chicken is a popular Indian dish that's made with lots of butter (hence the name) and heavy cream. It tastes amazing but may not work in a weight loss meal plan. Not to worry though—here is a lighter version that is just as tasty but made in a much lighter way. The cauliflower helps make the sauce creamy and is a great way to sneak in some extra vegetables. It's great served with cooked brown rice or quinoa.

2 pounds boneless, skinless chicken breasts, cut into 1-inch cubes

2 teaspoons ground cumin

1 teaspoon ground coriander

1 teaspoon garam masala

1 teaspoon sea salt

½ teaspoon freshly ground black pepper

½ teaspoon turmeric

1 tablespoon ghee or extra-virgin olive oil

1 small onion, chopped

3 garlic cloves, minced

½ tablespoon minced ginger

1 cup tomato sauce

1. In a large bowl, combine the chicken, cumin, coriander, garam masala, salt, pepper, and turmeric, mixing to combine. Cover the bowl, refrigerate, and marinate the chicken for at least 1 hour or as long as overnight.

2. Press the Sauté button and adjust to normal. Stir in the ghee. Once hot, add the onion and sauté for 2 minutes, until the onion is softened. Add the garlic and ginger and sauté for 1 minute. Add the marinated chicken and sauté for about 5 minutes, until the chicken is no longer pink. Add the tomato sauce and tomato paste, mix well, then add the cauliflower. Press the Cancel/Off button.

3. Lock the lid in place and seal the steam valve. Select Pressure/Manual and adjust the time to 8 minutes on high pressure.

4. After cooking, let the pressure release naturally for 10 minutes, then quick release any remaining pressure. Carefully remove the lid and set aside.

CONTINUED ▶

Light 'n' Easy Butter Chicken CONTINUED

2 tablespoons tomato paste

½ cauliflower head, cut into florets

ADD-INS

⅓ cup plain low-fat Greek yogurt

Juice of ½ lemon

2 tablespoons chopped fresh cilantro leaves

5. Using a silicone spatula, mash the cauliflower and allow to cool for about 5 minutes. Stir in the yogurt and lemon juice. Sprinkle with the cilantro and serve warm.

SHORTCUT: If you have the time, marinating the cubed chicken for at least 1 hour helps enhance the flavors. But if you're short on time, you can skip the marinating; just mix the chicken and spices and continue with the steps listed.

PER SERVING (½ cup butter chicken) Calories: 140; Total Fat: 3g; Fiber: 2g; Protein: 22g; Sodium: 301mg; Sugar: 3g

GLUTEN-FREE, NUT-FREE, ONE POT, 30 MINUTES OR LESS

Creamy Chicken and Broccoli Rice

Serves: 6 / **Prep Time:** 10 minutes / **Sauté:** 6 minutes / **Pressure Cook:** 6 minutes high pressure / **Release:** Quick / **Total Time:** 30 minutes

When my kids were younger, evenings were always a crazy time. So, it was usually some sort of casserole thrown in the oven for dinner. It was during that time that I realized how easy it is to change up a meal by modifying a few simple ingredients. This is my favorite modified version of the classic chicken and broccoli casserole. Serve with a tossed salad on the side.

1 tablespoon extra-virgin olive oil

1 small onion, chopped

1 cup chopped carrots

½ red bell pepper, chopped

½ cup chopped mushrooms

3 garlic cloves, minced

2 pounds boneless, skinless chicken breasts, cut into ½-inch cubes

½ teaspoon sea salt

½ teaspoon dried basil

¼ teaspoon freshly ground black pepper

1½ cups low-sodium chicken broth or water

1 cup quinoa, rinsed

ADD-INS

3 cups broccoli florets

½ cup shredded Parmesan cheese

1. Press the Sauté button and adjust to normal. Pour in the olive oil. Once hot, add the onion and sauté for 1 minute, until the onion is softened. Add the carrot, bell pepper, mushrooms, and garlic and sauté for 2 minutes, until the vegetables are softened. Add the chicken, salt, basil, and pepper and sauté for about 4 minutes, until the chicken is no longer pink. Add the broth and quinoa and mix well. Press the Cancel/Off button.

2. Lock the lid in place and seal the steam valve. Select Pressure/Manual and adjust the time to 6 minutes on high pressure.

3. After cooking, quick release the pressure. Carefully remove the lid and set aside.

4. Stir in the broccoli and Parmesan cheese, cover the pot, and let rest 5 minutes, until the broccoli is tender-crisp. Serve warm.

SHORTCUT: The broccoli in this recipe is tender-crisp. For a softer texture and reduced wait time, steam the broccoli florets and stir them in before serving.

PER SERVING (1 cup) Calories: 314; Total Fat: 8g; Fiber: 4g; Protein: 37g; Sodium: 404mg; Sugar: 2g

GLUTEN-FREE, NUT-FREE, ONE POT, 30 MINUTES OR LESS

Garlic-Lime Shrimp Scampi

Serves: 6 / **Prep Time:** 8 minutes / **Sauté:** 3 minutes / **Pressure Cook:** 1 minute high pressure/ **Release:** Quick / **Total Time:** 15 minutes

I love shrimp—I could eat them every day. But when my son was younger, we realized that he has an allergy to shellfish. To reduce his exposure, we stopped making shellfish at home. However, whenever he's out for dinner, I try to sneak in a shrimp meal. This easy shrimp scampi can be enjoyed with some spiralized zucchini, whole-grain pasta, brown rice, or salad.

- 2 tablespoons unsalted butter, divided
- 2 scallions, both white and green parts, chopped
- 4 garlic cloves, minced
- 1½ pounds shrimp, peeled and deveined
- ½ teaspoon sea salt
- ¼ teaspoon red pepper flakes (optional)
- ¼ cup low-sodium vegetable broth

ADD-INS

- 1 cup fresh baby spinach leaves
- ¼ cup chopped fresh cilantro leaves or parsley
- Juice of 1 lime
- 1 teaspoon grated lime zest

1. Press the Sauté button and adjust to normal. Add 1 tablespoon of butter. Once melted, add the scallions and garlic and sauté for 1 minute, until fragrant. Add the shrimp, salt, and red pepper flakes (if using). Add the broth and press the Cancel/Off button.

2. Lock the lid in place and seal the steam valve. Select Pressure/Manual and adjust the time to 1 minute on high pressure.

3. After cooking, quick release the pressure. Carefully remove the lid and set aside.

4. Using a slotted spoon, remove the shrimp and set aside. Press the Sauté button and adjust to normal. Stir in the remaining 1 tablespoon of butter and mix until combined. Simmer for about 2 minutes, until thickened, then add the spinach, cilantro, lime juice, lime zest, and cooked shrimp, mixing to coat. Serve warm.

VARIATION TIP: You can use frozen shrimp in this recipe, but increase the cook time from 1 to 3 minutes.

PER SERVING (6 to 8 shrimp) Calories: 122; Total Fat: 5g; Fiber: 0g; Protein: 16g; Sodium: 842mg; Sugar: 0g

DAIRY-FREE, GLUTEN-FREE, NUT-FREE, ONE POT, 30 MINUTES OR LESS

Lemon-Dill Salmon

Serves: 4 / **Prep Time:** 10 minutes / **Sauté:** 3 minutes / **Pressure Cook:** 3 minutes high pressure / **Release:** Quick / **Total Time:** 20 minutes

One of the main benefits of including salmon in your diet is that it is a high source of omega-3 fatty acids. The body is unable to produce omega-3 fatty acids, an important nutrient for brain development and overall good health. Make sure you purchase wild-caught salmon as opposed to farm raised.

2 pounds skin-on wild-caught salmon fillet
2 tablespoons chopped fresh dill
1 teaspoon sea salt, divided
½ teaspoon freshly ground black pepper, divided
1 teaspoon garlic powder, divided
Juice of ½ lemon
1 tablespoon extra-virgin olive oil
1 large sweet potato, peeled and cut in ½-inch cubes
½ teaspoon dried oregano

1. Rinse the salmon fillet and pat dry. Then place the fillet, skin-side down, on a piece of aluminum foil. Sprinkle it with the dill, ½ teaspoon of salt, ¼ teaspoon of pepper, and ½ teaspoon of garlic powder. Drizzle the lemon juice all over the salmon.

2. Press the Sauté button and adjust to normal. Pour in the olive oil. Once hot, add the sweet potato and sauté for 2 to 3 minutes, until the sweet potato starts to brown. Sprinkle with the remaining ½ teaspoon of salt, ¼ teaspoon of pepper, ½ teaspoon of garlic powder, and the oregano, tossing well. Press the Cancel/Off button.

3. Place a trivet into the pot, making sure it's resting flat on the bottom. Place the foil with the salmon on the trivet.

4. Lock the lid in place and seal the steam valve. Select Pressure/Manual and adjust the time to 3 minutes on high pressure.

5. After cooking, quick release the pressure. Carefully remove the lid and set aside.

CONTINUED ▶

Lemon-Dill Salmon CONTINUED

ADD-INS

½ lemon, sliced

2 cups broccoli, small florets

6. Place the lemon slices on top of cooked salmon and arrange the broccoli around it. Cover with the lid to allow the broccoli to steam for 5 minutes, until tender-crisp. Serve the salmon, broccoli, and sweet potatoes together.

SUBSTITUTION TIP: Dried dill can be used instead of fresh in this recipe; just decrease the amount to 1 tablespoon of dried leaves.

PER SERVING (⅓ pound salmon) Calories: 293; Total Fat: 13g; Fiber: 2g; Protein: 31g; Sodium: 681mg; Sugar: 2g

ALLERGY-FREE, ONE POT

Thai Red Chicken Curry

Serves: 6 / **Prep Time:** 15 minutes / **Sauté:** 10 minutes / **Pressure Cook:** 8 minutes high pressure / **Release:** Natural for 5 minutes, then quick / **Total Time:** 40 minutes

My husband and I love Thai food; it's our first choice for date-night meals. My favorite choice is always a red curry, and his favorite choice is cashew chicken. The downer is now that I've been able to re-create both of these meals in our electric pressure cooker, we need to get more creative with our date-night plans!

1 tablespoon extra-virgin olive oil
1 small onion, chopped
3 garlic cloves, minced
1 tablespoon minced ginger
½ teaspoon sea salt
2 pounds boneless, skinless chicken breasts, cut into 1-inch cubes
2 cups cubed eggplant
1 cup chopped carrots
3 tablespoons red curry paste, for mild to medium spice
½ cup low-sodium chicken broth

ADD-INS
1 red bell pepper, chopped
1 cup broccoli florets
1 (13.5-ounce) can full-fat coconut milk
Juice of 1 lime

1. Press the Sauté button and adjust to normal. Pour in the olive oil. Once hot, add the onion and sauté for 2 to 3 minutes, until the onion is softened. Add the garlic, ginger, and salt and sauté for 1 minute. Add the chicken and sauté until chicken is no longer pink, about 3 minutes. Add the eggplant and carrots and cook for 1 minute. Stir in the curry paste and broth. Press the Cancel/Off button.

2. Lock the lid in place and seal the steam valve. Select Pressure/Manual and adjust the time to 8 minutes on high pressure.

3. After cooking, let the pressure release naturally for 5 minutes, then quick release any remaining pressure. Carefully remove the lid and set aside.

4. Press the Sauté button and adjust to normal. Stir in the bell pepper and broccoli, and simmer for 2 minutes. Add the coconut milk and stir to combine. Press the Cancel/Off button.

5. Stir in the lime juice. Serve warm.

SUBSTITUTE TIP: If you like things a little spicy, add 1 or 2 fresh whole red chiles with the vegetables.

PER SERVING (¾ cup) Calories: 240; Total Fat: 13g; Fiber: 3g; Protein: 25g; Sodium: 206mg; Sugar: 3g

GLUTEN-FREE, NUT-FREE, ONE POT

Spicy Mexican Chicken

Serves: 6 / **Prep Time:** 10 minutes / **Sauté:** 7 minutes / **Pressure Cook:** 10 minutes high pressure / **Release:** Natural for 10 minutes, then quick / **Total Time:** 40 minutes

I make a pot of this chicken for meal prep then use it through the week as an add-in to various recipes like salads, burritos, and rice dishes. This chicken also freezes well, making it a lifesaver on those busy evenings when you're thinking about takeout.

1 tablespoon extra-virgin olive oil
1 small onion, sliced
1 red bell pepper, sliced
2 jalapeños, chopped (leave seeds in for more heat)
3 garlic cloves, minced
½ teaspoon sea salt
1 (10-ounce) can diced tomatoes, drained
2 tablespoons chili powder
1 teaspoon ground cumin
1 teaspoon dried oregano
2 pounds boneless, skinless chicken breasts
½ cup low-sodium chicken broth

ADD-INS
¼ cup plain low-fat Greek yogurt
Juice of 1 lime
2 tablespoons chopped fresh cilantro

1. Press the Sauté button and adjust to normal. Pour in the olive oil. Once hot, add the onion and sauté for 2 to 3 minutes, until the onion is softened. Add the bell peppers, jalapeños, garlic, and salt and sauté for 1 minute. Add the tomatoes, chili powder, cumin, and oregano, stirring to combine. Add the chicken in a single layer and pour in the broth. Press the Cancel/Off button.

2. Lock the lid in place and seal the steam valve. Select Pressure/Manual and adjust the time to 10 minutes on high pressure.

3. After cooking, let the pressure release naturally for 10 minutes, then quick release any remaining pressure. Carefully remove the lid and set aside.

4. Transfer the chicken to a cutting board, press the Sauté button, and adjust to normal. Simmer for 3 minutes to reduce the sauce as you shred the chicken with two forks.

5. Add the yogurt and stir to combine, then add the shredded chicken and press the Cancel/Off button. Stir in the lime juice and cilantro. Serve warm.

PER SERVING (½ cup) Calories: 139; Total Fat: 3g; Fiber: 2g; Protein: 22g; Sodium: 253mg; Sugar: 3g

DAIRY-FREE

Cashew Chicken

Serves: 6 / **Prep Time:** 15 minutes / **Sauté:** 6 minutes / **Pressure Cook:** 8 minutes high pressure / **Release:** Natural for 5 minutes, then quick / **Total Time:** 40 minutes

Here is my husband's favorite Thai meal. He makes me laugh every time we go to a Thai restaurant. He'll look over the menu, point out a couple of items that sound good that he may try, then when it comes time to place our order, he asks for . . . cashew chicken!

FOR THE CASHEW CHICKEN

- ½ cup low-sodium chicken broth or water
- ¼ cup low-sodium soy sauce
- 2 tablespoons oyster sauce
- 2 tablespoons rice vinegar
- 2 tablespoons honey
- ½ tablespoon sesame oil
- 2 garlic cloves, minced
- 1 teaspoon minced ginger
- 1 teaspoon red pepper flakes (optional)
- 2 pounds boneless, skinless chicken breast, cut into ½-inch cubes
- 1 tablespoon extra-virgin olive oil

1. **To make the cashew chicken:** In a medium bowl, whisk together the broth, soy sauce, oyster sauce, vinegar, honey, sesame oil garlic, ginger, and red pepper flakes (if using). In a separate medium bowl, combine 2 tablespoons of the prepared sauce and the chicken, mixing to combine.

2. **To make the white rice:** In an oven-safe bowl, combine the water, rice, salt, and olive oil and set aside.

3. Press the Sauté button and adjust to high. Pour in the olive oil. Once hot, add the chicken and sauté for 2 to 3 minutes, until the chicken is no longer pink. Pour in the remaining prepared sauce and mix well. Press the Cancel/Off button.

4. Place a long-legged trivet into the pot and arrange the chicken to allow the trivet to rest flat on the bottom. Place the bowl of rice on the trivet.

5. Lock the lid in place and seal the steam valve. Select Pressure/Manual and adjust the time to 8 minutes on high pressure.

CONTINUED ▶

Cashew Chicken CONTINUED

FOR THE WHITE RICE

3 cups water

1½ cups white basmati rice, rinsed

1 teaspoon sea salt

1 teaspoon extra-virgin olive oil

ADD-INS

2 tablespoons water

1 tablespoon cornstarch or arrowroot powder

1 red bell pepper, chopped

1 cup halved sugar snap peas

½ onion, sliced

½ cup raw or roasted cashews

2 tablespoons chopped fresh cilantro leaves

6. After cooking, let the pressure release naturally for 5 minutes, then quick release any remaining pressure. Carefully remove the lid and set aside. Using oven mitts, remove the dish and place on a heat-resistant surface. Fluff the rice with a fork and cover to keep warm.

7. Press the Sauté button and adjust to normal. In a small bowl, mix together the water and cornstarch and pour the slurry into the pot. Add the bell pepper, peas, and onion and simmer for about 3 minutes, until the sauce thickens. Press the Cancel/Off button.

8. Top with the cashews and cilantro and serve warm with the rice.

VARIATION TIP: If you do not have a long-legged stand or would rather enjoy the cashew chicken with brown rice or Cauliflower Fried Rice (see page 58), just omit the rice portion of this recipe.

PER SERVING (½ cup) Calories: 313; Total Fat: 8g; Fiber: 1g; Protein: 25g; Sodium: 488mg; Sugar: 5g

ALLERGY-FREE, ONE POT

Mediterranean Turkey-Quinoa Bowl

Serves: 6 to 8 / **Prep Time:** 10 minutes / **Sauté:** 7 minutes / **Pressure Cook:** 6 minutes high pressure / **Release:** Natural for 10 minutes, then quick / **Total Time:** 40 minutes

We generally don't eat a lot of turkey at our place. Even during the holidays, chicken is our go-to. I have made this recipe with ground chicken and it always turns out great, but I had a friend try it with turkey and it was a hit with her family.

1 tablespoon extra-virgin olive oil
1½ pounds ground turkey
1 cup halved cherry tomatoes
1 red onion, chopped
4 garlic cloves, minced
2 teaspoons dried oregano
1 teaspoon sea salt
½ teaspoon dried dill
½ teaspoon freshly ground black pepper
1 (15-ounce) can low-sodium chickpeas, rinsed
1½ cups low-sodium chicken broth or water
1¼ cups quinoa, rinsed
1 red bell pepper, chopped

ADD-INS
1 cup chopped fresh spinach
Juice of 1 lemon

1. Press the Sauté button and adjust to high. Pour in the olive oil. Add the turkey and sauté, stirring and breaking into pieces, for 5 minutes, until the turkey is no longer pink. Add the tomatoes, onion, garlic, oregano, salt, dill, and pepper and sauté for 2 minutes, until the tomatoes begin to soften. Add the chickpeas, broth, quinoa, and bell pepper. Press the Cancel/Off button.

2. Lock the lid in place and seal the steam valve. Select Pressure/Manual and adjust the time to 6 minutes on high pressure.

3. After cooking, let the pressure release naturally for 10 minutes, then quick release any remaining pressure. Carefully remove the lid and set aside.

4. Stir in the spinach and lemon juice and let rest for 5 minutes, until the spinach softens. Serve warm.

SHORTCUT: To chop cherry tomatoes faster, take two plastic lids, place one lid flat with the top side of the lid facing up. Arrange the tomatoes evenly on the lid. Place the second lid on top of the cherry tomatoes with the top side of the lid facing down. Place one hand firmly on top of the top lid and, with a serrated knife, slice through the tomatoes between the lids.

PER SERVING (1 cup) Calories: 310; Total Fat: 11g; Fiber: 5g; Protein: 23g; Sodium: 359mg; Sugar: 3g

DAIRY-FREE, GLUTEN-FREE, NUT-FREE, 30 MINUTES OR LESS

Saucy Italian Fish and Quinoa

Serves: 6 / **Prep Time:** 10 minutes / **Pressure Cook:** 3 minutes high pressure / **Release:** Natural for 8 minutes, then quick / **Sauté:** 2 minutes / **Total Time:** 25 minutes

The mouthwatering flavors in this dish work well with a white flaky fish like halibut, cod, haddock, and tilapia. Whichever fish you choose, aim to get wild caught as opposed to farm raised, as it's hard to confirm the quality of the farms and the feed that the fish were given. Fish feeding from their natural habitat will obviously taste the best.

FOR THE QUINOA
- 2 cups water or low-sodium vegetable or chicken broth
- 1½ cups quinoa, rinsed
- 1 teaspoon sea salt
- 1 teaspoon extra-virgin olive oil

FOR THE ITALIAN FISH
- ½ cup low-sodium vegetable or chicken broth
- 6 (3- to 4-ounce) whitefish fillets
- 2 cups halved cherry tomatoes
- 1 red bell pepper, sliced
- ½ green bell pepper, sliced
- ½ red onion, sliced
- ½ cup sliced pitted olives
- 2 teaspoons Italian seasoning
- ½ teaspoon sea salt

1. **To make the quinoa:** In an oven-safe bowl, combine the water, quinoa, salt, and olive oil, and set aside.

2. **To make the Italian fish:** In the pressure cooker pot, add the broth and arrange the fillets on the bottom. Evenly distribute the tomatoes, bell peppers, onion, and olives. Sprinkle on the Italian seasoning, salt, red pepper flakes (if using), and black pepper and drizzle with the olive oil.

3. Place a long-legged trivet in the pot, making sure it's resting flat on the bottom. Place the bowl with the quinoa on the trivet.

4. Lock the lid in place and seal the steam valve. Select Pressure/Manual and adjust the time to 3 minutes on high pressure.

5. After cooking, let the pressure release naturally for 8 minutes, then quick release any remaining pressure. Carefully remove the lid and set aside. Using oven mitts, remove the bowl of quinoa, place on a heat-resistant surface, and cover to keep warm. Remove the fish fillets and set aside.

½ teaspoon red pepper flakes (optional)

¼ teaspoon freshly ground black pepper

1 tablespoon extra-virgin olive oil

ADD-INS

Juice of 1 lime

3 tablespoons chopped fresh basil

6. Press the Sauté button, adjust to normal, and simmer for 2 minutes. Press the Cancel/Off button. Stir in the lime juice and basil. Taste and adjust the seasonings if necessary.

7. To serve, place a portion of quinoa on a plate. Add a piece of fish on top and spoon the sauce and vegetables over the fish.

SUBSTITUTION TIP: Frozen fish fillets can be used instead of fresh. Just decrease the water amount to ¼ cup (water will be released from frozen fillets) and increase the cook time to 4 minutes.

PER SERVING (1 fish fillet, ½ cup quinoa) Calories: 345; Total Fat: 9g; Fiber: 5g; Protein: 28g; Sodium: 751mg; Sugar: 8g

NUT-FREE, ONE POT, 30 MINUTES OR LESS

Parmesan Turkey Meatballs

Serves: 6 / **Prep Time:** 10 minutes / **Pressure Cook:** 10 minutes high pressure / **Release:** Natural for 5 minutes, then quick / **Total Time:** 30 minutes

Mix things up a little and make ground turkey or chicken meatballs instead of beef. Serve on spiralized zucchini for a low-calorie, low-carb option.

- 1½ pounds ground turkey
- ¼ cup chopped onion
- ¼ cup bread crumbs
- 2 large eggs
- 2 tablespoons shredded Parmesan cheese
- 1 tablespoon Worcestershire sauce
- 1 tablespoon Italian seasoning
- 3 garlic cloves, minced
- 1 teaspoon sea salt
- ½ teaspoon freshly ground black pepper
- 1 tablespoon extra-virgin olive oil
- 1 (24-ounce) jar marinara sauce
- ⅓ cup water

1. In a large bowl, using damp hands to prevent the meat from sticking, mix together the turkey, onion, bread crumbs, egg, Parmesan cheese, Worcestershire sauce, Italian seasoning, garlic, salt, and pepper until combined. Portion out 1½ to 2 tablespoons of the turkey mixture and roll into a ball or use an ice-cream scoop. Place the meatballs on a flat plate or tray.

2. In the pressure cooker pot, spread the olive oil around to coat the bottom of the pot. Add the meatballs, one at a time, to the bottom of the pot. For the second layer, place each meatball between two on the bottom layer. Pour the marinara sauce and water into the pot.

3. Lock the lid in place and seal the steam valve. Select Pressure/Manual and adjust the time to 10 minutes on high pressure.

4. After cooking, let the pressure release naturally for 5 minutes, then quick release any remaining pressure. Carefully remove the lid and set aside.

5. Carefully stir the meatballs and serve warm.

HEALTH BOOST: For a gluten-free and more nutritious option, use ¼ cup of rolled oats instead of bread crumbs.

PER SERVING (5 meatballs) Calories: 292; Total Fat: 15g; Fiber: 2g; Protein: 27g; Sodium: 670mg; Sugar: 5g

DAIRY-FREE, GLUTEN-FREE, NUT-FREE, 30 MINUTES OR LESS

Orange Shrimp Stir-Fry

Serves: 6 / **Prep Time:** 15 minutes / **Sauté:** 5 minutes / **Pressure Cook:** 2 minutes high pressure / **Release:** Quick / **Total Time:** 25 minutes

I think stir-fries are one of the quickest and healthiest meals, especially when following a weight loss lifestyle meal plan. You have a protein source, lots of vegetables, and a light sauce sautéed together and served with some whole grains or just enjoyed on its own.

¼ cup orange juice

¼ cup low-sodium chicken broth

3 tablespoons low-sodium soy sauce

2 teaspoons apple cider vinegar

2 teaspoons honey

3 garlic cloves, minced

1 teaspoon minced ginger

1 teaspoon sesame oil

1 tablespoon extra-virgin olive oil

1 red bell pepper, chopped

1 red onion, sliced

1 cup halved sugar snap peas

1. In a medium bowl, combine the orange juice, broth, soy sauce, vinegar, honey, garlic, ginger, and sesame oil, mixing to combine.

2. Press the Sauté button and adjust to normal. Stir in the bell peppers, onion, and peas and sauté for 2 minutes. Add the prepared sauce and shrimp, tossing to combine. Press the Cancel/Off button.

3. Lock the lid in place and seal the steam valve. Select Pressure/Manual and adjust the time to 2 minutes on high pressure.

4. After cooking, quick release the pressure. Carefully remove the lid and set aside.

CONTINUED ▶

Orange Shrimp Stir-Fry CONTINUED

1 pound shrimp, peeled and deveined

ADD-INS

1 tablespoon cornstarch or arrowroot powder

2 tablespoons water

1 cup broccoli florets

2 tablespoons chopped fresh cilantro leaves

5. Press the Sauté button and adjust to normal. As the mixture comes to a simmer, in a small bowl, mix together the cornstarch and water until smooth and pour it into the pot. Add the broccoli, stir, and simmer for 2 to 3 minutes, until the sauce has thickened and the broccoli is tender-crisp. Press the Cancel/Off button.

6. Sprinkle on the cilantro and serve.

SHORTCUT: Frozen shrimp can be used in this recipe along with a frozen blend of vegetables; just increase the cook time to 3 minutes. The mixture may need to thicken at the end for a little longer, as frozen shrimp and vegetables will release additional liquid.

PER SERVING (⅔ cup) Calories: 125; Total Fat: 4g; Fiber: 2g; Protein: 12g; Sodium: 693mg; Sugar: 5g

Pot Roast and Potatoes, page 167

CHAPTER NINE

Beef, Lamb, and Pork

Meat Loaf and Mashed Potatoes 158

Sesame Mongolian Beef 160

Sloppy Joe Stuffed Potatoes 161

Warm 'n' Cozy Beef Stew 163

Cuban Beef Picadillo 164

Shredded Chipotle Beef 165

Pot Roast and Potatoes 167

One-Pot Spaghetti and Meat Sauce 169

Spicy Beef Curry 171

Tzatziki Lamb Meatballs 172

Mediterranean Lamb Chops 174

Moroccan Lamb Stew 176

Pork Carnitas 178

Pork and Broccoli 179

Pork Barbacoa 181

NUT-FREE

Meat Loaf and Mashed Potatoes

Serves: 4 to 6 / **Prep Time:** 15 minutes / **Pressure Cook:** 25 minutes high pressure / **Release:** Quick / **Total Time:** 45 minutes

This recipe may look like it has a lot of ingredients and steps involved—and it does—but just imagine having your meat loaf and mashed potatoes cooked together in one pan, at the same time! I promise taking the time to read over the steps will be totally worth it, and you can thank me later when you realize how easy this meal is to throw together.

FOR THE MEAT LOAF

- 1½ pounds lean ground beef
- 1 small onion, chopped
- 2 large eggs
- ⅓ cup rolled oats
- ¼ cup chopped red bell pepper
- 1 tablespoon Worcestershire sauce
- 1 tablespoon pure maple syrup
- 4 garlic cloves, minced
- 2 teaspoons Italian seasoning
- 1 teaspoon sea salt
- ½ teaspoon freshly ground black pepper

FOR THE MASHED POTATOES

- 2½ pounds Yukon gold potatoes, peeled and quartered

1. **To make the meat loaf:** In a large bowl, place all the meat loaf ingredients and mix until just combined, avoiding overmixing. Cut a piece of aluminum foil that is large enough to fit inside the pressure cooker pot. Shape the meat loaf into an oval shape that is wide enough to fit on the trivet/stand. Place the shaped loaf onto the piece of foil and fold up the sides so the loaf is nestled into the foil. Set aside.

2. **To make the mashed potatoes:** In the pressure cooker pot, combine the potatoes, broth, and garlic powder. Place the trivet in the pot and arrange the potatoes so that the trivet rests flat on the bottom. Carefully place the wrapped meat loaf onto the trivet, but do not cover the loaf with foil.

3. Lock the lid in place and seal the steam valve. Select Pressure/Manual and adjust the time to 25 minutes on high pressure.

4. **To make the glaze:** Meanwhile, in a small bowl, whisk together the all the glaze ingredients and set aside.

5. After cooking, quick release the pressure. Carefully remove the lid and set aside.

- 1½ cups low-sodium vegetable or chicken broth
- 1 teaspoon garlic powder
- ¼ cup low-fat milk
- 2 tablespoons cream cheese
- 2 tablespoons unsalted butter
- 1 tablespoon dried or chopped fresh chives (optional)

FOR THE GLAZE
- ¼ cup tomato sauce
- 1 tablespoon honey
- 2 teaspoons Worcestershire sauce
- 1 teaspoon apple cider vinegar
- ½ teaspoon Dijon mustard

6. Place a baking sheet near the pressure cooker and, holding the foil, carefully transfer the meat loaf to the baking sheet. There will be liquid gathered around the meat loaf within the foil; try to avoid dripping any and make sure that the edges of the foil are still securely wrapped around the loaf. Spread the prepared glaze over the top of the meat loaf. The meat loaf can be left like this, or broil it for 5 to 10 minutes until the glaze starts bubbling.

7. Remove the trivet from the pot and add the milk, cream cheese, and butter. Use a silicone potato masher to mash the potatoes. If there is too much liquid in the potatoes, press the Sauté button, adjust to low, and allow the water to evaporate as you continue to stir to prevent burning. Stir in the chives (if using).

8. Slice the meat loaf and serve with mashed potatoes.

SUBSTITUTION TIP: There are a few easy substitutions that can be made in this recipe. Bread crumbs can replace the oats, half-and-half can replace the milk for creamier mashed potatoes, and in the glaze, regular ketchup can replace tomato sauce and Worcestershire sauce.

PER SERVING (1-inch slice of meat loaf and ⅓ cup mashed potatoes) Calories: 382; Total Fat: 12g; Fiber: 4g; Protein: 32g; Sodium: 447mg; Sugar: 8g

ALLERGY-FREE

Sesame Mongolian Beef

Serves: 6 / **Prep Time:** 10 minutes / **Sauté:** 10 minutes / **Pressure Cook:** 12 minutes high pressure / **Release:** Quick / **Total Time:** 35 minutes

Here's a lighter take on a popular Asian dish. Traditionally, Mongolian beef is made with a lot of brown sugar. In this heathier version, I add maple syrup as a natural sweetener and pile in broccoli and red bell peppers for extra fiber, vitamin C, and color.

½ cup water

⅓ cup coconut aminos

3 tablespoons pure maple syrup

4 garlic cloves, minced

1½ teaspoons sesame oil

1 teaspoon minced ginger

1 teaspoon apple cider vinegar

½ teaspoon freshly ground black pepper

1 tablespoon extra-virgin olive oil

1½ pounds flank steak, cut in strips

ADD-INS

2 tablespoons water

1 tablespoon cornstarch

2 cups broccoli florets

1 red bell pepper, sliced

1 scallion, sliced

1 tablespoon sesame seeds

1. In a medium bowl, whisk together the water, coconut aminos, maple syrup, garlic, sesame oil, ginger, vinegar, and black pepper until smooth.

2. Press the Sauté button and adjust to high. Pour in the olive oil. Once hot, add the steak and sauté for 5 minutes, until all sides are seared and no longer pink. Pour in the prepared sauce and stir to combine. Press the Cancel/Off button.

3. Lock the lid in place and seal the steam valve. Select Pressure/Manual and adjust the time to 12 minutes on high pressure.

4. After cooking, quick release the pressure. Carefully remove the lid and set aside.

5. In a small bowl, mix together the water and cornstarch until smooth. Press the Sauté button, adjust to normal, and stir in the slurry. Add the broccoli and bell pepper and simmer for 4 to 5 minutes, until the sauce is thickened to the desired consistency and the vegetables are tender. Press the Cancel/Off button.

6. Sprinkle on the scallions and sesame seeds before serving.

PER SERVING (½ cup) Calories: 253; Total Fat: 10g; Fiber: 2g; Protein: 27g; Sodium: 579mg; Sugar: 8g

GLUTEN-FREE, NUT-FREE, ONE POT, 30 MINUTES OR LESS

Sloppy Joe Stuffed Potatoes

Serves: 6 to 8 / **Prep Time:** 10 minutes / **Sauté:** 6 minutes / **Pressure Cook:** 12 minutes high pressure / **Release:** Quick / **Total Time:** 30 minutes

I think sweet potatoes need more love. They are a starchy root vegetable with a distinct sweet flavor profile that come in a variety of shapes and colors. Sweet potatoes are high in various vitamins and minerals along with fiber and antioxidants that help promote good gut health. This beef mixture can be enjoyed with sweet potatoes, but it can also be added to a wrap, brown rice, or a salad bowl.

FOR THE SLOPPY JOES

- 1 tablespoon extra-virgin olive oil
- 1½ pounds lean ground beef
- 1 small onion, chopped
- 1 red bell pepper, chopped
- 1 cup chopped carrots
- 2 garlic cloves, minced
- 2 tablespoons coconut aminos
- 1 tablespoon pure maple syrup
- ½ tablespoon apple cider vinegar
- 1 (15-ounce) can diced tomatoes, drained
- 1 cup tomato sauce

1. **To make the sloppy joes:** Press the Sauté button and adjust to high. Pour in the olive oil. Once hot, add the beef and sauté, stirring and breaking into large pieces, for about 4 minutes, until the meat is no longer pink. Drain the fat, if needed.

2. Add the onion, bell pepper, carrots, and garlic and sauté for 2 minutes, until the vegetables begin to soften. Stir in the coconut aminos, maple syrup, and vinegar, stirring to combine. Add the tomatoes, tomato sauce, oregano, salt, and black pepper. Press the Cancel/Off button.

3. **To make the sweet potatoes:** Place a trivet in the pot, making sure it's resting flat on the bottom. Arrange the sweet potatoes on the trivet.

4. Lock the lid in place and seal the steam valve. Select Pressure/Manual and adjust the time to 12 minutes on high pressure.

CONTINUED ▶

Sloppy Joe Stuffed Potatoes CONTINUED

1 teaspoon dried oregano

½ teaspoon sea salt

½ teaspoon freshly ground black pepper

FOR THE SWEET POTATOES

4 medium sweet potatoes

ADD-INS

½ cup plain low-fat Greek yogurt

1 scallion, both white and green parts, chopped

5. After cooking, quick release the pressure. Carefully remove the lid and set aside. Remove the sweet potatoes, cover them, and set aside. Give the beef mixture a stir to combine all the ingredients and let it rest while you work on the potatoes.

6. Halve the sweet potatoes lengthwise and use a fork to gently mash the middle of each half. Scoop the beef mixture on top of the potatoes. Top with the yogurt and sprinkle with the scallion. Serve.

SUBSTITUTION TIP: For a decadent alternative, stuffed potatoes can be topped with 1 tablespoon of sour cream and 1 tablespoon of shredded cheese instead of the yogurt, but this will also increase the fat and calorie count of the meal.

PER SERVING (½ sweet potato, ½ cup beef mixture) Calories: 233; Total Fat: 7g; Fiber: 5g; Protein: 22g; Sodium: 356mg; Sugar: 10g

ALLERGY-FREE, ONE POT

Warm 'n' Cozy Beef Stew

Serves: 6 / **Prep Time:** 10 minutes / **Sauté:** 7 minutes / **Pressure Cook:** 30 minutes high pressure / **Release:** Quick / **Total Time:** 50 minutes

The first recipe I ever made in my pressure cooker was a beef stew. I heard how easy it was and how tender the meat turns out. I was used to making stews in my slow cooker so was a little apprehensive about how it would taste, but wow! Tender meats, savory broth, and delicious vegetables ready to go in under an hour? It's a winning recipe.

- 2 pounds boneless stew beef
- 1 teaspoon sea salt
- ½ teaspoon black pepper
- 1 tablespoon extra-virgin olive oil
- 3 cups low-sodium beef broth or water, divided
- 1 pound small potatoes, halved
- 2 cups carrots, chopped
- 1 medium onion, chopped
- 2 tablespoons tomato paste
- 1 tablespoon Worcestershire sauce
- 3 garlic cloves, minced
- 1 teaspoon Italian seasoning
- 2 bay leaves
- 2 tablespoons water
- 1 tablespoon cornstarch
- 1 cup frozen peas
- 1 cup chopped fresh spinach

1. In a large bowl, toss the stew beef with the salt and pepper and set aside.

2. Press the Sauté button and adjust to high. Pour in the olive oil. Once hot, add the beef and sauté for about 4 minutes, until it is no longer pink and slightly seared.

3. Add 1½ cups of broth. Use a silicone spatula to deglaze the pot, scraping up any brown bits. Add the remaining 1½ cups of broth. Add the potatoes, carrots, onion, tomato paste, Worcestershire sauce, garlic, Italian seasoning, and bay leaves, stirring to combine. Press the Cancel/Off button.

4. Lock the lid in place and seal the steam valve. Select Pressure/Manual and adjust the time to 30 minutes on high pressure. After cooking, quick release the pressure. Carefully remove the lid and set aside.

5. In a small bowl, mix the water and cornstarch together. Add the slurry to the pot and stir. Add the peas and spinach. Simmer for 3 minutes, until the sauce has thickened. Remove and discard the bay leaves Serve warm.

PER SERVING (1¼ cup) Calories: 304; Total Fat: 9g; Fiber: 3g; Protein: 35g; Sodium: 576mg; Sugar: 4g

DAIRY-FREE, NUT-FREE, ONE POT, 30 MINUTES OR LESS

Cuban Beef Picadillo

Serves: 6 to 8 / **Prep Time:** 10 minutes / **Sauté:** 4 minutes / **Pressure Cook:** 8 minutes high pressure / **Release:** Natural for 5 minutes, then quick / **Total Time:** 30 minutes

Picadillo is a Cuban-based dish that is made with rich flavors and a surprise ingredient. This tasty beef mixture can be enjoyed with a bowl of cauliflower rice, brown rice, or salad or stuffed into a wrap.

- 2 pounds lean ground beef
- 3 garlic cloves, minced
- ½ teaspoon sea salt
- ½ teaspoon freshly ground black pepper
- 1 red onion, chopped
- 1 teaspoon ground cumin
- 1 teaspoon dried oregano
- 2 bay leaves
- 1 (15-ounce) can diced tomatoes, drained
- 1 red bell pepper, chopped
- ½ cup tomato sauce
- ⅓ cup sliced green olives
- 2 tablespoons Worcestershire sauce
- 1 tablespoon rice vinegar
- 1 tablespoon chopped jalapeño

ADD-INS

- ⅓ cup dried raisins
- ¼ cup chopped fresh cilantro
- Juice of ½ lime

1. Press the Sauté button and adjust to high. Once hot, Stir in the beef and sauté, stirring and breaking into pieces, for about 3 minutes, until the beef is no longer pink. Add the garlic, salt, and pepper, stirring to combine. Drain the fat, if necessary.

2. Add the onion, cumin, oregano, and bay leaves and sauté for 1 minute, until the onion has softened. Add the tomatoes, bell pepper, tomato sauce, olives, Worcestershire sauce, vinegar, and jalapeño, stirring to combine. Press the Cancel/Off button.

3. Lock the lid in place and seal the steam valve. Select Pressure/Manual and adjust the time to 8 minutes on high pressure.

4. After cooking, let the pressure release naturally for 5 minutes, then quick release any remaining pressure. Carefully remove the lid and set aside.

5. Add the raisins, cilantro, and lime juice. Remove and discard the bay leaves. Serve warm.

HEALTH BOOST: For a leaner meal, use ground turkey or ground chicken instead of ground beef, and follow the same cook time as above.

PER SERVING (½ cup) Calories: 158; Total Fat: 5g; Fiber: 2g; Protein: 21g; Sodium: 208mg; Sugar: 6g

ALLERGY-FREE, ONE POT

Shredded Chipotle Beef

Serves: 6 / **Prep Time:** 5 minutes / **Sauté:** 4 minutes / **Pressure Cook:** 40 minutes high pressure / **Release:** Natural for 10 minutes, then quick / **Total Time:** 1 hour 5 minutes

I love cooking beef in my electric pressure cooker; it is always tender and juicy. Here is a tasty shredded beef recipe that is sure to heat up your next Taco Tuesday dinner. We're not spicy eaters at our house, but if you enjoy spice, increase the pepper amounts to taste and remember you can always add more after. Serve this along with brown rice or wrapped in corn tortillas. Enjoy with some plain Greek yogurt, guacamole, or pico de gallo.

1 tablespoon extra-virgin olive oil

2 pounds stew beef, cubed

¾ cup low-sodium beef broth or water

2 tablespoons chopped chipotle pepper in adobo sauce, with seeds

4 garlic cloves, minced

1 tablespoon coconut aminos or low-sodium soy sauce

1 tablespoon apple cider vinegar

Juice of 1 lime

½ teaspoon sea salt

½ teaspoon freshly ground black pepper

1 tablespoon chili powder

2 teaspoons onion powder

2 teaspoons ground cumin

1 teaspoon dried oregano

1. Press the Sauté button and adjust to high. Pour in the olive oil. Once hot, add the beef and sauté for about 4 minutes, until the beef is no longer pink and beginning to sear. Add the broth and use a silicone spatula to deglaze the pot, scraping up any brown bits. Add the chipotle pepper, garlic, coconut aminos, vinegar, lime juice, salt, black pepper, chili powder, onion powder, cumin, and oregano, stirring to combine. Press the Cancel/Off button.

2. Lock the lid in place and seal the steam valve. Select Pressure/Manual and adjust the time to 40 minutes on high pressure.

3. After cooking, let the pressure release naturally for 10 minutes, then quick release any remaining pressure. Carefully remove the lid and set aside.

4. Using a slotted spoon, transfer the cooked beef to a cutting board and shred with two forks. Place the beef back into the pot and mix with the sauce. Add the lime juice, taste, and add more adobo sauce or chipotle if desired.

CONTINUED ▶

Shredded Chipotle Beef CONTINUED

ADD-INS

Juice of 1 lime

1 cup shredded lettuce

½ cup chopped red onion

¾ cup fresh or thawed frozen corn kernels

¼ cup chopped fresh cilantro leaves

5. Serve the shredded beef topped with the lettuce, onion, corn, and cilantro.

SUBSTITUTION TIP: If you don't have chipotle pepper in adobo sauce, try this recipe with pickled jalapeño and jalapeño brine for a similar flavor profile.

PER SERVING (1 cup) Calories: 245; Total Fat: 9g; Fiber: 2g; Protein: 34g; Sodium: 481mg; Sugar: 1g

DAIRY-FREE, NUT-FREE

Pot Roast and Potatoes

Serves: 6 to 8 / **Prep Time:** 10 minutes / **Sauté:** 14 minutes / **Pressure Cook:** 60 minutes high pressure / **Release:** Natural for 10 minutes, then quick / **Total Time:** 1 hour 40 minutes

Who needs to wait for Sunday to enjoy a pot roast? Traditionally, this meal is slow-cooked and takes a while, which is one of the reasons it would be usually be enjoyed on Sundays, when people have some extra time to prepare dinner.

1 teaspoon sea salt
½ teaspoon freshly ground black pepper
1 teaspoon onion powder
1 teaspoon dried thyme
1 (3-pound) chuck roast
2 cups low-sodium beef broth or water
2 tablespoons balsamic vinegar or apple cider vinegar
1 tablespoon Worcestershire sauce
1 tablespoon tomato paste
2 garlic cloves, minced
1 tablespoon extra-virgin olive oil
1 pound baby potatoes
4 carrots, peeled and cut into 1-inch pieces
1 large onion, quartered
2 thyme sprigs

1. In a small bowl, whisk together the salt, pepper, onion powder, and thyme. Sprinkle the spice mixture all over the roast and press down lightly. In a medium bowl, whisk together the broth, vinegar, Worcestershire sauce, tomato paste, and garlic.

2. Press the Sauté button and adjust to high. Pour in the olive oil. Once hot, add the seasoned roast. Sear for 3 minutes, then use silicone tongs to gently turn the roast over and sear the other side for 3 minutes. Repeat this process until all sides have been seared. Use the tongs to carefully remove the roast from the pot and set aside. Add the prepared sauce and use a silicone spatula to deglaze the pot, scraping up any brown bits. Press the Cancel/Off button.

3. Place the seared roast back into the pot. Arrange the potatoes, carrots, and onion around the roast. Add the thyme on top. Lock the lid in place and seal the steam valve. Select Pressure/Manual and adjust the time to 60 minutes on high pressure.

4. After cooking, let the pressure release naturally for 10 minutes, then quick release any remaining pressure. Carefully remove the lid and set aside.

CONTINUED ▶

Pot Roast and Potatoes CONTINUED

ADD-INS

2 tablespoons water

1 tablespoon arrowroot powder or cornstarch

2 tablespoons chopped fresh parsley

5. Using tongs, carefully remove the roast and place it on a plate to rest. Remove and discard the thyme. Using a slotted spoon, transfer the potatoes, carrots, and onion to a serving dish. Press the Sauté button, adjust to normal, and bring the liquid left in the pot to a simmer. In a small bowl, mix together the water and arrowroot powder until smooth. Add the slurry and simmer for about 2 minutes, or until the gravy reaches the desired consistency. Spoon the gravy into a dish.

6. Using two forks, shred the roast beef and add it to the platter with the cooked vegetables. Serve with the gravy.

SHORTCUT: Want dinner ready even faster? Cut the raw roast into 2 or 3 pieces, then follow the steps as listed but reduce the cook time to 40 minutes.

PER SERVING (½ cup shredded roast) Calories: 260; Total Fat: 10g; Fiber: 2g; Protein: 30g; Sodium: mg; Sugar: 3g

NUT-FREE, ONE POT, 30 MINUTES OR LESS

One-Pot Spaghetti and Meat Sauce

Serves: 6 / **Prep Time:** 10 minutes / **Sauté:** 6 minutes / **Pressure Cook:** 4 minutes high pressure / **Release:** Natural for 5 minutes, then quick / **Total Time:** 30 minutes

Spaghetti has always been an easy go-to dinner at our house, one I know everyone will enjoy. As easy as this meal is to prepare on the stove, it's even easier in an electric pressure cooker. As a bonus, you only use one pot! As you've probably figured out by now, I try to pack in as many vegetables into my recipes as I can, and this recipe is no different. Use the vegetables listed below or change them up to your favorites.

1 pound lean ground beef
1 medium onion, chopped
4 garlic cloves, minced
1 teaspoon Italian seasoning
½ teaspoon sea salt
½ teaspoon red pepper flakes (optional)
½ cup finely chopped carrots
½ cup finely chopped zucchini
½ cup chopped mushrooms
1 pound whole-grain spaghetti
1 (24-ounce) jar tomato sauce
3 cups water

ADD-INS
¼ cup chopped fresh basil leaves
¼ cup grated Parmesan cheese

1. Press the Sauté button and adjust to high. Once hot, Stir in the ground beef and sauté, stirring and breaking into pieces, for 3 to 4 minutes, until the beef is no longer pink. Drain the fat, if necessary. Add the onion, garlic, Italian seasoning, salt, and red pepper flakes (if using) and sauté for 1 minute. Add the carrots, zucchini, and mushrooms and sauté 1 minute, until the vegetables soften. Press the Cancel/Off button.

2. Break a handful of the spaghetti noodles in half and arrange in the pot in one direction. Break another handful in half and arrange in the pot in the opposite direction, repeating until all the pasta is in the pot. This crisscross pattern helps prevent the pasta from clumping together. Pour the tomato sauce over the noodles and add the water. Do not stir.

3. Lock the lid in place and seal the steam valve. Select Pressure/Manual and adjust the time to 4 minutes high pressure (or half the suggested cooking time minus one additional minute on the pasta package).

CONTINUED ▶

One-Pot Spaghetti and Meat Sauce CONTINUED

4. After cooking, let the pressure release naturally for 5 minutes, then quick release any remaining pressure. Carefully remove the lid and set aside.

5. Stir the sauce, pasta, and meat together until everything is tossed and combined. Test the pasta. If it's a little hard, place the lid on the pot and let the spaghetti rest an additional 2 minutes. Serve the spaghetti warm topped with the basil and Parmesan cheese.

SHORTCUT: To help speed up prep time, add your vegetables to a mini-chopper or food processor and pulse. Pulse according to how you want your vegetables (just a little for chunky vegetables or a lot to blend the vegetables completely so they are unnoticeable in the sauce). It's perfect if you have any picky eaters; they won't even notice them in there.

PER SERVING (1½ cup) Calories: 427; Total Fat: 6g; Fiber: 9g; Protein: 30g; Sodium: 348mg; Sugar: 6g

ALLERGY-FREE, ONE POT

Spicy Beef Curry

Serves: 6 / **Prep Time:** 10 minutes / **Sauté:** 10 minutes / **Pressure Cook:** 20 minutes high pressure / **Release:** Natural for 10 minutes, then quick / **Total Time:** 55 minutes

In this recipe, I'm using all the delicious curry flavors that I grew up with and adding in some fresh vegetables to bump up the nutrients and fiber. Don't be afraid of the name of the recipe; if you're not a fan of spicy foods, like me, you can reduce the amount of chili powder to your taste.

- 1 tablespoon extra-virgin olive oil
- 1 medium onion, chopped
- 1½ pounds stew beef, cut into 1-inch cubes
- 1 large tomato, chopped
- 3 or 4 garlic cloves, minced
- 1 teaspoon minced ginger
- ½ teaspoon turmeric
- 1 teaspoon ground cumin
- ½ teaspoon ground coriander
- 1 teaspoon sea salt
- ½ teaspoon chili powder or cayenne pepper
- 1 tablespoon tomato paste
- 1 teaspoon garam masala
- 1½ cups water

ADD-INS
- 1 cup broccoli florets
- 1 cup chopped fresh spinach
- Juice of 1 lemon
- ¼ cup chopped fresh cilantro

1. Press the Sauté button and adjust to normal. Pour in the olive oil. Once hot, add the onion and sauté for about 5 minutes, until it starts to brown. Add the beef and sauté for 3 minutes, until the beef is no longer pink. Add the tomato, garlic, ginger, turmeric, cumin, coriander, salt, chili powder, tomato paste, garam masala, and water, stirring to combine. Press the Cancel/Off button.

2. Lock the lid in place and seal the steam valve. Select Pressure/Manual and adjust the time to 20 minutes on high pressure.

3. After cooking, let the pressure release naturally for 10 minutes, then quick release any remaining pressure. Carefully remove the lid and set aside.

4. Press the Sauté button and adjust to normal. Stir in the broccoli and spinach and simmer for 2 minutes. Stir in the lemon juice and cilantro before serving.

HEALTH BOOST: Traditionally curries are served with warm naan or rice, but for a lower carbohydrate, lower calorie, and more nutritious option, serve with cauliflower rice or warm quinoa.

PER SERVING (¾ cup curry) Calories: 189; Total Fat: 7g; Fiber: 2g; Protein: 26g; Sodium: 478mg; Sugar: 2g

GLUTEN-FREE, NUT-FREE

Tzatziki Lamb Meatballs

Serves: 6 / **Prep Time:** 10 minutes / **Pressure Cook:** 6 minutes high pressure / **Release:** Natural for 5 minutes, then quick / **Sauté:** 10 minutes / **Total Time:** 35 minutes

These flavorful and easy-to-make meatballs can be enjoyed in a variety of different ways. Add them to a large Greek salad or tossed salad and use the tzatziki sauce as a dressing. Add a little spaghetti sauce to the meatballs and enjoy them on some cooked spaghetti squash. In a multigrain pita, add meatballs, tzatziki sauce, and fresh lettuce. These meatballs also freeze great; make a batch for meal prep and have them ready to go at any time.

FOR THE MEATBALLS

1½ pounds lean ground lamb
1 red onion, minced
½ cup rolled oats or bread crumbs
2 large eggs, lightly beaten
2 tablespoons chopped fresh mint leaves
4 garlic cloves, minced
2 teaspoons dried oregano
1½ teaspoons ground cumin
1½ teaspoons sea salt
1 teaspoon freshly ground black pepper
1 teaspoon ground cinnamon
1 cup water
2 tablespoons extra-virgin olive oil

1. **To make the meatballs:** In a large bowl, use damp hands to combine the lamb, onion, oats, eggs, mint, garlic, oregano, cumin, salt, pepper, and cinnamon. Use a tablespoon to measure out equal amounts of the lamb mixture and roll it into balls.

2. Pour the water into the pressure cooker pot and place a trivet inside the pot. Place a small, flat oven-safe plate (that fits inside the pot) on the trivet and arrange the meatballs on the plate. When adding the second layer, place the meatballs between two on the bottom and repeat for the third layer.

3. Lock the lid in place and seal the steam valve. Select Pressure/Manual and adjust the time to 6 minutes on high pressure.

4. **To make the tzatziki sauce:** While meatballs are cooking, in a small bowl, whisk all the sauce ingredients together. Place the sauce in the refrigerator to let flavors to combine until ready to eat.

FOR THE TZATZIKI SAUCE

¼ cup shredded cucumber (water squeezed out)

1 cup plain Greek yogurt

Juice of 1 lemon

2 tablespoons extra-virgin olive oil

1 garlic clove, minced

1 teaspoon dried dill

½ teaspoon dried oregano

½ teaspoon sea salt

5. After cooking, let the pressure release naturally for 5 minutes, then quick release any remaining pressure. Carefully remove the lid and set aside. Remove the plate with the meatballs and the trivet and set both aside. Carefully remove the pot from the cooker, pour out any remaining water, dry the inside of the pot, and place it back into the cooker.

6. Press the Sauté button and adjust to normal. Pour in the olive oil. Once hot, add the meatballs, one at a time, until they cover the bottom of the pot. Sear the meatballs for 2 minutes, then carefully turn each meatball and sear the other side for 2 minutes. Remove and set aside. Repeat the process until all the meatballs have been seared.

7. Serve the meatballs topped with tzatziki sauce.

SHORTCUT: If you would like to speed up dinner, skip sautéing the meatballs. Instead, put the cooked meatballs in a single layer on a baking sheet. Broil them on high in the oven for 1 minute, then turn the meatballs and broil the other side for 1 minute.

PER SERVING (5 meatballs) Calories: 487; Total Fat: 37g; Fiber: 2g; Protein: 26g; Sodium: 908mg; Sugar: 3g

GLUTEN-FREE, NUT-FREE

Mediterranean Lamb Chops

Serves: 6 / **Prep Time:** 15 minutes, plus 30 minutes to marinate / **Sauté:** 8 minutes / **Pressure Cook:** 6 minutes high pressure / **Release:** Natural for 5 minutes, then quick / **Total Time:** 40 minutes

I've always been a little intimidated with the thought of cooking lamb chops at home. I was never sure how they would turn out. I thought I would give them a try in my electric pressure cooker, and I couldn't believe how easy it was to make this decadent meal. Want to impress at your next dinner party? Give this easy, healthy recipe a try.

FOR THE LAMB CHOPS

4 pounds lean lamb chops (6 to 8 pieces)
1 shallot or ¼ red onion, minced
4 garlic cloves, minced
Juice of 1 lemon
2½ tablespoons extra-virgin olive oil, divided
1 teaspoon dried oregano
½ teaspoon sea salt
1 cup low-sodium beef broth or water
1 tablespoon tomato paste
¼ cup chopped fresh parsley

FOR THE FETA AND TOMATO QUINOA

1¼ cups water
1 cup quinoa, rinsed
1 (15-ounce) can diced tomatoes, drained

1. **To make the lamb chops:** Rinse and pat the lamp chops dry. In a medium bowl, whisk together the shallot, garlic, lemon juice, ½ tablespoon of olive oil, the oregano, and salt. Rub the marinade mixture on both sides of the lamb chops and let them rest for about 30 minutes.

2. **To make the feta and tomato quinoa:** In an oven-safe bowl, mix together the water, quinoa, tomatoes, olive oil, salt, garlic powder, and oregano and set aside.

3. Press the Sauté button and adjust to high. Pour in 1 tablespoon of olive oil. Once hot, add half the lamb chops to the pot and avoid overlapping them. Sear on one side for 2 minutes, then turn them over to sear the other side for 2 minutes. Remove the seared chops and set aside. Add the remaining 1 tablespoon of olive oil. Once hot, repeat the searing process with remaining lamb chops, removing them from the pot when done.

- **1 teaspoon extra-virgin olive oil**
- **1 teaspoon sea salt**
- **1 teaspoon garlic powder**
- **1 teaspoon dried oregano**
- **½ cup chopped fresh baby spinach leaves**
- **¼ cup crumbled feta cheese**

4. Add the broth. Use a silicone spatula to deglaze the pot, scraping up any brown bits. Add the tomato paste and stir until combined. Arrange the seared lamb chops in the pot in layers. Place a long-legged trivet in the pot and make sure it rests flat on the bottom.

5. Place the prepared quinoa bowl on top of the trivet, ensuring that it's level. Press the Cancel/Off button.

6. Lock the lid in place and seal the steam valve. Select Pressure/Manual and adjust the time to 6 minutes on high pressure.

7. After cooking, let the pressure release naturally for 5 minutes, then quick release any remaining pressure. Carefully remove the lid and set aside.

8. Remove the cooked quinoa and stir in the spinach and feta cheese. Set the bowl aside. Carefully transfer the lamb chops to a serving dish. Drizzle broth from the pan over the chops. Sprinkle with the parsley and serve warm with the quinoa.

VARIATION TIP: Lamb chops can also be served with Creamy Mashed Cauliflower (see page 59), or with a large Greek salad for a more nutritious option.

PER SERVING (1 lamb chop, ¾ cup quinoa) Calories: 624; Total Fat: 30g; Fiber: 4g; Protein: 66g; Sodium: 973mg; Sugar: 3g

ALLERGY-FREE, ONE-POT

Moroccan Lamb Stew

Serves: 6 to 8 / **Prep Time:** 10 minutes / **Sauté:** 4 minutes / **Pressure Cook:** 50 minutes high pressure / **Release:** Natural for 10 minutes, the quick / **Total Time:** 1 hour 20 minutes

Like most other stews, this one is packed full of hearty and nutritious ingredients to make you feel warm and cozy all over. I know some people enjoy stews in the winter, but this delicious combination of flavors should be enjoyed year-round. Enjoy stew on its own or with cauliflower rice or warm quinoa.

- **2 tablespoons extra-virgin olive oil**
- **3 pounds lean lamb shoulder, cut into 1½-inch cubes**
- **1 large onion, chopped**
- **2 cups chopped carrots (1-inch pieces)**
- **4 garlic cloves, minced**
- **1 teaspoon minced ginger**
- **2 teaspoons ground allspice**
- **1 teaspoon turmeric**
- **1 teaspoon sea salt**
- **½ teaspoon red pepper flakes**
- **2 tablespoons white vinegar**

1. Press the Sauté button and adjust to high. Pour in the olive oil. Once hot, add the lamb and sear on one side for 2 minutes, then stir and sear on the other side for 2 minutes. Add the onion, carrots, garlic, ginger, allspice, turmeric, salt, red pepper flakes, vinegar, honey, tomato paste, broth, raisins, olives, and chickpeas, stirring once to combine. Press the Cancel/Off button.

2. Lock the lid in place and seal the steam valve. Select Pressure/Manual and adjust the time to 50 minutes on high pressure.

3. After cooking, let the pressure release naturally for 10 minutes, then quick release any remaining pressure. Carefully remove the lid and set aside.

1 tablespoon honey

3 tablespoons tomato paste

2½ cups low-sodium beef broth or water

¼ cup raisins

¼ cup sliced pitted green olives

1 (15-ounce) can low-sodium chickpeas, rinsed

ADD-INS

Juice of ½ lemon

4. Stir to combine. Remove and discard the bay leaves. Stir in the lemon juice before serving.

VARIATION TIP: If you're not a fan of Moroccan flavors, then try the same recipe as the Warm 'n' Cozy Beef Stew (see page 163), but use stew lamb meat instead.

PER SERVING (1 cup) Calories: 460; Total Fat: 22g; Fiber: 5g; Protein: 43g; Sodium: 416mg; Sugar: 11g

ALLERGY-FREE, ONE POT

Pork Carnitas

Serves: 8 / **Prep Time:** 10 minutes / **Pressure Cook:** 1 hour high pressure / **Release:** Natural for 10 minutes, then quick / **Total Time:** 1 hour 25 minutes

Use pork shoulder or butt roast in this recipe and the results will be meltingly tender meat. While we don't crisp the meat after it's been cooked, if you'd like the edges of the pulled pork crispy, simply place the shredded meat and its juices on a broiler pan and broil on high for three to four minutes. Swap in lettuce cups for the more traditional tortillas and top with chopped cilantro, chopped onion, and salsa. —*Recipe contributed by Sandy Gluck*

- 2 pounds boneless pork roast, cut into 3 pieces
- 1 cup freshly squeezed orange juice
- 3 tablespoons distilled white vinegar
- 2 tablespoons extra-virgin olive oil
- 4 large garlic cloves, peeled and smashed
- 2 bay leaves
- 2 teaspoons ancho chile powder
- 1 teaspoon crumbled dried oregano
- 1 teaspoon kosher salt
- ¾ teaspoon freshly ground black pepper

1. In the pressure cooker pot, combine all the ingredients and mix well.

2. Lock the lid in place and seal the steam valve. Select Pressure/Manual and adjust the time to 1 hour (60 minutes) on high pressure.

3. After cooking, let the pressure release naturally for 10 minutes, then quick release any remaining pressure. Carefully remove the lid and set aside.

4. Remove and discard the bay leaves. Using two forks, shred the pork. Serve immediately, or store the shredded pork and any juices in an airtight container and refrigerate for up to four days or freeze for up to two months.

Substitution Tip: Ancho chile powder, made from poblano chiles, is mildly hot and smoky. If you can't find it, use 1¾ teaspoons of regular chili powder and ¼ teaspoon of red pepper flakes.

PER SERVING Calories: 197; Total Fat: 8g; Fiber: 0g; Protein: 27g; Sodium: 347mg; Sugar: 3g

DAIRY-FREE, NUT-FREE

Pork and Broccoli

Serves: 8 / **Prep Time:** 20 minutes / **Sauté:** 6 minutes / **Pressure Cook:** 8 minutes, then 1 minute high pressure / **Release:** Natural for 5 minutes, then quick / **Total Time:** 45 minutes

Pork and broccoli is a spin on beef and broccoli, a staple on Chinese American restaurant menus. The cornstarch slurry added at the end of cooking gives a rich, velvety finish to the dish. The recipe calls for broccoli florets, but you can use the stems as well; pare them with a knife to remove the tough outer skin and use along with the florets. —*Recipe contributed by Sandy Gluck*

¼ cup water

2 tablespoons cornstarch

2 tablespoons toasted sesame oil

2 pounds boneless pork chops, cut into ½-inch-thick slices

5 scallions, both white and green parts, divided

3 tablespoons minced fresh ginger

3 garlic cloves, minced

½ cup low-sodium chicken broth

¼ cup oyster sauce

2 tablespoons low-sodium soy sauce

2 teaspoons sugar

1 pound broccoli florets (about 3½ cups)

1. In a small bowl, make a slurry by whisking together the water and cornstarch. Set aside.

2. Press the Sauté button and adjust to high. Pour in the sesame oil. Once hot, add the pork and sauté for 3 minutes, stirring occasionally, until the meat is lightly browned. Add the whites of the scallions, ginger, and garlic and sauté for 1 minute. Press the Cancel/Off button.

3. Add the broth. Use a wooden spoon to deglaze the pot, scraping up any brown bits. Add the oyster sauce, soy sauce, and sugar and stir to combine.

4. Lock the lid in place and seal the steam valve. Select the Pressure/Manual and adjust the time to 8 minutes on high pressure. After cooking, let the pressure release naturally for 5 minutes, then quick release any remaining pressure. Carefully remove the lid and set aside.

CONTINUED ▶

Pork and Broccoli CONTINUED

5. Add the broccoli florets. Lock the lid and seal the steam valve. Select Pressure/Manual and adjust the time to 1 minute on high pressure. After cooking, quick release the pressure. Carefully remove the lid and set aside.

6. Press the Sauté button and adjust to normal. Use a slotted spoon to transfer the pork and broccoli to a serving plate. Once the liquid is simmering, whisk in the cornstarch slurry and let the sauce cook, uncovered, for 2 minutes, or until it starts to thicken.

7. Return the pork and broccoli to the pot and stir to combine. Press the Cancel/Off button.

8. Serve the dish garnished with the scallion greens. Store leftovers in an airtight container and refrigerate for up to four days.

Shortcut: For easy slicing, place the pork in the freezer for 30 minutes to firm it up and then slice the meat across the grain.

PER SERVING Calories: 218; Total Fat: 8g; Fiber: 2g; Protein: 27g; Sodium: 450mg; Sugar: 2g

ALLERGY-FREE, ONE POT

Pork Barbacoa

Serves: 8 / **Prep Time:** 10 minutes / **Sauté:** 3 minutes / **Pressure Cook:** 30 minutes high pressure / **Release:** Natural for 10 minutes, then quick / **Total Time:** 55 minutes

Hailing from Mexico, barbacoa is traditionally made with beef or goat, but it is equally delicious made with pork. Try topping a salad of crunchy greens with the meat mixture and garnishing it with diced avocado, sour cream, or plain low-fat yogurt and a handful of crushed corn tortilla chips. —*Recipe contributed by Sandy Gluck*

- 2 tablespoons extra-virgin olive oil
- 2 pounds pork tenderloin, cut into 2-inch chunks
- 1 medium onion, chopped
- 3 large garlic cloves, thinly sliced
- 2 chipotles in adobo, finely chopped (1 tablespoon)
- 2 teaspoons ground coriander
- 1 teaspoon ground cumin
- 1 teaspoon kosher salt
- ¾ teaspoon crumbled dried oregano
- 1 cup low-sodium chicken broth
- ¼ cup freshly squeezed lime juice
- ¾ cup coarsely chopped fresh cilantro leaves and tender stems

1. Press the Sauté button and adjust to high. Pour in the olive oil. Once hot, add the pork, onion, garlic, chipotles, coriander, cumin, salt, and oregano and sauté, stirring occasionally, for 3 minutes, until the meat is lightly browned. Press the Cancel/Off button.

2. Add the broth and lime juice. Use a wooden spoon to deglaze the pot, scraping up any brown bits.

3. Lock the lid in place and seal the steam valve. Select Pressure/Manual and adjust the time to 30 minutes on high pressure. After cooking, let the pressure naturally release for 10 minutes, then quick release any remaining pressure. Carefully remove the lid and set aside.

4. Stir in the cilantro. If you want to shred the pork, use two forks to pull apart each piece.

5. Serve immediately or store the pork in an airtight container and refrigerate for up to four days or freeze up to two months.

PER SERVING Calories: 164; Total Fat: 6g; Fiber: 0g; Protein: 24g; Sodium: 280mg; Sugar: 1g

Fudgy Chocolate Brownies, page 186

CHAPTER TEN

Desserts and Drinks

Zesty Lemon Cheesecake **184**

Fudgy Chocolate Brownies **186**

Pineapple Carrot Cake **188**

Cinnamon Apple Crumble **190**

Vanilla-Cardamom Rice Pudding **192**

Chocolate Lava Cakes **193**

Cinnamon Apple Cake **195**

Banana Bread with Chocolate Chips **196**

Summer Berry Compote **197**

Strawberry-Banana Mason Jar Cake **198**

Cranberry-Apple Crumble **200**

Tropical Tapioca Pudding **201**

Berry Swirl Cheesecake **202**

Turmeric Latte **204**

Masala Chai **205**

GLUTEN-FREE, NUT-FREE, VEGETARIAN

Zesty Lemon Cheesecake

Serves: 6 / **Prep Time:** 10 minutes / **Pressure Cook:** 30 minutes high pressure / **Release:** Natural for 15 minutes, then quick / **Total Time:** 1 hour

Living a healthy lifestyle and eating well does not mean you have to give up your favorite desserts. With a few simple modifications, you can still enjoy desserts and stay on track. On any weight loss plan you want to start the first 2 weeks avoiding all sweets to help curb your cravings and then introduce natural sweeteners like fruits, honey, and maple syrup, cutting out all processed and refined sugars.

FOR THE ICING

- 1 cup plain whole-milk Greek yogurt
- ⅓ cup Swerve icing sugar
- 1 teaspoon vanilla extract
- 1 teaspoon grated lemon zest
- ½ teaspoon agar powder

FOR THE CHEESECAKE

- 8 ounces plain cream cheese, at room temperature
- ½ cup pure maple syrup
- ⅓ cup ricotta cheese
- 1 tablespoon freshly squeezed lemon juice
- ½ teaspoon vanilla extract
- 1 large egg

1. Lightly grease a 7-inch springform pan with cooking spray.

2. **To make the icing:** In a medium bowl, whisk together all the icing ingredients until well combined. Place the bowl in the refrigerator to set.

3. **To make the cheesecake:** In another medium bowl, using a hand blender on medium, beat the cream cheese, maple syrup, ricotta cheese, lemon juice, and vanilla until smooth. Taste for sweetness and adjust as needed. Add the egg and mix until just combined, avoiding overmixing. Stir in 1 teaspoon of lemon zest. Pour the mixture into the prepared pan and cover with aluminum foil or a silicone lid.

4. Pour the water into the pressure cooker pot and place the trivet inside. Place the covered springform pan on the trivet.

5. Lock the lid in place and seal the steam valve. Select Pressure/Manual and adjust the time to 30 minutes on high pressure.

1½ teaspoons grated lemon zest, divided

1 cup water

6. After cooking, let the pressure release naturally for 15 minutes, then quick release any remaining pressure. Carefully remove the lid and set aside.

7. Remove the cheesecake pan and cover. Let the cheesecake rest for 2 to 3 hours until completely cooled. Remove the springform sleeve, cover the top of the cake with the chilled icing, and sprinkle the remaining ½ teaspoon of lemon zest over top. Place the iced cheesecake in the refrigerator for up to 3 hours before serving.

SUBSTITUTION TIP: If you can't find Swerve sweetener, use ½ teaspoon of liquid Stevia instead. Stevia is much sweeter than other sweeteners and a little goes a long way.

PER SERVING Calories: 262; Total Fat: 17g; Fiber: 0g; Protein: 6g; Sodium: 184mg; Sugar: 19g

GLUTEN-FREE, NUT-FREE, VEGETARIAN

Fudgy Chocolate Brownies

Serves: 6 / **Prep Time:** 10 minutes / **Sauté:** 10 / **Pressure Cook:** 6 minutes high pressure / **Release:** Natural for 10 minutes, then quick / **Total Time:** 40 minutes

Chocolate! I have always been a sucker for chocolate, but the amount of sugar found in chocolate desserts have made me cut back on one of my favorite treats. But no more. It's so easy to create delicious chocolate treats with natural sweeteners that taste just as decadent as the ones loaded with refined sugar. The only sugar in these brownies are in the dark chocolate chips. The rest of the sweetness comes from applesauce. Make your own with the recipe included in this book (see page 105).

FOR THE BROWNIES

Olive oil cooking spray

1 cup water

¾ cup dark chocolate chips

½ cup unsweetened applesauce

2 large eggs, at room temperature

½ teaspoon pure vanilla extract

¼ cup oat flour

3 tablespoons cocoa powder, plus more for dusting

1 teaspoon baking powder

⅛ teaspoon sea salt

FOR THE ICING

½ cup dark chocolate chips

2 tablespoons coconut oil

1. Grease a 7-inch springform pan with cooking spray and dust with cocoa powder.

2. **To make the brownies:** Pour the water into the pressure cooker pot and place a trivet inside. Press the Sauté button and adjust to normal, bringing the water to a simmer. In a small bowl, place the chocolate chips. Set the bowl on the trivet and wait for the chocolate chips to melt, about 5 minutes, then remove bowl and set aside.

3. In a large bowl, whisk together the applesauce, eggs, and vanilla until smooth. Add the oat flour, cocoa powder, baking powder, and salt and mix until combined. Fold in the melted chocolate. Pour the mixture into the prepared pan and cover with aluminum foil or a silicone lid. Place the pan on top of the trivet.

4. Lock the lid in place and seal the steam valve. Select Pressure/Manual and adjust the time to 6 minutes on high pressure.

5. After cooking, quick release the pressure. Carefully remove the lid and set aside. Remove the pan and set aside to cool for 10 minutes before flipping the cake on to a serving platter.

6. **To make the icing:** In a small bowl, combine the chocolate chips and coconut oil. Press the Sauté button, adjust to normal, and bring the water inside the pot to a simmer. Place the bowl into the pot on the trivet to melt the chocolate chips, about 5 minutes. Remove the bowl and stir until smooth. Drizzle the icing over the cooled cake.

HEALTH BOOST: To make this cake completely refined sugar-free, use dark chocolate chips that are naturally sweetened with stevia or coconut sugar.

PER SERVING Calories: 375; Total Fat: 27g; Fiber: 6g; Protein: 7g; Sodium: 147mg; Sugar: 13g

DAIRY-FREE, GLUTEN-FREE, VEGETARIAN

Pineapple Carrot Cake

Serves: 6 / **Prep Time:** 10 minutes / **Pressure Cook:** 50 minutes high pressure / **Release:** Natural for 5 minutes, then quick / **Total Time:** 1 hour 10 minutes

This carrot cake is bursting with flavor and all kinds of goodness, a welcome addition to any healthy-eating plan. It's made with lots of naturally sweetened ingredients and warm spices. Just imagine how delicious your house is going to smell with this cooking in your electric pressure cooker. Serve with a scoop of vanilla Greek yogurt or coconut yogurt.

Olive oil cooking spray

1½ cups all-purpose gluten-free flour or whole-wheat flour, plus more for dusting

1 teaspoon apple pie spice blend

1 teaspoon baking powder

½ teaspoon baking soda

¼ teaspoon sea salt

¼ cup pure maple syrup

¼ cup unsweetened almond milk

2 large eggs

2 tablespoons extra-virgin olive oil

1 cup shredded carrots, squeezed dry

½ cup finely chopped pineapple

½ cup chopped dates

¼ cup chopped walnuts

1½ cups water

1. Grease a 7-inch springform pan or cake pan well with cooking spray and dust with flour.

2. In a large bowl, combine the flour, apple pie spice, baking powder, baking soda, and salt. In a separate medium bowl, whisk together the maple syrup, almond milk, eggs, and olive oil until just combined. Do not overmix. Pour the wet ingredients into the dry ingredients and mix well, then fold in the carrots, pineapple, dates, and walnuts.

3. Pour the batter into the prepared pan, spreading it evenly. Cover the pan with aluminum foil or a silicone lid.

4. Pour the water into the pressure cooker pot. Place a trivet in the pot and set the covered pan on the trivet.

5. Lock the lid in place and seal the steam valve. Select Pressure/Manual and adjust the time to 50 minutes on high pressure.

6. After cooking, let the pressure release naturally for 5 minutes, then quick release any remaining pressure. Carefully remove the lid and set aside.

7. Carefully remove the pan, uncover, and set the cake aside to rest for 10 minutes. Remove the cake from the pan and serve warm.

HEALTH BOOST: To make this cake fully vegan, substitute flax eggs for eggs. To make two flax eggs, mix 2 tablespoons of ground flaxseed with ¼ cup of warm water and let it rest for at least 15 minutes before adding it to the recipe.

PER SERVING Calories: 290; Total Fat: 10g; Fiber: 6g; Protein: 6g; Sodium: 308mg; Sugar: 20g

GLUTEN-FREE, NUT-FREE, VEGETARIAN, 30 MINUTES OR LESS

Cinnamon Apple Crumble

Serves: 4 / **Prep Time:** 10 minutes / **Pressure Cook:** 10 minutes high pressure /
Release: Natural for 5 minutes, then quick / **Total Time:** 30 minutes

Anyone else love apple pie? Unfortunately, most store-bought varieties are high in sugars, calories, and carbs—all the things we want to avoid. Here is an amazingly simple low sugar and low-carb version that is packed full of the traditional apple pie spices that will make your house smell delicious. Plus, this version is so fun to enjoy topped with vanilla Greek yogurt and extra cinnamon.

4 or 5 small apples
⅓ cup oat flour
¼ cup coconut sugar or brown sugar
1 teaspoon ground cinnamon
¼ teaspoon ground nutmeg
½ teaspoon pure vanilla extract
2 tablespoons unsalted butter, quartered
1 cup water

1. Use a paring knife to slice the top ½ inch off each of the apples and set the tops aside. Core the inside of each apple. Then use a small spoon to remove some of the apple from the sides, transferring these pieces to a large bowl and making sure to leave the bottoms intact as a supportive base. Set the cored apples aside. Take the tops, cut any apple from around the stem, chop them, and add the pieces to the bowl.

2. Add the oat flour, coconut sugar, cinnamon, and nutmeg, stirring to combine. Add the vanilla and butter and, using clean hands, combine the ingredients together until the mixture is crumbly. Use a tablespoon to add the mixture into the cored apples, evenly distributing the filling among the apples.

3. Pour the water into the pressure cooker pot. Place a trivet in the pot and arrange the stuffed apples on top of the trivet, leaving a little room between the apples.

4. Lock the lid in place and seal the steam valve. Select Pressure/Manual and adjust the time to 10 minutes on high (or 12 minutes for softer apples). Time will also vary depending on the apples' size.

5. After cooking, let the pressure release naturally for 5 minutes, then quick release any remaining pressure. Carefully remove the lid and set aside.

6. Using silicone tongs, carefully transfer the apples to a serving dish and allow them to rest for about 5 minutes before serving.

VARIATION TIP: For a delicious seasonal treat, try this recipe with peaches. Follow the steps as listed but substitute peaches for apples and set the cook time to four minutes.

PER SERVING (1 apple) Calories: 174; Total Fat: 5g; Fiber: 4g; Protein: 1g; Sodium: 40mg; Sugar: 22g

DAIRY-FREE, GLUTEN-FREE, ONE POT, VEGAN, 30 MINUTES OR LESS

Vanilla-Cardamom Rice Pudding

Serves: 6 to 8 / **Prep Time:** 5 minutes / **Pressure Cook:** 8 minutes high pressure / **Release:** Natural for 10 minutes, then quick / **Total Time:** 25 minutes

I grew up eating a traditional Indian version of rice pudding known as *kheer*. So creamy and delightful, but not very healthy at all. Here is a lighter version of my mum's classic recipe. We're using maple syrup as the natural sweetener, but you can try this with whichever sweetener you prefer. We always lightly blend our rice pudding so it's creamier, but if you'd rather skip this step that's fine—it will still be delicious.

1½ cups water
1 cup basmati, Arborio, or jasmine rice, rinsed
⅛ teaspoon sea salt
1 (13.5-ounce) can full-fat coconut milk
⅓ cup pure maple syrup
½ teaspoon ground cardamom
½ teaspoon saffron (optional)
¼ teaspoon ground nutmeg
¼ teaspoon ground cinnamon

1. In the pressure cooker pot, combine the water, rice, and salt.

2. Lock the lid in place and seal the steam valve. Select Pressure/Manual and adjust the time to 8 minutes on high pressure.

3. After cooking, let the pressure release naturally for 10 minutes, then quick release any remaining pressure. Carefully remove the lid and set aside.

4. Add the coconut milk, maple syrup, cardamom, saffron (if using), nutmeg, and cinnamon, stirring until well combined. Remove the pot and place on a heat-resistant surface. Using a hand blender, blend the pudding to your desired consistency. (I like my pudding with a little texture so I don't blend it completely smooth.) Let the pudding cool about 20 minutes before serving and serve warm or serve it cold.

HEALTH BOOST: Try using brown rice instead of white in this recipe for added dietary fiber and nutrients. Follow the steps as listed except set the cook time to 22 minutes and natural release for 10 minutes.

PER SERVING (½ cup) Calories: 261; Total Fat: 14g; Fiber: 1g; Protein: 3g; Sodium: 63mg; Sugar: 10g

GLUTEN-FREE, NUT-FREE, VEGETARIAN, 30 MINUTES OR LESS

Chocolate Lava Cakes

Serves: 4 / **Prep Time:** 10 minutes / **Pressure Cook:** 8 minutes high pressure / **Release:** Quick / **Total Time:** 20 minutes

I know what you're thinking: How can you make chocolate lava cakes in an electric pressure cooker and what are they doing in a weight loss cookbook? Well, these decadent cakes are easier to make in an electric pressure cooker than in the oven. While the ingredients in this recipe have been modified to be healthier, it's just as rich and chocolaty as the original versions.

1 cup dark chocolate chunks or chips
⅓ cup coconut oil
2 large eggs
⅓ cup pure maple syrup
½ teaspoon pure vanilla extract
¼ cup brown rice flour
⅛ teaspoon sea salt
1 cup water

1. In a microwave-safe bowl, place the chocolate chunks and coconut oil and heat in the microwave for 30 seconds. Stir and place back in the microwave for 15 seconds, then remove and stir again. If there are still chunks of chocolate, place the bowl back in the microwave for another 15 seconds. The chocolate should be smooth and shiny.

2. In a large bowl, whisk together the eggs, maple syrup, and vanilla and stir in the brown rice flour and salt. Fold in the melted chocolate and stir until just combined.

3. Pour the chocolate mixture into four ramekins, about three-quarters full. Cover each bowl with a piece of aluminum foil to keep moisture out, if desired.

4. Pour the water into the pressure cooker pot and place a trivet inside. Place the ramekins onto the trivet. If they do not fit, arrange three on the base and add the last one on top of the three, in the middle.

CONTINUED ▶

Chocolate Lava Cakes CONTINUED

5. Lock the lid in place and seal the steam valve. Select Pressure/Manual and adjust the time to 8 minutes on high, or add an extra minute for a more cake-like texture.

6. After cooking, quick release the pressure. Carefully open and remove the lid, avoiding any extra water from falling into the pot.

7. Remove the ramekins from the pot. Serve lava cakes warm in the ramekins or gently run a butter knife around the edges of the bowl and turn upside down onto a plate.

SUBSTITUTE TIP: You can use whole-wheat flour instead of brown rice flour, but the resulting lava cakes will not be gluten-free. Use butter instead of coconut oil for a non-vegan option.

PER SERVING (1 lava cake) Calories: 501; Total Fat: 36g; Fiber: 4g; Protein: 7g; Sodium: 124mg; Sugar: 24g

DAIRY-FREE, GLUTEN-FREE, VEGAN

Cinnamon Apple Cake

Serves: 8 / **Prep Time:** 10 minutes / **Pressure Cook:** 25 minutes high pressure / **Release:** Natural for 10 minutes, then quick / **Total Time:** 50 minutes

I love my cinnamon—I sprinkle it on everything. Cinnamon can help balance blood sugar levels, making it a great spice for anyone dealing with diabetes. Cinnamon can also help curb sugar cravings and reduce inflammation in the body. So, get your cinnamon and sprinkle away!

Olive oil cooking spray
1½ cups brown rice flour or whole-wheat flour
½ cup rolled oats
2 teaspoons ground cinnamon
1 teaspoon baking powder
⅛ teaspoon sea salt
½ cup unsweetened applesauce
½ cup pure maple syrup
¼ cup unsweetened almond milk or unsweetened milk of choice
1 teaspoon pure vanilla extract
1 cup apples, chopped
¼ cup chopped walnuts
1 cup water

1. Grease a 7-inch springform pan with cooking spray.

2. In a large bowl, combine the brown rice flour, oats, cinnamon, baking powder, and salt, stirring to combine. Add the applesauce, maple syrup, almond milk, and vanilla, stirring until combined. Fold in the apples and walnuts. Pour the mixture into the prepared pan and cover with aluminum foil or a silicone lid.

3. Pour the water into the pressure cooker pot, place a trivet inside, and set the pan on the trivet.

4. Lock the lid in place and seal the steam valve. Select Pressure/Manual and adjust the time to 25 minutes on high pressure. After cooking, let the pressure release naturally for 10 minutes, then quick release any remaining pressure. Carefully remove the lid and set aside.

5. Remove the pan, uncover, and set aside to cool for 10 minutes before serving.

VARIATION TIP: When baking with apples, try to use Honeycrisp, Cortland, Gala, Golden Delicious, or Granny Smith.

PER SERVING Calories: 241; Total Fat: 4g; Fiber: 4g; Protein: 4g; Sodium: 94mg; Sugar: 16g

DESSERTS AND DRINKS

GLUTEN-FREE, VEGETARIAN

Banana Bread with Chocolate Chips

Serves: 8 / **Prep Time:** 10 minutes / **Pressure Cook:** 50 minutes high pressure /
Release: Natural for 10 minutes, then quick / **Total Time:** 1 hour 10 minutes

Have some bananas browning on your counter? I love baking with my ripe bananas. Ripe bananas make a great natural sweetener, and the riper the bananas, the sweeter they are. If you have too many bananas, freeze them to use at a later date.

Olive oil cooking spray
2 cups oat flour or whole-wheat flour
1 teaspoon baking soda
1 teaspoon baking powder
½ teaspoon ground cinnamon
¼ teaspoon sea salt
2 ripe bananas, mashed (about 1¼ cups)
2 large eggs, at room temperature
⅓ cup pure maple syrup
¼ cup coconut oil, melted and cooled
⅓ cup semi-sweet chocolate chips
¼ cup chopped walnuts
1½ cups water

1. Grease a 7-inch round baking pan with cooking spray.

2. In a medium bowl, combine the oat flour, baking soda, baking powder, cinnamon, and salt and stir until combined. In a large bowl, combine the bananas, eggs, maple syrup, and coconut oil and mix well. Add the bowl of dry ingredients into the bowl of wet ingredients and mix well. Fold in the chocolate chips and walnuts. Pour the batter into the prepared pan and cover with aluminum foil or a silicone lid.

3. Pour the water into the pressure cooker pot and place a trivet inside. Set the pan on the trivet.

4. Lock the lid in place and seal the steam valve. Select Pressure/Manual and adjust the time to 50 minutes on high pressure.

5. After cooking, let the pressure release naturally for 10 minutes, then quick release any remaining pressure. Carefully remove the lid and set aside.

6. Remove the pan from the pot, uncover, and let rest for 10 minutes before removing the cake from the pan.

PER SERVING Calories: 291; Total Fat: 13g; Fiber: 5g; Protein: 7g; Sodium: 297mg; Sugar: 14g

ALLERGY-FREE, ONE POT, VEGAN, 30 MINUTES OR LESS

Summer Berry Compote

Serves: 8 / **Prep Time:** 5 minutes / **Pressure Cook:** 3 minutes high pressure / **Release:** Natural for 5 minutes, then quick / **Total Time:** 15 minutes

Berries may be small, but they are packed full of nutrients and antioxidants. They are also low on the glycemic index, making them a welcome addition to your weight loss plan. As wonderful as berries are on their own, here is a simple compote that will allow you to enjoy the taste of berries in a variety of recipes, including yogurt parfaits, on top of pancakes or waffles, as a topping for cakes or puddings—endless possibilities!

3 cups mixed berries
⅓ cup pure maple syrup or honey
¼ cup water
1 teaspoon freshly squeezed lemon juice
1 teaspoon grated lemon zest
¼ teaspoon ground cinnamon
1 tablespoon chia seeds (optional)

1. In the pressure cooker pot, combine the berries, maple syrup, water, lemon juice and zest, and cinnamon.

2. Lock the lid in place and seal the steam valve. Select Pressure/Manual and adjust the time to 3 minutes on high pressure.

3. After cooking, let the pressure release naturally for 5 minutes, then quick release any remaining pressure. Carefully remove the lid and set aside.

4. For a thicker compote, stir in the chia seeds (if using). Let the compote cool for at least 20 minutes. Serve warm or cool on your favorite recipes. Store compote in an airtight container in the refrigerator for five to seven days.

SUBSTITUTIONS: Frozen berries are just as nutritious as fresh and can be a cheaper option when berries are not in season. This recipe can be made with frozen berries but omit the water, as the frozen fruit will release liquid. Also, increase the cook time to 4 minutes.

PER SERVING (¼ cup) Calories: 54; Total Fat: 0g; Fiber: 1g; Protein: 0g; Sodium: 2mg; Sugar: 11g

DAIRY-FREE, GLUTEN-FREE, VEGETARIAN, 30 MINUTES OR LESS

Strawberry-Banana Mason Jar Cake

Serves: 1 / **Prep Time:** 5 minutes / **Pressure Cook:** 15 minutes high pressure / **Release:** Natural for 5 minutes, then quick / **Total Time:** 30 minutes

I have a whole drawer full of Mason jars in my kitchen. I use these versatile jars for everything from storing foods to serving drinks to making dressings, and now I use them to make cake! These cakes can be made right in the jar (note that the recipe below is per jar). All you have to do is add these simple ingredients into each jar and you can make up to four or five at a time, depending on the size of the jars you use and how well they fit inside your electric pressure cooker.

⅓ cup almond flour or oat flour
1 large egg
1½ tablespoons pure maple syrup or honey
½ teaspoon baking powder
¼ teaspoon pure vanilla extract
⅛ teaspoon sea salt
3 tablespoons mashed ripe banana
3 tablespoons chopped strawberries
1 cup water

1. In an 8-ounce Mason jar, add the almond flour, egg, maple syrup, baking powder, salt, and vanilla and whisk with a fork until well combined. Stir in the bananas and strawberries. Cover the jar with a piece of aluminum foil.

2. Pour the water into the pressure cooker pot, place a trivet inside the pot, and place the Mason jar onto the trivet.

3. Lock the lid in place and seal the steam valve. Select Pressure/Manual and adjust the time to 15 minutes on high (or 18 minutes for a firmer cake texture).

4. After cooking, let the pressure release naturally for 5 minutes, then quick release any remaining pressure. Carefully remove the lid and set aside.

5. Use tongs or oven mitts to carefully remove the jar from the pot; the jar will be hot. Set the jar aside to cool for 10 minutes. Serve from the jar.

VARIATION TIP: There are a few different variations to this recipe that you can try. Omit the bananas and strawberries and try any of the following:

MIXED BERRY: ¼ cup of mixed berries or single berry of choice

CHOCOLATE BANANA: ¼ cup of mashed ripe banana and 2 tablespoons of semi-sweet or dark chocolate chips

APPLE CINNAMON: ¼ cup of chopped apples and ½ teaspoon of ground cinnamon

BANANA BREAD: ¼ cup of mashed ripe banana and 2 tablespoons of chopped walnuts

DOUBLE CHOCOLATE: 1 tablespoon of cocoa powder, ½ tablespoon of water, and 2 tablespoons of semi-sweet or dark chocolate chips

PER SERVING (1 Mason jar) Calories: 355; Total Fat: 8g; Fiber: 5g; Protein: 12g; Sodium: 394mg; Sugar: 27g

DAIRY-FREE, GLUTEN-FREE, VEGAN

Cranberry-Apple Crumble

Serves: 6 / **Prep Time:** 15 minutes / **Pressure Cook:** 20 minutes high pressure / **Release:** Natural for 5 minutes, then quick / **Total Time:** 45 minutes

I think desserts that combine sweet with tart are so refreshing. The filling for this crumble is a combination of sweet apples and tart cranberries with a hint of cinnamon—so warming and delicious.

FOR THE FILLING

- 3 cups cubed apples
- 1½ cups frozen cranberries
- ½ tablespoon lemon juice
- ⅓ cup coconut sugar
- 1 tablespoon arrowroot powder
- 1 teaspoon cinnamon
- 1 teaspoon lemon zest
- ½ teaspoon ground ginger
- ¼ teaspoon sea salt
- 1 cup water

FOR THE TOPPING

- 1 cup rolled oats
- ⅓ cup shredded unsweetened coconut
- ⅓ cup chopped walnuts
- ¼ cup coconut sugar
- 1 teaspoon cinnamon
- ⅛ teaspoon sea salt
- ⅓ cup coconut oil, plus more for greasing
- 1 cup water

1. Lightly grease a 7-inch oven-safe dish with coconut oil.

2. **To make the filling:** In a medium bowl, mix together all the filling ingredients until well combined. Pour the filling into the prepared dish and set aside.

3. **To make the topping:** In a separate medium bowl, mix the oats, coconut, walnuts, coconut sugar, cinnamon, and salt and stir. Add the coconut oil and use a fork to combine all ingredients until moistened. Add the topping over the filling, using a spatula and spread. Cover the dish with aluminum foil.

4. Pour the water into the pressure cooker pot, place the trivet in the pot, and set the crumble dish on top. Lock the lid in place and seal the steam valve. Select Pressure/Manual and adjust the time to 20 minutes on high pressure.

5. After cooking, let the pressure release naturally for 5 minutes, then quick release any remaining pressure. Remove the lid and set aside. Remove the dish from the pot and cool for 10 minutes. Serve warm.

PER SERVING (½ cup) Calories: 376; Total Fat: 18g; Fiber: 6g; Protein: 6g; Sodium: 155mg; Sugar: 52g

DAIRY-FREE, GLUTEN-FREE, VEGAN, 30 MINUTES OR LESS

Tropical Tapioca Pudding

Serves: 6 / **Prep Time:** 5 minutes / **Pressure Cook:** 10 minutes high pressure /
Release: Natural for 5 minutes, then quick / **Total Time:** 25 minutes

Tapioca is a starch that's sourced from the root of cassava plants. If you're a fan of tapioca pudding, you can still enjoy this creamy dessert on a weight loss plan by making it at home, which lets you control the ingredients and exercise portion control.

1 (13.5-ounce) can full-fat coconut milk
⅓ cup pure maple syrup
½ teaspoon pure vanilla extract
⅛ teaspoon sea salt
⅓ cup small fine tapioca pearls, rinsed well
1 cup water

ADD-INS

½ cup chopped ripe mangos
¼ cup shredded unsweetened dried coconut, divided
2 tablespoons sliced almonds

1. In an oven-safe dish, combine the coconut milk, maple syrup, vanilla, and salt and mix well. Stir in the tapioca pearls.

2. Pour the water into the pressure cooker pot, place a trivet inside the pot, and set the bowl with the tapioca mixture on the trivet.

3. Lock the lid in place and seal the steam valve. Select Pressure/Manual and adjust the time to 10 minutes on high pressure.

4. After cooking, let the pressure release naturally for 5 minutes, then quick release any remaining pressure. Carefully remove the lid and set aside.

5. Remove the bowl from the pot and set on a heat-resistant surface. Stir in the mangos and 2 tablespoons of coconut. Set the pudding aside to rest and cool for 10 minutes.

6. Cover the dish and place in the refrigerator to cool completely. Serve the pudding topped with the remaining 2 tablespoons of coconut and the almonds.

HEALTH BOOST: To make your tapioca pudding more nutritious, always try to add fresh fruits to provide a natural sweetener.

PER SERVING (½ cup) Calories: 224; Total Fat: 15g; Fiber: 1g; Protein: 2g; Sodium: 63mg; Sugar: 13g

GLUTEN-FREE, NUT-FREE, VEGETARIAN

Berry Swirl Cheesecake

Serves: 8 / **Prep Time:** 15 minutes / **Pressure Cook:** 30 minutes high pressure / **Release:** Natural for 8 minutes, then quick / **Total Time:** 55 minutes

Cheesecakes are one of the most popular desserts to prepare in an electric pressure cooker because they are so easy to make and have a moist, silky texture when completed. This decadent dessert can be a part of your healthy lifestyle as long as you include the right ingredients, natural sweeteners, whole grains, and fresh fruits where you can.

FOR THE CRUST

- 1 cup oat flour
- ¼ teaspoon ground cinnamon
- ⅛ teaspoon sea salt
- 4 tablespoons unsalted butter, melted
- 2 tablespoons coconut sugar

FOR THE FILLING

- ¾ cup plain full-fat Greek yogurt
- 4 ounces plain cream cheese, at room temperature
- ⅓ cup pure maple syrup
- ½ teaspoon vanilla extract
- 1 large egg
- ¼ cup frozen berries, thawed and mashed
- 1 cup water

1. **To make the crust:** In a medium bowl, combine all the crust ingredients and mix until the oat flour is moist. Press the mixture firmly into the base of a 7-inch springform pan.

2. **To make the filling:** In a medium bowl, using a hand blender or stand mixer on medium, blend the yogurt, cream cheese, maple syrup, and vanilla. Add the egg and mix until combined, avoiding overmixing that can result in a cracked cake.

3. Pour the batter into the prepared pan, being sure all the crust is covered. Add teaspoonfuls of mashed berries around the top of the mixture and use a butter knife to gently swirl the berries through the top of the cake.

4. Pour the water into the pressure cooker pot, place a trivet in the pot, and carefully set the pan on the trivet.

5. Lock the lid in place and seal the steam valve. Select Pressure/Manual and adjust the time to 30 minutes on high pressure.

6. After cooking, let the pressure release naturally for 8 minutes, then quick release any remaining pressure. Carefully remove the lid and set aside.

7. Using oven mitts, remove the pan and set aside. Use a paper towel to soak up any water that may have gathered on the surface of the cake. Allow the cake to cool for up to 2 hours, then cover the cake and place it in the refrigerator to cool and settle for at least 3 hours.

VARIATION TIP: Try a chocolate swirl cheesecake by omitting fresh berries and swirling in 3 tablespoons of melted chocolate chips. To melt the chocolate chips, add 3 tablespoons of semi-sweet chocolate chips and 1 teaspoon of olive oil to a bowl. Pour 1 cup of water into the pressure cooker pot and press the Sauté button. Set the trivet in the pot and place the bowl with the chocolate chips on the trivet. Melt the chocolate chips while preparing the rest of the cheesecake, occasionally stirring the chips. Remove the bowl once melted. Drizzle the melted chocolate on top of the cheesecake filling in the pan and use a butter knife to swirl.

PER SERVING Calories: 225; Total Fat: 13g; Fiber: 1g; Protein: 4g; Sodium: 115mg; Sugar: 13g

DAIRY-FREE, GLUTEN-FREE, ONE POT, VEGAN, 30 MINUTES OR LESS

Turmeric Latte

Serves: 6 / **Prep Time:** 5 minutes / **Pressure Cook:** 2 minutes high pressure / **Release:** Natural for 5 minutes, then quick / **Total Time:** 15 minutes

Turmeric lattes are a wonderful cold-weather drink, and they're full of warming, immune-boosting ingredients like turmeric, ginger, and cinnamon. This simple vegan version is full of flavorful spices and sweetened with dates. It tastes so good that you'll want to sip it all year-round.

6 cups water

1 cup raw cashews, rinsed

5 dates, pitted and quartered

1 tablespoon coconut oil

½ tablespoon minced peeled fresh ginger

½ tablespoon ground turmeric

1 teaspoon ground cinnamon, plus more for serving

1 teaspoon ground cardamom

⅛ teaspoon freshly ground black pepper

⅛ sea salt

1. In the pressure cooker pot, combine all the ingredients. Lock the lid in place and seal the steam valve. Select Pressure/Manual and adjust the time to 2 minutes on high pressure.

2. After cooking, let the pressure release naturally for 5 minutes, then quick release any remaining pressure. Carefully remove the lid and set aside.

3. Using a hand blender, blend all the ingredients together until smooth and frothy. Serve warm with a sprinkle of ground cinnamon.

SUBSTITUTION TIP: Instead of using dates as a natural sweetener in this latte, try adding 3 tablespoons of honey. However, the honey will change this to a non-vegan drink.

PER SERVING (1 cup) Calories: 179; Total Fat: 13g; Fiber: 2g; Protein: 5g; Sodium: 55mg; Sugar: 5g

GLUTEN-FREE, NUT-FREE, ONE POT, VEGETARIAN, 30 MINUTES OR LESS

Masala Chai

Serves: 6 / **Prep Time:** 5 minutes / **Pressure Cook:** 2 minutes high pressure / **Release:** Natural for 8 minutes, then quick / **Sauté:** 4 minutes / **Total Time:** 20 minutes

Chai was a staple in our house growing up. Even now when we go to my parents' house, we know there will be a fresh pot of chai after dinner. One thing my mom always complained about was that the chai would boil over and ruin the stovetop, and that's one reason why making it in an electric pressure cooker is so great. You just add all the ingredients, set it, and forget it.

4 cups water

4 black tea bags

1 cinnamon stick

4 or 5 cardamom pods, gently pinched flat

½ teaspoon pure vanilla extract

¼ teaspoon ground ginger

2 cups whole milk

Sweetener of choice

1. In the pressure cooker pot, combine the water, tea bags, cinnamon stick, cardamom pods, vanilla, and ginger.

2. Lock the lid in place and seal the steam valve. Select Pressure/Manual and adjust the time to 2 minutes on high pressure.

3. After cooking, let the pressure release naturally for 8 minutes, then quick release any remaining pressure. Carefully remove the lid and set aside.

4. Press the Sauté button and adjust to low. Pour in the milk and simmer for 3 to 4 minutes, until the chai reaches the desired color. Press the Cancel/Off button. Skim a hand strainer through the pot to collect and dispose of the tea bags and whole spices. Serve warm, allowing drinkers to add sweetener to their own tastes.

HEALTH BOOST: For a vegan, lower fat, and lower calorie option, substitute unsweetened almond milk for whole milk.

PER SERVING (1 cup) Calories: 51; Total Fat: 3g; Fiber: 0g; Protein: 3g; Sodium: 35mg; Sugar: 4g

Measurement Conversions

VOLUME EQUIVALENTS (LIQUID)

US STANDARD	US STANDARD (OUNCES)	METRIC (APPROXIMATE)
2 tablespoons	1 fl. oz.	30 mL
¼ cup	2 fl. oz.	60 mL
½ cup	4 fl. oz.	120 mL
1 cup	8 fl. oz.	240 mL
1½ cups	12 fl. oz.	355 mL
2 cups or 1 pint	16 fl. oz.	475 mL
4 cups or 1 quart	32 fl. oz.	1 L
1 gallon	128 fl. oz.	4 L

OVEN TEMPERATURES

FAHRENHEIT	CELSIUS (APPROXIMATE)
250°F	120°C
300°F	150°C
325°F	165°C
350°F	180°C
375°F	190°C
400°F	200°C
425°F	220°C
450°F	230°C

VOLUME EQUIVALENTS (DRY)

US STANDARD	METRIC (APPROXIMATE)
⅛ teaspoon	0.5 mL
¼ teaspoon	1 mL
½ teaspoon	2 mL
¾ teaspoon	4 mL
1 teaspoon	5 mL
1 tablespoon	15 mL
¼ cup	59 mL
⅓ cup	79 mL
½ cup	118 mL
⅔ cup	156 mL
¾ cup	177 mL
1 cup	235 mL
2 cups or 1 pint	475 mL
3 cups	700 mL
4 cups or 1 quart	1 L

WEIGHT EQUIVALENTS

US STANDARD	METRIC (APPROXIMATE)
½ ounce	15 g
1 ounce	30 g
2 ounces	60 g
4 ounces	115 g
8 ounces	225 g
12 ounces	340 g
16 ounces or 1 pound	455 g

Index

A

Allergy-free
- Baba Ganoush, 44–45
- Baked Sweet Potatoes, 56
- Beet Hummus, 46–47
- Blueberry Chia Jam, 39
- Carrot-Ginger Soup, 92
- Cauliflower-Potato Curry, 113
- Chana Masala, 110–111
- Chili-Lime Brown Rice, 57
- Chili-Lime Chicken and Rice, 132
- Cinnamon Applesauce, 105
- Coconut-Lentil Curry, 117–118
- Coconut-Lime Quinoa, 55
- Coconut-Quinoa Curry, 127
- Creamy Coconut Yogurt, 25–26
- Creamy Root Vegetable Soup, 94
- Easy Homemade Ketchup, 102
- Garlic-Basil Marinara Sauce, 104
- Healing Bone Broth, 86
- Hearty Lentil Stew, 121
- Honey-Garlic Brussels Sprouts, 50
- Honey-Garlic Chicken Lettuce Wraps, 64
- Lemon-Cilantro Chicken, 137–138
- Lemony Green Beans, 53
- Mediterranean Turkey-Quinoa Bowl, 149
- Moroccan Lamb Stew, 176–177
- Mushroom and Wild Rice Soup, 96
- One-Pot Mexican Rice and Beans, 114
- Pork Barbacoa, 181
- Pork Carnitas, 178
- Roasted Chicken and Veggies, 135–136
- Root Vegetable Medley, 51
- Saucy Garden-Fresh Salsa, 48
- Sesame Mongolian Beef, 160
- Shredded Beef Lettuce Cups, 82
- Shredded Chipotle Beef, 165–166
- Spiced Roasted Cauliflower Head, 60
- Spicy Beef Curry, 171
- Spicy Black Bean and Rice Salad, 76
- Spicy Cranberry Sauce, 106
- Steak Fajita Wraps, 69–70
- Summer Berry Compote, 197
- Sweet Potato and Corn Soup, 90
- Sweet Potato and Quinoa Chili, 101
- Sweet Potato Quinoa Salad, 80
- Tangy Potato Salad, 65–66
- Tex-Mex Butternut Squash Soup, 87–88
- Tex-Mex Chicken Salad Bowl, 75
- Tex-Mex Lentil Bowl, 81
- Thai Lentil Soup, 89
- Thai Red Chicken Curry, 145
- Turmeric Latte Quinoa Oats, 23
- Turmeric Lentil Soup, 91
- Two-Bean Rice Bowl, 67–68
- Vegan Lentil Chili, 99
- Veggie and Lentil Bolognese, 112
- Veggie Rice Pilaf, 128
- Warm 'n' Cozy Beef Stew, 163

Altitude adjustments, 13

Apples
- Carrot-Ginger Soup, 92
- Cinnamon Apple Cake, 195
- Cinnamon Apple Crumble, 190–191
- Cinnamon Applesauce, 105
- Cranberry-Apple Crumble, 200

Arugula
- Beet and Feta Salad, 71

Avocados
- Avocado Egg Salad, 79
- Fajitas Fiesta Eggs, 35–36

B

Baba Ganoush, 44–45
Baked Sweet Potatoes, 56
Balanced plate, 7

Bananas
    Banana Bread with Chocolate Chips, 196
    Strawberry-Banana Mason Jar Cake, 198–199
Beans
    Beef and Bean Chili, 97
    Chicken Tortilla Soup, 95
    Chili-Lime Chicken and Rice, 132
    Mexican Black Bean and Quinoa Bowl, 73
    Mushroom and Wild Rice Soup, 96
    Mushroom-Turkey Chili, 100
    One-Pot Mexican Rice and Beans, 114
    Quinoa and Lentil Stuffed Peppers, 116
    Spicy Black Bean and Rice Salad, 76
    Sweet Potato and Quinoa Chili, 101
    Tex-Mex Breakfast Scramble, 30
    Tex-Mex Butternut Squash Soup, 87–88
    Tex-Mex Chicken Salad Bowl, 75
    Two-Bean Rice Bowl, 67–68
    Vegan Lentil Chili, 99
    White Chicken Chili, 98
Beef
    Beef and Bean Chili, 97
    Cuban Beef Picadillo, 164
    Healing Bone Broth, 86
    Meat Loaf and Mashed Potatoes, 158–159
    One-Pot Spaghetti and Meat Sauce, 169–170
    Pot Roast and Potatoes, 167–168
    Sesame Mongolian Beef, 160
    Shredded Beef Lettuce Cups, 82
    Shredded Chipotle Beef, 165–166
    Sloppy Joe Stuffed Potatoes, 161–162
    Spicy Beef Curry, 171
    Steak Fajita Wraps, 69–70
    Warm 'n' Cozy Beef Stew, 163
Beet and Feta Salad, 71
Beet Hummus, 46–47
Berries
    Berry Swirl Cheesecake, 202–203
    Blueberry Chia Jam, 39
    Cranberry-Apple Crumble, 200
    Maple-Almond Granola, 40
    Maple-Blueberry Pancake Bites, 31–32
    Spicy Cranberry Sauce, 106
    Strawberry-Banana Mason Jar Cake, 198–199
    Summer Berry Compote, 197
    Sweet and Savory Wild Rice, 126
    Very Berry Cauli-Oats, 22
Beverages
    Masala Chai, 205
    Turmeric Latte, 204
Blueberry Chia Jam, 39
Bowls
    Mediterranean Chickpea Bowl, 74
    Mediterranean Turkey-Quinoa Bowl, 149
    Mexican Black Bean and Quinoa Bowl, 73
    Tex-Mex Chicken Salad Bowl, 75
    Tex-Mex Lentil Bowl, 81
    Two-Bean Rice Bowl, 67–68
Breakfast Casserole, 38
Broccoli
    Creamy Chicken and Broccoli Rice, 141
    Lemon-Dill Salmon, 143–144
    Orange Shrimp Stir-Fry, 153–154
    Pork and Broccoli, 179–180
    Spicy Beef Curry, 171
    Thai Red Chicken Curry, 145
Brussels Sprouts, Honey-Garlic, 50
Buttery Mashed Potatoes, 54

C

Cabbage
    Vegetable Pad Thai, 119–120
Carrots
    Beef and Bean Chili, 97
    Carrot-Ginger Soup, 92
    Cauliflower Fried Rice, 58
    Cauli-Queso Dip, 49
    Creamy Chicken and Broccoli Rice, 141
    Creamy Root Vegetable Soup, 94
    Healing Bone Broth, 86
    Hearty Lentil Stew, 121
    Meatless Shepherd's Pie, 122–123

INDEX

Carrots (continued)
- Moroccan Lamb Stew, 176–177
- Mushroom and Wild Rice Soup, 96
- One-Pot Spaghetti and Meat Sauce, 169–170
- Orange-Ginger Salmon Dinner, 133–134
- Pineapple Carrot Cake, 188–189
- Pot Roast and Potatoes, 167–168
- Roasted Chicken and Veggies, 135–136
- Root Vegetable Medley, 51
- Shredded Beef Lettuce Cups, 82
- Sloppy Joe Stuffed Potatoes, 161–162
- Sweet Potato and Corn Soup, 90
- Sweet Potato and Quinoa Chili, 101
- Thai Red Chicken Curry, 145
- Vegetable Barley Soup, 93
- Vegetable Pad Thai, 119–120
- Veggie and Lentil Bolognese, 112
- Warm 'n' Cozy Beef Stew, 163
- White Chicken Chili, 98

Cashew Chicken, 147–148

Cauliflower
- Cauliflower Fried Rice, 58
- Cauliflower-Potato Curry, 113
- Cauli-Queso Dip, 49
- Creamy Mashed Cauliflower, 59
- Creamy Vegan Alfredo Sauce, 103
- Light 'n' Easy Butter Chicken, 139–140
- Meatless Shepherd's Pie, 122–123
- rice, 5
- Spiced Roasted Cauliflower Head, 60
- Very Berry Cauli-Oats, 22

Cauli-Queso Dip, 49

Chana Masala, 110–111

Cheese. See also Cream cheese
- Beet and Feta Salad, 71
- Breakfast Casserole, 38
- Cauli-Queso Dip, 49
- Creamy Chicken and Broccoli Rice, 141
- Creamy Mashed Cauliflower, 59
- Creamy Mushroom Penne, 124–125
- Greek Chicken Salad Lettuce Wraps, 72
- Mediterranean Chickpea Bowl, 74
- Mediterranean Lamb Chops, 174–175
- One-Pot Spaghetti and Meat Sauce, 169–170
- Parmesan Spaghetti Squash, 52
- Parmesan Turkey Meatballs, 152
- Quinoa and Lentil Stuffed Peppers, 116
- Spinach and Feta Egg Muffins, 27
- Sweet and Savory Wild Rice, 126
- Tex-Mex Breakfast Scramble, 30
- Vegetable Risotto, 115

Chia seeds
- Blueberry Chia Jam, 39
- Summer Berry Compote, 197
- Turmeric Latte Quinoa Oats, 23
- Very Berry Cauli-Oats, 22

Chicken
- Cashew Chicken, 147–148
- Chicken Tortilla Soup, 95
- Chili-Lime Chicken and Rice, 132
- Creamy Chicken and Broccoli Rice, 141
- Greek Chicken Salad Lettuce Wraps, 72
- Honey-Garlic Chicken Lettuce Wraps, 64
- Lemon-Cilantro Chicken, 137–138
- Light 'n' Easy Butter Chicken, 139–140
- Mediterranean Chicken Shawarma, 77–78
- Roasted Chicken and Veggies, 135–136
- Spicy Mexican Chicken, 146
- Tex-Mex Chicken Salad Bowl, 75
- Thai Red Chicken Curry, 145
- White Chicken Chili, 98

Chickpeas
- Beet Hummus, 46–47
- Chana Masala, 110–111
- Coconut-Quinoa Curry, 127
- Meatless Shepherd's Pie, 122–123
- Mediterranean Chickpea Bowl, 74

Mediterranean Turkey-Quinoa Bowl, 149
Moroccan Lamb Stew, 176–177
Sweet and Savory Wild Rice, 126
Sweet Potato Quinoa Salad, 80
Two-Bean Rice Bowl, 67–68
Chili-Lime Brown Rice, 57
Chili-Lime Chicken and Rice, 132
Chilis
   Beef and Bean Chili, 97
   Mushroom-Turkey Chili, 100
   Sweet Potato and Quinoa Chili, 101
   Vegan Lentil Chili, 99
   White Chicken Chili, 98
Chocolate
   Banana Bread with Chocolate Chips, 196
   Chocolate Lava Cakes, 193–194
   Fudgy Chocolate Brownies, 186–187
Cinnamon Apple Cake, 195
Cinnamon Apple Crumble, 190–191
Cinnamon Applesauce, 105
Coconut
   Cranberry-Apple Crumble, 200
   Tropical Tapioca Pudding, 201
Coconut aminos, 5
Coconut milk/cream
   Carrot-Ginger Soup, 92
   Coconut-Lentil Curry, 117–118
   Coconut-Lime Quinoa, 55
   Coconut-Quinoa Curry, 127
   Creamy Coconut Yogurt, 25–26
   Creamy Mushroom Penne, 124–125
   Mushroom and Wild Rice Soup, 96
   Spinach-and-Tofu Curry, 129
   Sweet Potato and Corn Soup, 90
   Thai Red Chicken Curry, 145
   Tropical Tapioca Pudding, 201
   Vanilla-Cardamom Rice Pudding, 192
Corn
   Beef and Bean Chili, 97
   Chicken Tortilla Soup, 95
   Chili-Lime Chicken and Rice, 132
   Meatless Shepherd's Pie, 122–123
   Mexican Black Bean and Quinoa Bowl, 73
   Mushroom-Turkey Chili, 100
   Quinoa and Lentil Stuffed Peppers, 116
   Shredded Chipotle Beef, 165–166
   Spicy Black Bean and Rice Salad, 76
   Sweet Potato and Corn Soup, 90
   Sweet Potato and Quinoa Chili, 101
   Tex-Mex Butternut Squash Soup, 87–88
   Tex-Mex Chicken Salad Bowl, 75
   Two-Bean Rice Bowl, 67–68
   Veggie Rice Pilaf, 128
   White Chicken Chili, 98
Cranberry-Apple Crumble, 200
Cream cheese
   Berry Swirl Cheesecake, 202–203
   Meat Loaf and Mashed Potatoes, 158–159
   Zesty Lemon Cheesecake, 184–185
Creamy Chicken and Broccoli Rice, 141
Creamy Coconut Yogurt, 25–26
Creamy Mashed Cauliflower, 59
Creamy Mushroom Penne, 124–125
Creamy Root Vegetable Soup, 94
Creamy Vegan Alfredo Sauce, 103
Cuban Beef Picadillo, 164
Cucumbers
   Greek Chicken Salad Lettuce Wraps, 72
   Mediterranean Chickpea Bowl, 74
   Tzatziki Lamb Meatballs, 172–173
Curries
   Cauliflower-Potato Curry, 113
   Chana Masala, 110–111
   Coconut-Lentil Curry, 117–118
   Coconut-Quinoa Curry, 127
   Spicy Beef Curry, 171
   Spinach-and-Tofu Curry, 129
   Thai Red Chicken Curry, 145

D

Dairy-free
- Avocado Egg Salad, 79
- Beef and Bean Chili, 97
- Cashew Chicken, 147–148
- Cauliflower Fried Rice, 58
- Cinnamon Apple Cake, 195
- Cranberry-Apple Crumble, 200
- Creamy Vegan Alfredo Sauce, 103
- Cuban Beef Picadillo, 164
- Egg and Sweet Potato Hash, 33
- Eggy Ratatouille, 28–29
- Fajitas Fiesta Eggs, 35–36
- Lemon-Dill Salmon, 143–144
- Maple-Almond Granola, 40
- Maple-Blueberry Pancake Bites, 31–32
- Mexican Black Bean and Quinoa Bowl, 73
- Orange-Ginger Salmon Dinner, 133–134
- Orange Shrimp Stir-Fry, 153–154
- Perfect Poached Eggs, 24
- Perfectly Boiled Eggs, 37
- Pineapple Carrot Cake, 188–189
- Pork and Broccoli, 179–180
- Pot Roast and Potatoes, 167–168
- Saucy Italian Fish and Quinoa, 150–151
- Spinach-and-Tofu Curry, 129
- Strawberry-Banana Mason Jar Cake, 198–199
- Tropical Tapioca Pudding, 201
- Turmeric Latte, 204
- Vanilla-Cardamom Rice Pudding, 192
- Vegetable Barley Soup, 93
- Vegetable Pad Thai, 119–120
- Very Berry Cauli-Oats, 22

Dates
- Pineapple Carrot Cake, 188–189
- Turmeric Latte, 204

Desserts
- Banana Bread with Chocolate Chips, 196
- Berry Swirl Cheesecake, 202–203
- Chocolate Lava Cakes, 193–194
- Cinnamon Apple Cake, 195
- Cinnamon Apple Crumble, 190–191
- Cranberry-Apple Crumble, 200
- Fudgy Chocolate Brownies, 186–187
- Pineapple Carrot Cake, 188–189
- Strawberry-Banana Mason Jar Cake, 198–199
- Summer Berry Compote, 197
- Tropical Tapioca Pudding, 201
- Vanilla-Cardamom Rice Pudding, 192
- Zesty Lemon Cheesecake, 184–185

Dips and spreads
- Baba Ganoush, 44–45
- Beet Hummus, 46–47
- Blueberry Chia Jam, 39
- Cauli-Queso Dip, 49
- Saucy Garden-Fresh Salsa, 48

E

Easy Homemade Ketchup, 102

Eggplants
- Baba Ganoush, 44–45
- Eggy Ratatouille, 28–29
- Thai Red Chicken Curry, 145

Eggs
- Avocado Egg Salad, 79
- Breakfast Casserole, 38
- Cauliflower Fried Rice, 58
- Egg and Sweet Potato Hash, 33
- Eggy Ratatouille, 28–29
- Fajitas Fiesta Eggs, 35–36
- Maple-Pecan French Toast, 34
- Perfect Poached Eggs, 24
- Perfectly Boiled Eggs, 37
- Spinach and Feta Egg Muffins, 27
- Tex-Mex Breakfast Scramble, 30

Electric pressure cookers
- accessories, 14
- altitude adjustments, 13
- benefits of, 2–4
- care and cleaning, 12–13
- frozen foods in, 4
- functions, 10–11
- safety, 12

Exercise, 6

F

Fajitas Fiesta Eggs, 35–36

Fish
- Lemon-Dill Salmon, 143–144

Orange-Ginger Salmon Dinner, 133–134
Saucy Italian Fish and Quinoa, 150–151
Flours, 5
Fudgy Chocolate Brownies, 186–187

G

Garlic-Basil Marinara Sauce, 104
Garlic-Lime Shrimp Scampi, 142
Gluten-free
    Avocado Egg Salad, 79
    Banana Bread with Chocolate Chips, 196
    Beet and Feta Salad, 71
    Berry Swirl Cheesecake, 202–203
    Breakfast Casserole, 38
    Buttery Mashed Potatoes, 54
    Cauliflower Fried Rice, 58
    Cauli-Queso Dip, 49
    Chocolate Lava Cakes, 193–194
    Cinnamon Apple Cake, 195
    Cinnamon Apple Crumble, 190–191
    Cranberry-Apple Crumble, 200
    Creamy Chicken and Broccoli Rice, 141
    Creamy Mashed Cauliflower, 59
    Creamy Mushroom Penne, 124–125
    Creamy Vegan Alfredo Sauce, 103
    Egg and Sweet Potato Hash, 33
    Eggy Ratatouille, 28–29
    Fajitas Fiesta Eggs, 35–36
    Fudgy Chocolate Brownies, 186–187
    Garlic-Lime Shrimp Scampi, 142
    Greek Chicken Salad Lettuce Wraps, 72
    Lemon-Dill Salmon, 143–144
    Light 'n' Easy Butter Chicken, 139–140
    Maple-Almond Granola, 40
    Maple-Blueberry Pancake Bites, 31–32
    Masala Chai, 205
    Meatless Shepherd's Pie, 122–123
    Mediterranean Chicken Shawarma, 77–78
    Mediterranean Chickpea Bowl, 74
    Mediterranean Lamb Chops, 174–175
    Mexican Black Bean and Quinoa Bowl, 73
    Mushroom-Turkey Chili, 100
    Orange-Ginger Salmon Dinner, 133–134
    Orange Shrimp Stir-Fry, 153–154
    Parmesan Spaghetti Squash, 52
    Perfect Poached Eggs, 24
    Perfectly Boiled Eggs, 37
    Pineapple Carrot Cake, 188–189
    Quinoa and Lentil Stuffed Peppers, 116
    Saucy Italian Fish and Quinoa, 150–151
    Sloppy Joe Stuffed Potatoes, 161–162
    Spicy Mexican Chicken, 146
    Spinach and Feta Egg Muffins, 27
    Spinach-and-Tofu Curry, 129
    Strawberry-Banana Mason Jar Cake, 198–199
    Sweet and Savory Wild Rice, 126
    Tex-Mex Breakfast Scramble, 30
    Tropical Tapioca Pudding, 201
    Turmeric Latte, 204
    Tzatziki Lamb Meatballs, 172–173
    Vanilla-Cardamom Rice Pudding, 192
    Vegetable Pad Thai, 119–120
    Vegetable Risotto, 115
    Very Berry Cauli-Oats, 22
    White Chicken Chili, 98
    Zesty Lemon Cheesecake, 184–185
Greek Chicken Salad Lettuce Wraps, 72
Green beans
    Lemony Green Beans, 53
    Tangy Potato Salad, 65–66
Greens. *See also specific*
    Tex-Mex Lentil Bowl, 81

H

Healing Bone Broth, 86
Hearty Lentil Stew, 121
Honey-Garlic Brussels Sprouts, 50
Honey-Garlic Chicken Lettuce Wraps, 64
Hydration, 7

K

Kale
- Hearty Lentil Stew, 121
- Spinach-and-Tofu Curry, 129
- Sweet Potato Quinoa Salad, 80
- Vegetable Risotto, 115

Keep warm/cancel/off function, 11

L

Lamb
- Mediterranean Lamb Chops, 174–175
- Moroccan Lamb Stew, 176–177
- Tzatziki Lamb Meatballs, 172–173

Lemongrass
- Thai Lentil Soup, 89

Lemons
- Lemon-Cilantro Chicken, 137–138
- Lemon-Dill Salmon, 143–144
- Lemony Green Beans, 53
- Zesty Lemon Cheesecake, 184–185

Lentils
- Coconut-Lentil Curry, 117–118
- Hearty Lentil Stew, 121
- Tex-Mex Lentil Bowl, 81
- Thai Lentil Soup, 89
- Turmeric Lentil Soup, 91
- Vegan Lentil Chili, 99
- Veggie and Lentil Bolognese, 112

Lettuce
- Avocado Egg Salad, 79
- Greek Chicken Salad Lettuce Wraps, 72
- Honey-Garlic Chicken Lettuce Wraps, 64
- Mediterranean Chicken Shawarma, 77–78
- Shredded Beef Lettuce Cups, 82
- Shredded Chipotle Beef, 165–166
- Steak Fajita Wraps, 69–70
- Tex-Mex Chicken Salad Bowl, 75

Light 'n' Easy Butter Chicken, 139–140

Limes
- Chili-Lime Brown Rice, 57
- Chili-Lime Chicken and Rice, 132
- Coconut-Lime Quinoa, 55
- Garlic-Lime Shrimp Scampi, 142

M

Mangos
- Tropical Tapioca Pudding, 201

Manual/pressure function, 11
Maple-Almond Granola, 40
Maple-Blueberry Pancake Bites, 31–32
Maple-Pecan French Toast, 34
Masala Chai, 205
Meal plans, 16–19
Meat Loaf and Mashed Potatoes, 158–159
Meatless Shepherd's Pie, 122–123
Mediterranean Chicken Shawarma, 77–78
Mediterranean Chickpea Bowl, 74
Mediterranean Lamb Chops, 174–175
Mediterranean Turkey-Quinoa Bowl, 149
Mexican Black Bean and Quinoa Bowl, 73
Moroccan Lamb Stew, 176–177

Mung beans
- Thai Lentil Soup, 89
- Turmeric Lentil Soup, 91

Mushrooms
- Breakfast Casserole, 38
- Coconut-Lentil Curry, 117–118
- Creamy Chicken and Broccoli Rice, 141
- Creamy Mushroom Penne, 124–125
- Eggy Ratatouille, 28–29
- Meatless Shepherd's Pie, 122–123
- Mushroom and Wild Rice Soup, 96
- Mushroom-Turkey Chili, 100
- One-Pot Spaghetti and Meat Sauce, 169–170
- Sweet and Savory Wild Rice, 126
- Vegetable Barley Soup, 93
- Vegetable Risotto, 115
- Veggie and Lentil Bolognese, 112

N

Noodles
- Vegetable Pad Thai, 119–120

Nut-free
- Avocado Egg Salad, 79
- Beef and Bean Chili, 97
- Beet and Feta Salad, 71
- Berry Swirl Cheesecake, 202–203

Breakfast Casserole, 38
Buttery Mashed Potatoes, 54
Cauliflower Fried Rice, 58
Chicken Tortilla Soup, 95
Chocolate Lava Cakes, 193–194
Cinnamon Apple Crumble, 190–191
Creamy Chicken and Broccoli Rice, 141
Creamy Mashed Cauliflower, 59
Creamy Mushroom Penne, 124–125
Cuban Beef Picadillo, 164
Egg and Sweet Potato Hash, 33
Eggy Ratatouille, 28–29
Fajitas Fiesta Eggs, 35–36
Fudgy Chocolate Brownies, 186–187
Garlic-Lime Shrimp Scampi, 142
Greek Chicken Salad Lettuce Wraps, 72
Lemon-Dill Salmon, 143–144
Light 'n' Easy Butter Chicken, 139–140
Masala Chai, 205
Meat Loaf and Mashed Potatoes, 158–159
Meatless Shepherd's Pie, 122–123
Mediterranean Chicken Shawarma, 77–78
Mediterranean Chickpea Bowl, 74
Mediterranean Lamb Chops, 174–175
Mexican Black Bean and Quinoa Bowl, 73
Mushroom-Turkey Chili, 100
One-Pot Spaghetti and Meat Sauce, 169–170
Orange-Ginger Salmon Dinner, 133–134
Orange Shrimp Stir-Fry, 153–154
Parmesan Spaghetti Squash, 52
Parmesan Turkey Meatballs, 152
Perfect Poached Eggs, 24
Perfectly Boiled Eggs, 37
Pork and Broccoli, 179–180
Pot Roast and Potatoes, 167–168
Quinoa and Lentil Stuffed Peppers, 116
Saucy Italian Fish and Quinoa, 150–151
Sloppy Joe Stuffed Potatoes, 161–162
Spicy Mexican Chicken, 146
Spinach and Feta Egg Muffins, 27
Spinach-and-Tofu Curry, 129
Sweet and Savory Wild Rice, 126
Tex-Mex Breakfast Scramble, 30
Tzatziki Lamb Meatballs, 172–173
Vegetable Barley Soup, 93
Vegetable Risotto, 115
White Chicken Chili, 98
Zesty Lemon Cheesecake, 184–185
Nuts
Banana Bread with Chocolate Chips, 196
Cashew Chicken, 147–148
Cauli-Queso Dip, 49
Cinnamon Apple Cake, 195
Cranberry-Apple Crumble, 200
Creamy Vegan Alfredo Sauce, 103
Maple-Almond Granola, 40
Maple-Pecan French Toast, 34
Pineapple Carrot Cake, 188–189
Tropical Tapioca Pudding, 201
Turmeric Latte, 204
Vegetable Pad Thai, 119–120

O

Oats, 5
Cinnamon Apple Cake, 195
Cranberry-Apple Crumble, 200
Maple-Almond Granola, 40
Meat Loaf and Mashed Potatoes, 158–159
Turmeric Latte Quinoa Oats, 23
Tzatziki Lamb Meatballs, 172–173
Very Berry Cauli-Oats, 22
Oils, 5
Olives
Cuban Beef Picadillo, 164
Egg and Sweet Potato Hash, 33
Greek Chicken Salad Lettuce Wraps, 72
Mediterranean Chickpea Bowl, 74

Olives (*continued*)
   Moroccan Lamb Stew, 176–177
   Saucy Italian Fish and Quinoa, 150–151

One pot
   Beef and Bean Chili, 97
   Blueberry Chia Jam, 39
   Buttery Mashed Potatoes, 54
   Carrot-Ginger Soup, 92
   Cauliflower Fried Rice, 58
   Cauliflower-Potato Curry, 113
   Cauli-Queso Dip, 49
   Chili-Lime Brown Rice, 57
   Cinnamon Applesauce, 105
   Coconut-Lime Quinoa, 55
   Coconut-Quinoa Curry, 127
   Creamy Chicken and Broccoli Rice, 141
   Creamy Mushroom Penne, 124–125
   Creamy Root Vegetable Soup, 94
   Creamy Vegan Alfredo Sauce, 103
   Cuban Beef Picadillo, 164
   Easy Homemade Ketchup, 102
   Eggy Ratatouille, 28–29
   Garlic-Basil Marinara Sauce, 104
   Garlic-Lime Shrimp Scampi, 142
   Healing Bone Broth, 86
   Hearty Lentil Stew, 121
   Lemon-Dill Salmon, 143–144
   Lemony Green Beans, 53
   Masala Chai, 205
   Mediterranean Turkey-Quinoa Bowl, 149
   Moroccan Lamb Stew, 176–177
   Mushroom-Turkey Chili, 100
   One-Pot Mexican Rice and Beans, 114
   One-Pot Spaghetti and Meat Sauce, 169–170
   Parmesan Spaghetti Squash, 52
   Parmesan Turkey Meatballs, 152
   Pork Barbacoa, 181
   Pork Carnitas, 178
   Root Vegetable Medley, 51
   Saucy Garden-Fresh Salsa, 48
   Shredded Chipotle Beef, 165–166
   Sloppy Joe Stuffed Potatoes, 161–162
   Spicy Beef Curry, 171
   Spicy Cranberry Sauce, 106
   Spicy Mexican Chicken, 146
   Spinach-and-Tofu Curry, 129
   Summer Berry Compote, 197
   Sweet and Savory Wild Rice, 126
   Sweet Potato and Corn Soup, 90
   Sweet Potato and Quinoa Chili, 101
   Tex-Mex Butternut Squash Soup, 87–88
   Tex-Mex Lentil Bowl, 81
   Thai Lentil Soup, 89
   Thai Red Chicken Curry, 145
   Turmeric Latte, 204
   Turmeric Latte Quinoa Oats, 23
   Turmeric Lentil Soup, 91
   Vanilla-Cardamom Rice Pudding, 192
   Vegan Lentil Chili, 99
   Vegetable Risotto, 115
   Veggie and Lentil Bolognese, 112
   Veggie Rice Pilaf, 128
   Warm 'n' Cozy Beef Stew, 163
   White Chicken Chili, 98

One-Pot Mexican Rice and Beans, 114
One-Pot Spaghetti and Meat Sauce, 169–170
Orange-Ginger Salmon Dinner, 133–134
Orange Shrimp Stir-Fry, 153–154

P

Parmesan Spaghetti Squash, 52
Parmesan Turkey Meatballs, 152
Parsnips
   Root Vegetable Medley, 51
Pasta
   Creamy Mushroom Penne, 124–125
   One-Pot Spaghetti and Meat Sauce, 169–170
Peanut butter
   Vegetable Pad Thai, 119–120
Peas
   Cashew Chicken, 147–148

Cauliflower Fried Rice, 58
Creamy Mushroom Penne, 124–125
Hearty Lentil Stew, 121
Meatless Shepherd's Pie, 122–123
Orange-Ginger Salmon Dinner, 133–134
Orange Shrimp Stir-Fry, 153–154
Tangy Potato Salad, 65–66
Vegetable Barley Soup, 93
Vegetable Pad Thai, 119–120
Vegetable Risotto, 115
Veggie Rice Pilaf, 128
Warm 'n' Cozy Beef Stew, 163

Peppers
Breakfast Casserole, 38
Cashew Chicken, 147–148
Cauli-Queso Dip, 49
Creamy Chicken and Broccoli Rice, 141
Creamy Mushroom Penne, 124–125
Cuban Beef Picadillo, 164
Eggy Ratatouille, 28–29
Fajitas Fiesta Eggs, 35–36
Meat Loaf and Mashed Potatoes, 158–159
Mediterranean Turkey-Quinoa Bowl, 149
Mexican Black Bean and Quinoa Bowl, 73
One-Pot Mexican Rice and Beans, 114
Orange Shrimp Stir-Fry, 153–154
Pork Barbacoa, 181
Quinoa and Lentil Stuffed Peppers, 116

Saucy Garden-Fresh Salsa, 48
Saucy Italian Fish and Quinoa, 150–151
Sesame Mongolian Beef, 160
Shredded Chipotle Beef, 165–166
Sloppy Joe Stuffed Potatoes, 161–162
Spicy Black Bean and Rice Salad, 76
Spicy Mexican Chicken, 146
Spinach and Feta Egg Muffins, 27
Steak Fajita Wraps, 69–70
Sweet and Savory Wild Rice, 126
Sweet Potato and Corn Soup, 90
Sweet Potato and Quinoa Chili, 101
Tangy Potato Salad, 65–66
Tex-Mex Breakfast Scramble, 30
Tex-Mex Butternut Squash Soup, 87–88
Tex-Mex Chicken Salad Bowl, 75
Thai Red Chicken Curry, 145
Veggie Rice Pilaf, 128
Perfect Poached Eggs, 24
Perfectly Boiled Eggs, 37
Pineapple Carrot Cake, 188–189
Pork and Broccoli, 179–180
Pork Barbacoa, 181
Pork Carnitas, 178
Portion control, 3
Potatoes. *See also* Sweet potatoes

Breakfast Casserole, 38
Buttery Mashed Potatoes, 54
Cauliflower-Potato Curry, 113
Hearty Lentil Stew, 121
Meat Loaf and Mashed Potatoes, 158–159
Pot Roast and Potatoes, 167–168
Roasted Chicken and Veggies, 135–136
Root Vegetable Medley, 51
Tangy Potato Salad, 65–66
Warm 'n' Cozy Beef Stew, 163
Pot Roast and Potatoes, 167–168
Pumpkin seeds
Maple-Almond Granola, 40
Sweet and Savory Wild Rice, 126

Q

Quinoa
Coconut-Lime Quinoa, 55
Coconut-Quinoa Curry, 127
Creamy Chicken and Broccoli Rice, 141
Mediterranean Lamb Chops, 174–175
Mediterranean Turkey-Quinoa Bowl, 149
Mexican Black Bean and Quinoa Bowl, 73
Orange-Ginger Salmon Dinner, 133–134
Quinoa and Lentil Stuffed Peppers, 116

INDEX 217

Quinoa (continued)
- Saucy Italian Fish and Quinoa, 150–151
- Sweet Potato and Quinoa Chili, 101
- Sweet Potato Quinoa Salad, 80
- Thai Lentil Soup, 89
- Turmeric Latte Quinoa Oats, 23
- Turmeric Lentil Soup, 91

R

Raisins
- Cuban Beef Picadillo, 164
- Moroccan Lamb Stew, 176–177

Recipes, about, 15

Rice
- Cashew Chicken, 147–148
- Chana Masala, 110–111
- Chili-Lime Brown Rice, 57
- Chili-Lime Chicken and Rice, 132
- Coconut-Lentil Curry, 117–118
- Mushroom and Wild Rice Soup, 96
- One-Pot Mexican Rice and Beans, 114
- Spicy Black Bean and Rice Salad, 76
- Sweet and Savory Wild Rice, 126
- Two-Bean Rice Bowl, 67–68
- Vanilla-Cardamom Rice Pudding, 192
- Vegetable Risotto, 115
- Veggie Rice Pilaf, 128

Roasted Chicken and Veggies, 135–136

Root Vegetable Medley, 51

S

Salads. *See also* Bowls
- Avocado Egg Salad, 79
- Beet and Feta Salad, 71
- Spicy Black Bean and Rice Salad, 76
- Sweet Potato Quinoa Salad, 80
- Tangy Potato Salad, 65–66
- Tex-Mex Chicken Salad Bowl, 75

Salmon
- Lemon-Dill Salmon, 143–144
- Orange-Ginger Salmon Dinner, 133–134

Sauces
- Cinnamon Applesauce, 105
- Creamy Vegan Alfredo Sauce, 103
- Easy Homemade Ketchup, 102
- Garlic-Basil Marinara Sauce, 104
- Saucy Garden-Fresh Salsa, 48
- Spicy Cranberry Sauce, 106
- Veggie and Lentil Bolognese, 112

Saucy Garden-Fresh Salsa, 48

Saucy Italian Fish and Quinoa, 150–151

Sauté function, 11

Sesame Mongolian Beef, 160

Shredded Beef Lettuce Cups, 82

Shredded Chipotle Beef, 165–166

Shrimp
- Garlic-Lime Shrimp Scampi, 142
- Orange Shrimp Stir-Fry, 153–154

Sleep, 6

Sloppy Joe Stuffed Potatoes, 161–162

Slow cook function, 11

Soups. *See also* Chilis
- Carrot-Ginger Soup, 92
- Chicken Tortilla Soup, 95
- Creamy Root Vegetable Soup, 94
- Healing Bone Broth, 86
- Mushroom and Wild Rice Soup, 96
- Sweet Potato and Corn Soup, 90
- Tex-Mex Butternut Squash Soup, 87–88
- Thai Lentil Soup, 89
- Turmeric Lentil Soup, 91
- Vegetable Barley Soup, 93

Spiced Roasted Cauliflower Head, 60

Spicy Beef Curry, 171

Spicy Black Bean and Rice Salad, 76

Spicy Cranberry Sauce, 106

Spicy Mexican Chicken, 146

Spinach
- Beet and Feta Salad, 71
- Breakfast Casserole, 38
- Chana Masala, 110–111
- Coconut-Lentil Curry, 117–118
- Coconut-Quinoa Curry, 127
- Creamy Mushroom Penne, 124–125
- Egg and Sweet Potato Hash, 33
- Garlic-Lime Shrimp Scampi, 142

Meatless Shepherd's Pie, 122–123
Mediterranean Turkey-Quinoa Bowl, 149
Spicy Beef Curry, 171
Spinach and Feta Egg Muffins, 27
Spinach-and-Tofu Curry, 129
Turmeric Lentil Soup, 91
Veggie Rice Pilaf, 128
Warm 'n' Cozy Beef Stew, 163

Squash. *See also* Zucchini
Creamy Root Vegetable Soup, 94
Parmesan Spaghetti Squash, 52
Tex-Mex Butternut Squash Soup, 87–88

Steak Fajita Wraps, 69–70
Steam function, 11
Stews. *See also* Chilis; Curries
Hearty Lentil Stew, 121
Moroccan Lamb Stew, 176–177
Warm 'n' Cozy Beef Stew, 163

Strawberry-Banana Mason Jar Cake, 198–199
Stress, 6
Substitutions, 5
Sugars, 5, 7
Summer Berry Compote, 197
Sweet and Savory Wild Rice, 126

Sweet potatoes
Baked Sweet Potatoes, 56

Sweeteners, 5
Coconut-Quinoa Curry, 127
Creamy Root Vegetable Soup, 94
Egg and Sweet Potato Hash, 33
Lemon-Dill Salmon, 143–144
Root Vegetable Medley, 51
Sloppy Joe Stuffed Potatoes, 161–162
Sweet Potato and Corn Soup, 90
Sweet Potato and Quinoa Chili, 101
Sweet Potato Quinoa Salad, 80

T

Tahini
Baba Ganoush, 44–45
Beet Hummus, 46–47
Spiced Roasted Cauliflower Head, 60

Tangy Potato Salad, 65–66
Tapioca Pudding, Tropical, 201

Tea
Masala Chai, 205

Tex-Mex Breakfast Scramble, 30
Tex-Mex Butternut Squash Soup, 87–88
Tex-Mex Chicken Salad Bowl, 75
Tex-Mex Lentil Bowl, 81
Thai Lentil Soup, 89
Thai Red Chicken Curry, 145

30 minutes or less
Avocado Egg Salad, 79
Blueberry Chia Jam, 39
Buttery Mashed Potatoes, 54
Carrot-Ginger Soup, 92
Cauliflower Fried Rice, 58
Cauliflower-Potato Curry, 113
Cauli-Queso Dip, 49
Chili-Lime Chicken and Rice, 132
Chocolate Lava Cakes, 193–194
Cinnamon Apple Crumble, 190–191
Cinnamon Applesauce, 105
Creamy Chicken and Broccoli Rice, 141
Creamy Mashed Cauliflower, 59
Creamy Mushroom Penne, 124–125
Creamy Vegan Alfredo Sauce, 103
Cuban Beef Picadillo, 164
Easy Homemade Ketchup, 102
Egg and Sweet Potato Hash, 33
Eggy Ratatouille, 28–29
Fajitas Fiesta Eggs, 35–36
Garlic-Basil Marinara Sauce, 104
Garlic-Lime Shrimp Scampi, 142
Greek Chicken Salad Lettuce Wraps, 72
Honey-Garlic Brussels Sprouts, 50
Honey-Garlic Chicken Lettuce Wraps, 64
Lemon-Dill Salmon, 143–144
Lemony Green Beans, 53
Maple-Blueberry Pancake Bites, 31–32
Masala Chai, 205
Meatless Shepherd's Pie, 122–123
Mexican Black Bean and Quinoa Bowl, 73

30 minutes or less (*continued*)
- One-Pot Spaghetti and Meat Sauce, 169–170
- Orange-Ginger Salmon Dinner, 133–134
- Orange Shrimp Stir-Fry, 153–154
- Parmesan Spaghetti Squash, 52
- Parmesan Turkey Meatballs, 152
- Perfect Poached Eggs, 24
- Perfectly Boiled Eggs, 37
- Quinoa and Lentil Stuffed Peppers, 116
- Saucy Italian Fish and Quinoa, 150–151
- Sloppy Joe Stuffed Potatoes, 161–162
- Spiced Roasted Cauliflower Head, 60
- Spicy Cranberry Sauce, 106
- Spinach and Feta Egg Muffins, 27
- Steak Fajita Wraps, 69–70
- Strawberry-Banana Mason Jar Cake, 198–199
- Summer Berry Compote, 197
- Sweet Potato and Corn Soup, 90
- Sweet Potato and Quinoa Chili, 101
- Sweet Potato Quinoa Salad, 80
- Tex-Mex Butternut Squash Soup, 87–88
- Tex-Mex Chicken Salad Bowl, 75
- Tex-Mex Lentil Bowl, 81
- Thai Lentil Soup, 89
- Tropical Tapioca Pudding, 201
- Turmeric Latte, 204
- Turmeric Latte Quinoa Oats, 23
- Turmeric Lentil Soup, 91
- Vanilla-Cardamom Rice Pudding, 192
- Vegetable Pad Thai, 119–120
- Vegetable Risotto, 115

Tofu-and-Spinach Curry, 129

Tomatoes
- Chana Masala, 110–111
- Chicken Tortilla Soup, 95
- Chili-Lime Chicken and Rice, 132
- Coconut-Lentil Curry, 117–118
- Coconut-Quinoa Curry, 127
- Cuban Beef Picadillo, 164
- Easy Homemade Ketchup, 102
- Eggy Ratatouille, 28–29
- Garlic-Basil Marinara Sauce, 104
- Greek Chicken Salad Lettuce Wraps, 72
- Hearty Lentil Stew, 121
- Meatless Shepherd's Pie, 122–123
- Mediterranean Chickpea Bowl, 74
- Mediterranean Lamb Chops, 174–175
- Mediterranean Turkey-Quinoa Bowl, 149
- Mushroom-Turkey Chili, 100
- One-Pot Mexican Rice and Beans, 114
- Quinoa and Lentil Stuffed Peppers, 116
- Saucy Garden-Fresh Salsa, 48
- Saucy Italian Fish and Quinoa, 150–151
- Sloppy Joe Stuffed Potatoes, 161–162
- Spicy Beef Curry, 171
- Spicy Black Bean and Rice Salad, 76
- Spicy Mexican Chicken, 146
- Spinach-and-Tofu Curry, 129
- Tex-Mex Breakfast Scramble, 30
- Two-Bean Rice Bowl, 67–68
- Vegan Lentil Chili, 99
- Vegetable Barley Soup, 93
- Veggie and Lentil Bolognese, 112
- Veggie Rice Pilaf, 128

Tropical Tapioca Pudding, 201

Turkey
- Mediterranean Turkey-Quinoa Bowl, 149
- Mushroom-Turkey Chili, 100
- Parmesan Turkey Meatballs, 152

Turmeric Latte, 204
Turmeric Latte Quinoa Oats, 23
Turmeric Lentil Soup, 91
Two-Bean Rice Bowl, 67–68
Tzatziki Lamb Meatballs, 172–173

V

Vanilla-Cardamom Rice Pudding, 192

Vegan
- Baba Ganoush, 44–45
- Baked Sweet Potatoes, 56
- Beet Hummus, 46–47
- Blueberry Chia Jam, 39
- Carrot-Ginger Soup, 92
- Cauliflower-Potato Curry, 113
- Chana Masala, 110–111
- Chili-Lime Brown Rice, 57
- Cinnamon Apple Cake, 195
- Cinnamon Applesauce, 105
- Coconut-Lentil Curry, 117–118
- Coconut-Lime Quinoa, 55
- Coconut-Quinoa Curry, 127
- Cranberry-Apple Crumble, 200
- Creamy Coconut Yogurt, 25–26
- Creamy Root Vegetable Soup, 94
- Creamy Vegan Alfredo Sauce, 103
- Easy Homemade Ketchup, 102
- Garlic-Basil Marinara Sauce, 104
- Hearty Lentil Stew, 121
- Lemony Green Beans, 53
- Maple-Almond Granola, 40
- Mexican Black Bean and Quinoa Bowl, 73
- Mushroom and Wild Rice Soup, 96
- One-Pot Mexican Rice and Beans, 114
- Root Vegetable Medley, 51
- Saucy Garden-Fresh Salsa, 48
- Spiced Roasted Cauliflower Head, 60
- Spicy Cranberry Sauce, 106
- Spinach-and-Tofu Curry, 129
- Summer Berry Compote, 197
- Sweet Potato and Corn Soup, 90
- Sweet Potato and Quinoa Chili, 101
- Sweet Potato Quinoa Salad, 80
- Tex-Mex Butternut Squash Soup, 87–88
- Tex-Mex Lentil Bowl, 81
- Thai Lentil Soup, 89
- Tropical Tapioca Pudding, 201
- Turmeric Latte, 204
- Turmeric Latte Quinoa Oats, 23
- Turmeric Lentil Soup, 91
- Two-Bean Rice Bowl, 67–68
- Vanilla-Cardamom Rice Pudding, 192
- Vegan Lentil Chili, 99
- Vegetable Barley Soup, 93
- Vegetable Pad Thai, 119–120
- Veggie and Lentil Bolognese, 112
- Veggie Rice Pilaf, 128
- Very Berry Cauli-Oats, 22

Vegan Lentil Chili, 99

Vegetable Barley Soup, 93

Vegetable Pad Thai, 119–120

Vegetable Risotto, 115

Vegetables. *See also specific*
- Tex-Mex Chicken Salad Bowl, 75
- Thai Lentil Soup, 89
- Turmeric Lentil Soup, 91

Vegetarian. *See also* Vegan
- Avocado Egg Salad, 79
- Banana Bread with Chocolate Chips, 196
- Beet and Feta Salad, 71
- Berry Swirl Cheesecake, 202–203
- Breakfast Casserole, 38
- Buttery Mashed Potatoes, 54
- Cauliflower Fried Rice, 58
- Cauli-Queso Dip, 49
- Chocolate Lava Cakes, 193–194
- Cinnamon Apple Crumble, 190–191
- Creamy Mashed Cauliflower, 59
- Creamy Mushroom Penne, 124–125
- Egg and Sweet Potato Hash, 33
- Eggy Ratatouille, 28–29
- Fajitas Fiesta Eggs, 35–36
- Fudgy Chocolate Brownies, 186–187
- Honey-Garlic Brussels Sprouts, 50
- Maple-Blueberry Pancake Bites, 31–32
- Maple-Pecan French Toast, 34
- Masala Chai, 205
- Meatless Shepherd's Pie, 122–123
- Mediterranean Chickpea Bowl, 74

Vegetarian (*continued*)
- Parmesan Spaghetti Squash, 52
- Perfect Poached Eggs, 24
- Perfectly Boiled Eggs, 37
- Pineapple Carrot Cake, 188–189
- Quinoa and Lentil Stuffed Peppers, 116
- Spicy Black Bean and Rice Salad, 76
- Spinach and Feta Egg Muffins, 27
- Strawberry-Banana Mason Jar Cake, 198–199
- Sweet and Savory Wild Rice, 126
- Tangy Potato Salad, 65–66
- Tex-Mex Breakfast Scramble, 30
- Vegetable Risotto, 115
- Zesty Lemon Cheesecake, 184–185

Veggie and Lentil Bolognese, 112
Veggie Rice Pilaf, 128
Very Berry Cauli-Oats, 22

W

Warm 'n' Cozy Beef Stew, 163
Weight loss, 7
White Chicken Chili, 98
Whitefish
- Saucy Italian Fish and Quinoa, 150–151

Wraps
- Avocado Egg Salad, 79
- Greek Chicken Salad Lettuce Wraps, 72
- Honey-Garlic Chicken Lettuce Wraps, 64
- Mediterranean Chicken Shawarma, 77–78
- Pork Carnitas, 178
- Shredded Beef Lettuce Cups, 82
- Steak Fajita Wraps, 69–70

Y

Yogurt
- Berry Swirl Cheesecake, 202–203
- Creamy Coconut Yogurt, 25–26
- Light 'n' Easy Butter Chicken, 139–140
- Mediterranean Chicken Shawarma, 77–78
- Sloppy Joe Stuffed Potatoes, 161–162
- Spicy Mexican Chicken, 146
- Tzatziki Lamb Meatballs, 172–173
- White Chicken Chili, 98
- Zesty Lemon Cheesecake, 1 84–185

Z

Zesty Lemon Cheesecake, 184–185
Zucchini
- Coconut-Lentil Curry, 117–118
- Eggy Ratatouille, 28–29
- One-Pot Spaghetti and Meat Sauce, 169–170
- Vegetable Risotto, 115

Acknowledgments

There are so many people in my life that I am grateful for daily.

To my husband, thank you for everything! Your endless love, support, and encouragement gives me the confidence to believe I can do anything.

To my children, we have been so blessed with the two of you. Your faith in me while I worked on this project, and in everything I do, means more to me then you will ever know.

To my parents, thank you for your unconditional love, support, and prayers, which I know have helped pave this path for me. To my siblings, I love you all, thanks for your willingness to try all my creations.

To my mother-in-law and family, thanks for always being so supportive in all that I do.

To my friends, thank you for always making me laugh out loud, encouraging me to go after what I want, and just being there.

To my niece Shahin, thank you for introducing me to the Instant Pot; and my friend Anar, for cohosting Instant Pot workshops for our friends and community with me.

To my social media family and friends, this is all thanks to you and the amazing relationships that we have been able to cultivate.

A very special thanks to my friend Shannon, for all your help, support, and words of encouragement. This has been a dream come true, thanks to you!

Thank you to Sandy Gluck for kindly sharing your pork recipes for us to include in this cookbook.

To the Callisto Media team, thank you for taking a chance on me. Elizabeth, thank you for all your patience with my endless questions and concerns. Alyson, I am so grateful for your kindness and positive words of encouragement that helped me believe that I could do this.

About the Author

Sukaina Bharwani is a holistic nutritionist and a wellness recipe creator. She has a passion for everything health and wellness and shares that passion with others through social media, her website, and workshops. Sukaina has gluten and refined sugar sensitivities and believes that eating healthy, with or without restrictions, can be easy, delicious, and not leave you feeling like you're missing out.

To find out more about Sukaina and her recipes follow her on Instagram at @healthandfoodjunkie or visit her website, HealthAndFoodJunkie.com.

www.ingramcontent.com/pod-product-compliance
Lightning Source LLC
Chambersburg PA
CBHW061418090426
42743CB00023B/3488